DAD, GOD, AND ME

*Remembering a Mennonite Pastor
and His Wayward Son*

RALPH FRIESEN

 FriesenPress

Suite 300 - 990 Fort St
Victoria, BC, V8V 3K2
Canada

www.friesenpress.com

ISBN
978-1-5255-6087-3 (Hardcover)
978-1-5255-6088-0 (Paperback)
978-1-5255-6089-7 (eBook)

1. BIOGRAPHY & AUTOBIOGRAPHY, PERSONAL MEMOIRS

Distributed to the trade by The Ingram Book Company

This book is dedicated to my siblings: Alvin, Donald, Mary Ann, Vernon and Norman. And to my mom, who managed to laugh in the face of adversity.

To Hannah —
my first reader, my deep
listener, my great encourager.

Love,
Ralph

Financial support provided by D. F. Plett Historical Research Foundation

Our family, 1946, a studio picture taken at Eatons.

All photos from Friesen family collection unless otherwise credited.

CONTENTS

INTRODUCTION

On a sunny Sunday morning in late August, 2007, my wife Hannah and I walked down to the Corner House Café. In our town, Nelson, B.C., the Corner House was both the nearest restaurant to us, and the place with a breakfast menu we liked best. As usual that morning, we talked about what we were reading, and Hannah told a story from a collection called *The First Man in My Life*. The writer's mother suffered a brain aneurysm and her father authorized an operation. The writer, aged just six at the time, and two older brothers and a baby sister went to see their mother in the hospital. She was distant, strange, barely recognizing them. Collectively, wordlessly, they all (except for the baby, who was confused) decided the same thing: this was not their mother. And, although the mother lived for another seven years, this was how it remained. Later the writer's father told her, "You became silent."

As I listened, I was reminded of my own experiences with my father. I started telling Hannah of my memories and was surprised by a sudden upwelling of sadness. There in the café, over bacon and eggs, I began to weep. Those tears were the seeds that developed into this book.

We were six children in my family—Alvin, Donald, Mary Ann, Vernon, Norman, and me, the youngest. When my father had his paralyzing stroke on August 11, 1958, we made our individual visits to the hospital to see him. We didn't go together.

To whom would it have occurred to bring all of us together and ask: "What does each of you need? What can you contribute? What shall be done now, now that you have lost your father?" (Or for my mother: "your husband.") To no one, apparently—it didn't happen. And this is one of the things that struck me at breakfast that day—that we each dealt with the situation alone.

Many years later, while studying to become a Marriage and Family Therapist, I attempted to re-create this situation in my "Self in the Family" class. Classmates played family members gathered for a fictional meeting, a year after the stroke. I was to be the therapist to my own family. Almost immediately I got stuck. I did not know how to help these people, all of them so resigned to events, all of them (except Mom) preoccupied with their own families, jobs, and so on. I was too close to the problem. Then I switched roles and became "myself" at age 14. When the instructor, as therapist, asked me, "What can you contribute?" I was struck dumb. I knew immediately that I had never been asked this question in connection with a family problem. I felt a surge of anxiety, and also of recognition, because the therapist's words implied belief in me, faith that I did have something to offer. I knew that this was true, and it changed my view of myself.

"Loss," I say of Dad, although he didn't die. But we treated him like an imposter. This paralyzed imitation of a man, whose brain didn't function properly anymore, was not our father. I believe we all thought that, without talking about it.

And we were wrong. Why was I crying at the Corner House? In my adolescence, after Dad's stroke, I was embarrassed by him. He tried to be of good cheer, despite the horrendous blow that had slammed his body and brain with such terrible force. I had always thought of this effort at cheerfulness as artificial—absurd, even. But now I was struck by his lonely courage. He carried on, as best he could. He must have known that we, his children, viewed him from a cool distance after his stroke, that we didn't try to understand his situation or connect with him. But he did not complain, or ask for sympathy. He was a brave man, far braver than I ever realized, and I had failed him. Understanding this for the first time, I wept that August morning.

When Mom died in 1983, Steinbach businessman and family friend Cornie Loewen met with us siblings regarding the settlement of the estate. He congratulated us on our spirit of cooperation. He saw that we had something, as a family. Whatever our differences, we were kindly disposed to each other.

There is for me in the memory of that estate meeting a hint of the guidance that we needed (and could not find among ourselves) after Dad's stroke; I'm still grateful to Cornie Loewen for bringing us together and giving us encouragement. Even today, with Mom and Dad gone, Vern gone, and Cornie Loewen gone too for that matter, and the Corner House Café transformed into a different restaurant, I wish for us to gather again and reconsider that time in our lives, more than 50 years ago. Perhaps this book is a kind of gathering, and reconsidering.

I have gathered everything I could find of my father—his diaries, a few letters, postcards, sermon notes, pictures. I have also drawn upon my mother's diaries and letters. I have interviewed my siblings and a number of people who knew my father as a businessman and as a church pastor. In this process, I have made discoveries, and have come to know Dad more completely than when he was alive.

I have also told my own story insofar as it intersects with his. So this is both a biography of a man, written by his son, and a memoir of parts of that son's boyhood. The task I set myself was not only to get to know my father better, but also to get to know myself better. Even if you know nothing about him, or me, you do know something about your own search for what has been lost, your own attempts at self-understanding. Our mutual searching, our need to know and understand—these things connect us.

CHAPTER 1:
"THE LORD SPOKE TO US"

"Dad's in the hospital." On a sunshine-filled Monday morning in August of 1958 I was still in bed when my mother came up the stairs and spoke these words. *In the hospital.* Why? But I wasn't completely surprised; he sometimes had gall bladder attacks, and he had angry-looking red sores on his shins. Also, he'd already been in the hospital a few weeks earlier, for a checkup of some kind, something to do with his heart.

"He's had a stroke," Mom said. Her round face, so often smiling, looked drawn and serious. A stroke? Even to my limited thirteen-year-old understanding, it didn't sound good. "In the middle of the night. He fell out of bed. The ambulance came."

What? Ambulance? I'd slept through all of it. My first thoughts on awakening had been the usual ones. Maybe I'd go out and bounce a sponge ball against the grey cinder block wall of the Penner's Transfer truck garage next door, or maybe I'd scout around the neighbourhood for a friend to hang out with, Harry or Earl or Bob, if I could duck out of whatever chores Mom might have for me to do.

But now this would be a different day. Dad was paralyzed on his left side, Mom said. I could not go to see him; only adults were allowed to be visitors in the hospital.

Mom was at the hospital off and on all that day, but according to her diary, somehow found time to start the laundry. Her sister, Aunt Marie, came over to help, and to can three big jars of cucumbers. My sister Mary Ann came from Winnipeg with her husband, and so did my brother Don and his wife. Even my aunt Catherine and uncle Peter Loewen came from Morris in the evening. The brothers who lived at home, Al, Vern, and Norm, did not let on that they were worried. As the youngest, I was used to picking up cues from them. I wondered how sick Dad was, anyway.

He was paralyzed, but there was some hope that he would get better. A little better, anyway. He could not walk . . . would he ever walk? The doctors didn't know. Or they weren't saying.

Mom had known something was wrong. When he drove into that stump beside the driveway a few months before, she should have known then, because he'd never done anything like that. She should have known . . . but what would she have done?

What could anyone have done? Invisible sabotage had been going on within my father's body. It might have had something to do with the food Dad loved, the *Verenike* with *Schmauntfat*, the *Foarmaworscht*, the *Tweeback* with butter . . . carbohydrates, fat, red meat. Mom had cooked the way she had learned at home, pretty much the same as all the other women in town.

I played Little League baseball, not well—but I loved it. My team was "The Blues," coached by my brother Norman, at the back. To my left is Patrick Friesen, who would later become my best friend.

Or maybe the problem had been exercise. Not enough of it. He sometimes had taken us swimming to Sherbrook Baths in Winnipeg but I didn't remember him actually swimming much; he would mostly sit at the side of the pool with his sore legs in the water. I saw that he had breasts, and felt ashamed. A man shouldn't look like that.

Once I had complained to Mom that he never did anything with me, like play catch with a baseball. Mom

5

had looked up from her mixing bowl. "He would like to play catch with you," she said. "He's just so busy. He hardly has the time." I had felt slightly pleased that she seemed to feel guilty, that I had the power to evoke that in her. And this was new information. I hadn't considered that Dad had ever given so much as a passing thought to spending time with me.

In her diary Mom wrote: "The Lord spoke to us in a real way during the night." Maybe she said something like that to us boys, too. So God had something to do with this event. He came like a thief in the night to give a message. We weren't ready. What did he mean for us to understand? I began to wrestle with that question.

CHAPTER 2:
RED ROCK: KEEPING SILENT

That same summer, in July, the religious question had already been burned into my consciousness. My parents, sensing that their youngest child had not made a definite decision for Christ, decided that I should go to Red Rock Lake Bible Camp.

They knew that I had been begging Al to let me go with him to see movies in Ste. Anne, a neighbouring French-Canadian village with a theatre. I

My brother Al, spiffy in his topcoat and leather gloves, with his Buick Century hardtop.

loved going along with my big brother in his green-and-white Buick Century hardtop, and I was totally indiscriminate in my tastes—any movie would do, Western or romance or war. It did not take long for Mom to discover these secret forays into the forbidden. She scolded both of us, me for seeking out un-Christian entertainment, and Al for being my enabler. Dad was not involved, but Mom must have talked to him.

You could go to Red Rock for free if you learned one hundred Bible verses off by heart. One hundred verses! Other children actually accomplished the task, but to me it seemed impossible, and I refused to try, and thought that might be the end of it. Also, my parents' expectations made me skittish. But they found another way: our well-off family friends, the Ed Loewens, stepped forward to pay for me.

The camp was located in the great Precambrian Canadian Shield, on a lake near the Manitoba-Ontario border. The lake's shoreline is irregular, with many bays and coves. Heavy forest and outcroppings of granite surround it.

The campers' cabins were basic, but the metal bunk beds were somehow familiar, like the ones my brothers slept in at home. Many of the children and counsellors were from Steinbach, so I did not have a big social adjustment to make. I liked swimming and boating. At evening services, the Parschauer sisters, daughters of visiting missionaries, sang gospel songs in their enchantingly sweet voices and I fantasized they might take an interest in me.

I planned on keeping my head down through the religious programs and maybe escape notice. This strategy seemed to work, until one evening shortly before we were scheduled to go home, I was called to the chapel. Entering, I noticed that the lights had been turned down, giving the rustic wood panelling an almost romantic atmosphere. A group of male counsellors were gathered. They closed the door when I came in; I was alone with them. They wanted to know about the state of my soul. I felt my heart beat faster, and moisture forming in my armpits. What should I tell them? I kept silent. They spoke of the wondrous sacrifice of Jesus, who had died for all sinners, including me. I had heard all this before, but in the semi-darkened room, surrounded by several determined, fervent churchmen, the words struck me forcefully, almost like physical blows. The men launched Bible verses at me, trying to penetrate my stubborn silence: "If we confess our sins, he is faithful and just to forgive us our sins and to cleanse us from all unrighteousness." And: "Whoever believes in him is not condemned, but whoever does not believe is condemned already, because he has not believed in the name of the only Son of God." And, more gently, but still somehow threateningly: "Behold, I stand at the door, and knock: if any man hear my voice, and open the door, I will come in."

"Confess that you are a sinner, Ralph," said one, a tall, burly man who worked at a local car dealership. Until now I had always thought him a good-natured sort. "Do it now. Right here. Let Jesus into your heart." Part of me wanted to do it, but my silence persisted, almost as if it had a will of its own. "Ralph, don't put your soul at risk. You have this opportunity; there may never be another one. And if you leave here having refused Christ, then it will be all the worse for you. Some sins cannot be forgiven."

The voices went on, earnest and persuasive. Desperately, I kept my silence. I did not dispute with them or try to justify myself. I turned my heart into stony ground; their words could not reach me, or, if they did, I would not show it. At last, exasperated, they let me go, telling me they would pray for me.

"Go ahead," I said, in a voice that came out too high-pitched. But I allowed a slight tone of proud defiance to come into that voice. Outside, breathing deeply and treading lightly, I walked on the great bedrock path to my cabin under a brilliant starlit sky and the black shadows of the tall, sweet-smelling pine trees.

Less than two weeks later, my dad had his stroke.

CHAPTER 3:
MY FATHER, BELOVED ENEMY

At the time of that Red Rock inquisition, and for many years after, I never thought that my dad had anything to do with it. Only decades later did I form the notion that my father had put me, his youngest son, in the hands of my enemies. He was not there to protect my person, my integrity, against violation by that rabid pack of evangelizers. More: by proxy he had aligned himself with my adversaries, against me. He was one of them. Such a notion—"Dad was my enemy"—has never been spoken in our family. It goes against what we've been taught, and what we feel. In general, we children remember him fondly and respectfully.

By personal example, Dad showed us the spiritual path he hoped we would take. But when he allowed or encouraged others—always these others were indoctrinated men on the hunt for souls—to browbeat us into accepting a fundamentalist formula for personal salvation, he unintentionally set up a deep conflict. Each of us children handled the problem in our own way, and it happens that of the six of us, three became Bible-believing, church-going Christians, as Dad would have wished. But the other three, including me, did not. So we have a situation of insiders and outsiders.

I have lived my long life outside that fold, and cannot imagine that this will change in whatever time is left to me. But I have never been at peace with this situation, because it means that I am cast out, or have cast myself out. Mom and Dad are dead, but we children still play parts in their religious story. Whatever our differences, all of us siblings get together, and when we do, we exchange hugs and say, "I love you," sincerely. But unspoken religious differences are present, like ghosts behind the walls.

Dad wanted us to follow him in his faith journey, but much of the time he was absent, so far away that we could not see or hear him. How would we follow this invisible, inaudible man? He made it hard. I decided to write his story, make him real, see if I could get hold of him this way.

Why not write about Mom, why not equal time for her? I can only say that she was there and Dad wasn't. I looked for what was missing.

Around 1980, when my wife Hannah and our young children Nathan and Zea were living in a duplex in Windsor Park, Winnipeg, Mom gave me Dad's diaries. Perhaps none of my siblings wanted them, or perhaps she thought I would have the greatest interest. Her little apartment in Steinbach was crowded, and she was never one to hang on to stuff, except for shoeboxes of old greeting cards gathering dust under her bed.

The diaries, a pile of 4 x 6–inch black notebooks, written in Dad's neat, small hand with a fountain pen, spanned the years 1930 to 1950. The entries were short and matter-of-fact, describing events and their time and place. I was disappointed not to find more personal revelations, emotions, and reflections. At the same time I was gratified, as the words allowed me partial entry into decades of my dad's life of which I knew almost nothing.

Dad's diary, 1930.

Over the years I interviewed people who had known Dad, and made notes. I found other notebooks of his, and a few letters. I visited church archives, locating minutes of ministerial meetings he had written. I collected pictures of him. After Mom died, I collected her diaries and letters, too.

Dad's writings include those he produced after his stroke. He copied several years of the diaries into my brother Norman's old coil-backed science scribblers. He also wrote new material in a 6 x 8–inch lined notebook. It was a good thing the notebook was lined. When he wrote letters on unlined paper the sentences tended to travel upwards or downwards on a comically steep slant. This was the same man who bought my aunt Marie a bread knife with a metal guide on it to help her cut slices evenly.

For a long time I did nothing with those post-stroke notes and letters, discounting them as the muddled meanderings of an unsound mind. But I kept them, and now I have incorporated them. My father was still my father after his stroke. For a long time I did not accept this simple state-ment. But now I do, and from this acceptance a new perspective emerges.

Dad hardly ever told stories of himself. Prior to his stroke most of his communication was in the form of giving orders. Usually he had a task for us. He was not harsh about it, but his way with us was hardly ever personal. So we grew up not knowing much about him, and thinking this was normal. We didn't think of our lack of knowledge as a deficit, really. Like the disused barn in our backyard, left over from our grandparents' time, it was just part of the environment we lived in and did not question.

After we had all left home, though, I found myself wondering about Dad and his untold life. I recognized a dim pain in my ignorance of him, in my not-knowing, in his absence from my life. Had it always been there, this Dad-shaped hole in my heart, to paraphrase Pascal's famous words about spiritual yearning? I carried this question within me; it ebbed and flowed with its own rhythm but never went away. Quite often, Dad appeared in my dreams.

As I read the diaries some of the void began to fill in. And now, when I am well past the age he reached—he died in 1966 at age sixty-three—I have written his story. I know him better now and I don't wait for him to answer my questions anymore. I have formulated my own answers.

I have written my story, too, insofar as it intersects with his. This account is about him, primarily, but it is also about me and my relationship with him, which continues now, long after his death. I have taken hold of him, and like Jacob wrestling with the angel until dawn, I have refused to release him until I receive a blessing.

Would Dad give his blessing to this account, if he could read it? I have tried to be faithful in giving it, both to him and myself. I have a dilemma, having sharply differed from him in the part of life that mattered most to him. Religion bound us together, and kept us apart. Maybe my revelations here would make him sad or angry. He valued unity, as do I, and I would love to be *einig*—it is the German word for united, agreed, reconciled, that comes to me—with him. But I cannot force the issue; I can only try to speak truth and receive whatever blessing comes from that. As it is, I feel closer to him now than when he was alive. Maybe even God cannot sepa-rate us.

Chapter 4:
The village of Steinbach

When my great-grandparents arrived at the site of their settlement in September of 1874, they found flat prairie with low, swampy areas, stands of poplar, and surrounding ranges of boreal forest. This land was part of the so-called East Reserve in Manitoba, set aside by the Dominion government specifically for immigrant Mennonites. The reserve was comprised of eight townships or about 18,000 acres east of the Red River and south of Winnipeg. Only a few years before, it had been part of the territory of Ojibway and Cree people, who, under pressure of the coming inflow of settlers, had signed a treaty giving up their claim.

The settlers—eighteen families altogether—immediately set about to create a replica of the arrangement they knew from the steppes of South Russia from whence they had come. They made a long main street, with individual dwellings and gardens on one side and long, narrow fields on the other. The street itself was at first a concept rather than a reality; it had to be hacked out of the poplar bush with Hudson's Bay Company axes purchased in Winnipeg. Trees grew so thick that the settlers had to lead their oxen, as there was not enough room to walk beside them. A buffalo trail ran alongside a creek on the east side of the street, and while the bison no longer passed through, Indigenous people still used the trail in the early years. Along the creek banks a blaze of wild flowers bloomed in various colours from spring to summer to fall.

The men cut into the virgin earth with ploughs. The women gave birth and cared for large families. The people endured long, deep-frozen winters and short summers with thick plagues of mosquitoes. But hardship was expected. To complain was to show weakness in your faith.

They called this place "Steinbach," meaning "stony brook," not just because of the creek, but also because that had been the name of their village in South Russia.

By the turn of the century, industrious villagers had drained off most of the swamps and sloughs, and had cleared much of the land, on which they grew wheat, barley, oats and potatoes. In the winter, many of the men camped in the surrounding woodland, cutting trees and bringing them back to the village for firewood or building material.

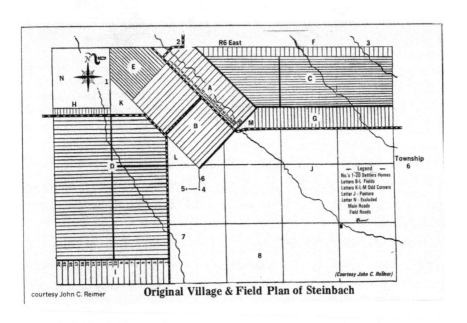

courtesy John C. Reimer   **Original Village & Field Plan of Steinbach**

\#

The Friesen homestead was near the centre of the village. Here my great-grandfather, Abraham S. Friesen, built a machine shop and woodworks factory set back maybe 100 metres from Main Street. My grandfather was put in charge of the machine shop, and in 1897 built a square wood-frame two-storey house, facing the street. The house, on a yard lined by maple trees planted by Great-grandfather, inserted itself confidently into the vast space of open prairie. It was simple, but a far cry from the earthen sod houses most settlers had built in 1874. In this house, on September 9, 1902, my father was born.

The Friesen estate, circa 1903. The dark building in the background houses the machine works and woodworks; the building to the right front is great-uncle J. R. Friesen's implement shop. It may also have housed great-uncle A. R. Friesen's general store, as the sign at the front clearly reads "Post Office," and he was the postmaster.

He was a small, weak thing, with doubtful prospects. His mother's sister Elisabeth looked at the frail infant and wondered aloud if he would survive. On a return visit a little later, she said, "I can hardly believe that he is still alive."

Waves of epidemics—diphtheria, scarlet fever, and croup or whooping cough—had struck the East Reserve with terrible force in the twenty-year period 1882 to 1902. From March to July, 1884, seventy deaths were recorded, almost all of them of infants and young children. During the winter of 1894 many local children became ill with scarlet fever. Two little daughters of Dad's great-uncle Klaas R. Reimer died and were buried in a single coffin. More than a hundred children died of whooping cough in 1900, literally choking to death.

Almost all Mennonite families were large, because children were needed to help make a livelihood. The death of little children was not necessarily thought of as a tragedy; it was simply how things were, how God had ordained it. But Dad escaped epidemics and survived childhood diseases. Later he commented: "The Lord saw fit that I should grow up and enjoy a fairly happy normal childhood among brothers & sisters."

"The Lord" was the God of the Mennonites, the God of the Bible, who had a purpose for every human being, and determined which ones would live, and which not. Dad's life was in God's hands, and God saw fit to spare him. God would have uses for this frail child.

Dad learned at an early age to obey his parents and do chores, with only brief opportunities for play. I think of him as shy and eager to please. But not without spirit: he learned to assert himself enough to make his mark.

His parents named him Peter—a biblical name very common among the Mennonites, and also the name of uncles on both sides of the family. There were four children ahead of him—Abraham, Nick, Johann, and Elisabeth, the first his elder by six years and the last by just seventeen months. Growing up, I knew of Uncle Abe and Uncle Nick; these were people we went to visit, or who came to visit us. Dad never mentioned an Uncle Johann or an Aunt Elisabeth. I only found out about their existence much later, when researching family history.

Their father, my grandfather Klaas R. Friesen, was in his early thirties at the time Dad was born, and in the midst of a busy and productive phase of his life. He invented and manufactured straw blowers, a labour-saving device which farmers could fit onto their threshing machines. His list of inventions included a bee-keeping container and a "gumming machine" for sharpening the large circular saws used in the lumber camps in the area. Although he had quit school at age twelve, he eventually acquired a steam engineer's certificate, and was widely recognized for his problem-solving abilities.

A photograph of the Friesen Machine Shop yard, taken in 1907 or so, shows the giant Case and Abell steam engine tractors and threshing machines brought there for repair. Grandfather rests his elbow casually against one of these massive machines. To the left, three men stand at the controls of a Case engine. One, wearing a broad-brimmed hat (it is probably Great-grandfather), pulls a handle, releasing a cloud of steam and a high-pitched blast of the whistle. In front of Grandfather is a triangle of barefoot boys; these must surely be his sons. The boy at the front wears too-short pants, a tight jacket, and a dark hat perched on the back of his head, leaving his blond bangs visible. His facial expression, so far as it can be made out, is composed and serious. I believe this child is my father.

The boys are straight-backed, arms clamped to their sides, standing at attention as befits the status of their father's enterprise in driving the village economy. They are not just farm boys; they are sons of a respected inventor and repair expert, situated near the centre of the village of which their grandfather had been the first mayor. They are familiar with the scream of steam engine whistles and the loud banging of hammers repairing steel drums. They know the smell of oil, of burning firewood, of fresh hay for the cow in the barn. And, in the house, the aroma of *Tweeback* newly out of the oven, or the stink of urine in the *Nachttopp* that has to be carried away and dumped out. They stink themselves, without being aware of it. Every Saturday they bathe and ready themselves for the long church services the next day.

Friesen Machine Shop yard, circa 1907.

Dad's mother Helena was a daughter of the *Aeltester*, or bishop, Abraham L. Dueck and Elisabeth Rempel Dueck, who had settled in Kleefeld, a village a few miles west of Steinbach. Helena's marriage to Grandfather would have been seen as suitable, as both families had traditions of church leadership dating back to Russia. The Duecks had a quiet temperament and the women seemed to fit unprotestingly into their assigned roles, and Grandmother was like that too.

The church had always favoured farming as the ideal occupation of a Christian, and some vestiges of farm life persisted in the Friesen household. A barn and some small outbuildings stood in the backyard, and the family kept chickens, a few pigs, and one cow. Grandmother also tended a large garden.

Dad grew up surrounded by relatives. Across the street from his father's house and shop lived his uncle, the tinsmith Klaas Brandt. Mrs. Brandt, Dad's aunt Helen, was a seamstress and ran a café for some years. She was a no-nonsense woman who taught her children and her nephews and nieces to strive, persevere, and avoid slacking. When she set Dad's dislocated finger when he was a young man, he fainted because of the pain.

An uncle, Peter R. Friesen, began as a business partner to Grandfather before branching out on his own. He moved to the U.S. and back with his family, and was mayor of Steinbach for a few years. Less conservative than Grandfather, he cut an elegant figure in his bowler hat, waistcoat with watch chain, and carefully trimmed beard. His daughters sought to become more educated than prescribed by the community norm.

On Friesen Avenue, named after Dad's grandparents, lived his aunt Elisabeth, wife of John D. Goossen, the secretary-treasurer of the municipality. Aunt Elisabeth was a passionate reader and a bit of a snob who considered her family to be superior to that of her eldest brother Abe, who moved away from Steinbach when Dad was just a boy, and fathered a family of eleven. The Goossen boys joined the armed forces in World War II, despite their parents' objections. Two would become engineers, the other a lawyer. One of the girls would get her PhD degree—the first woman from Steinbach to do so.

A block down Main Street another uncle, Jacob R. Friesen, ran a farm implement shop. In 1910 Jacob bought a car, one of the first in Steinbach.

The church, worried that the car would lead to worldly pride, threatened him with excommunication. He did not repent, and simply distanced himself from church life. Soon he established a garage and the first Ford car dealership west of Winnipeg. He was something of an intimidating man with a wry sense of humour and a love of travel. One of his sons would become the first person born in Steinbach to earn a medical degree.

One of the first factory-built cars to navigate Steinbach's streets or trails was this 1912 or 1913 Ford owned by A. A. Reimer. Mr. Reimer is at the wheel with Isaac T. Loewen in the front seat. The man at left in the rear is Jacob Schmidt. In the centre is J. R. Friesen and at right is P. S. Rempel.

Credit: Carillon News.

The extended Friesen family was not an easygoing lot. They were ambitious and possessed of a quiet pride, and carried an impression of themselves as a leading family in Steinbach. In them, Dad had plenty of role models for achievement, whether in business or education or in some profession.

As a seven-year-old, Dad wrote a Christmas wish to his parents in neat, well-formed German script. He promised to be a good, hardworking child and always to love and never disappoint his parents so that he might be worthy of heaven. He signed off as "your thankful son, Peter D. Friesen." Such pledges and wishes were common at the time, written proof that the child was committed to the right path. This signature, with the middle initial identifying him as the child of a mother whose surname was Dueck, he was to use all his life, with little variation.

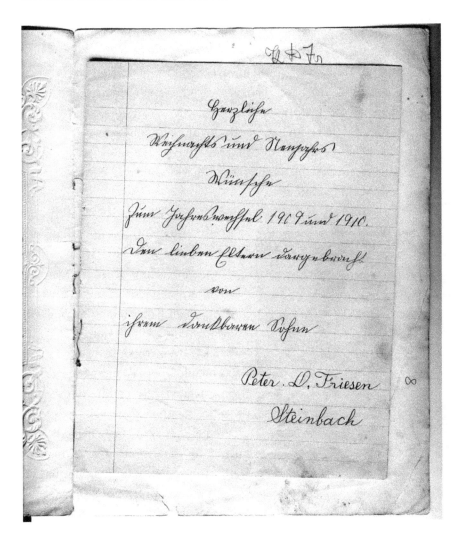

On his mother's side, Dad's grandparents died before he was born, so he never knew them. But he knew his paternal grandparents, and he loved this grandmother, Katharina. She and her husband lived on a farm in the Clearsprings area, just north of the village, where she grew lavish beds of peonies and looked after her large garden. In 1910 they moved back to

Steinbach to "a neat little house on Friesen Avenue" just down the street from Friesen Machine Shop. Dad had fond memories of staying there:

> When my parents left for a few days to visit my mother's relatives, my brother and I usually spent the time with our grandparents, which was always the most interesting and best experience of our young lives. Whenever Grandfather had to use a firm hand with rowdy youngsters, then Grandmother's loving, gentle manner usually prevailed on behalf of her grandchildren. She was the best, most loving, most sympathetic person that we had ever known or could imagine.

Dad's grandmother, Katharina Reimer Friesen.

Dad also judged his grandmother's fried potatoes to be "the best I've ever eaten, before or after." For this her grandsons loved her, and for saving them from spankings. She was "sympathetic"—the word suggests that she took time to listen to her grandchildren, in an era which generally dictated that children were not mature enough to have valid opinions. Perhaps her kindness helped Dad learn to value himself as a person, and, later, to dare to imagine that he had a special contribution to make.

#

The Friesen family, like most of Steinbach's population, were members of the Mennonite Kleine Gemeinde ("small church")—so called because it had broken away from the larger Mennonite community in South Russia in 1812, seeking greater purity of life and separation from worldly practices.

Practically the entire *Gemeinde* had traversed the Atlantic. They uprooted themselves because Canada promised them religious freedom, which they felt was endangered in Russia. They placed peace at the centre of their faith, believing that Christians should practise non-resistance even in the face of violence and warfare. They absolutely did not want to join the military. Eight hundred people settled in villages in southern Manitoba, while another thirty-six families went to Jansen, Nebraska.

In Steinbach, everyone knew everyone else, and most were related to each other. The 1901 census showed the population to be 366, most of these representing the original settler families and their descendants, although some Lutheran immigrants had by then found their way into the community. Almost everyone spoke Low German, with only a minority fluent in English. The village was almost medieval in that so much was prescribed, "given," according to the long-practised religion and culture of the people. There were rules, written or unwritten, for everything. It was as if the village had its own superego.

Preachers hammered at the importance of simplicity and humility. Houses, furniture, and dress, especially women's dress, were supposed to be plain. In the church, the men would meet on a regular basis to discuss problems amongst the membership. This arrangement was called *Bruderschaft*, or "brotherhood." Women did not attend such meetings, but could try to influence decisions through their husbands.

When innovations like the telephone, bicycles, or cars were introduced—this all happened in Dad's childhood—conservative elements in the community strongly opposed them. Even window curtains were condemned as too ostentatious. Violators of such prohibitions were subject to church discipline. Grandfather sometimes pushed the edges of prescribed behaviour; when he built the family home, the church reprimanded him for making the trim

Grandfather's excesses: window trim, chimney brickwork.

on the windows and the brickwork on the chimney unnecessarily decorative. By then it was too late for changes, though.

Every morning the village cowherd alerted people with blasts from his battered bugle as he gathered the cows from each family's lot and herded them down to the common pasture at the north end of Main Street.

Everything was arranged to support farming, the godliest livelihood. But an irrepressible entrepreneurial spirit flourished. In 1894, a visiting German-language reporter from Winnipeg marvelled at the village's industry, comparing Steinbach to "a small factory town with its smokestacks and the blowing and humming of steam boilers." He could have been describing the Friesen machine and woodworks business.

The village also boasted a flour mill, tannery, saddlery, cheese factory, several general stores, and a couple of guest houses. It lacked a doctor or dentist. Such services had to be provided by local amateur bonesetters, or *Trajchtmoaka*.

Main Street now was a broad, often muddy expanse cut with wagon tracks in summer and sleigh trails in winter. The original gardens and trees and fences which had lined the street in the early years were soon replaced by false-front buildings typical of the Canadian prairies. Wooden sidewalks made it easier for pedestrians to make their way.

For many years the Kleine Gemeinde had used the village school as a meeting house for their church services. In 1911 they erected a new church building at the south end of the village. Men and boys entered at one end of the church, and women and girls at the other, and inside, this division was maintained, with the males on the left side of the pulpit and the females on the right. The pulpit sat on a long platform on one side of the church, and at the beginning of Sunday services, an array of ministers and song leaders waited in an assembly room until the leading minister had given his formal greeting to the congregation: *Der Friede des Herrn sei mit euch allen* (may the peace of the Lord be with you all). Then they took their seats on the platform and the two-hour service began with slow singing of many verses of a hymn. As a child, in the days before Sunday school was introduced, Dad and his siblings would have had to sit through this exercise on hard, backless wooden benches.

After his stroke, Dad wrote down one story of his growing-up years. The Friesens were next-door neighbours to the village blacksmith Heinrich Kreutzer. Kreutzer was fast and efficient at his job, with a special gift for working with horses, and sometimes Dad would watch him at work:

When the horses were to have their teeth filed, a kind of form or brace was placed into the horse's mouth, forcing it to hold its mouth open, and then, using a file with a long handle, the teeth were given a vigorous working over. Then I usually had to throw up; it looked so disagreeable to me. Often, when Mr. Kreutzer set the sharp nail, ready to hammer it into the horse's hoof, I cried out in sympathy.

My soft-hearted father! We had no animals around our place when I was young, except for a cat whose job was to keep mice out of the house, and I don't remember seeing Dad handling any animal. I did not know he had compassion for them.

CHAPTER 5:
DISORDER AND
EARLY SORROW

What does a child know of death? My brother Don once held a solemn funeral for a neighbourhood dog, burying it in a shoebox in the garden. My older siblings remember Grandfather's open coffin in the kitchen, supported by chairs at either end. The child buries the dog-corpse, or smells the strange stink of the thing that once was Grandfather, and understands that the body is there but the person is not.

But to think that such a thing should ever happen to us—we may circle around the edges of such a thought, and then reject it. I remember an ordinary summer's day of my boyhood when I looked out on our yard, the robin on the fence, the serrated veiny leaves of the crabapple tree, and my own shadow on the dusty green grass, and I was struck with the realization that there was only one of me. "There's only one of me," I whispered. It was marvellous. I was me, and no one else. I knew that my uniqueness was contained or expressed in my physical being, and I knew that everybody dies.

Death broke into our house very suddenly one beautiful Saturday morning in early October, 1955, when I was ten. Mom and Dad came home with Aunt Marie, Mom's younger sister. My aunt uttered great, heartbreaking sobs as my parents led her through the kitchen, supporting her between them. She cried loudly, deeply, a sound I had never heard an adult make before. I was transfixed. At first I did not know why she was crying, and when I was told, the story seemed incredible to me. My uncle Jake was dead, of a heart attack.

That summer I had been at his farm, and he had taken the *Free Press* coloured comics away from me because they were sinful. That was how he was, strict. And healthy. I could hardly grasp that he was dead now, but the current of my aunt's great grief passed into my body, and I knew then that death was a real thing that could come very near, even if I was not ready to admit that it could ever come for me or my parents or siblings.

#

My father could have educated me on the subject from his own experience. The course of what he calls a fairly happy and normal childhood was interrupted when he was nine. His brother Johann, who was three years older with a birthday just two days after Dad's, suddenly fell sick with what Grandfather called "an inflammation of the brain"—probably meningitis. As Grandfather describes it in his journal:

> He had great pain in his head, neck and back. He was sick about a week. It began with an ear ache and progressed more into his head. A few days before his death he sang a good deal. Among others, he sang "The Great Physician Now Is Near" and "The Blessed Dear Jesus" . . . for us it was a blessing that he had sung such beautiful songs. And then after a few days he peacefully passed out of this world into eternity. So we hope that, before his demise, his soul remained preserved from harm. May God grant this through Jesus Christ. Amen!

Dad and his siblings watched helplessly in that week of Johann's dying, and learned that their parents were also helpless.

But he sang, my "uncle" Johann, though apparently out of his head, and from this my grandparents took a blessing. His headstone was engraved, in English: "John, Son of Klaas R. & Helena Friesen: The Lord is Thy Keeper." In death Johann had become anglicized to John, as if in anticipation of the more assimilated culture that was developing in the village.

They trusted that his soul "remained preserved from harm": it was the Kleine Gemeinde way of showing an attitude of humility, as we are not to assume or take for granted our own salvation. That is for God to decide. We can only hope.

Dad likely thought of his brother as somehow "held," after his passing, by the Lord. The church at that time did not teach that people, even if they had lived a virtuous life and confessed their faith, were transported immediately to heaven when they died. Rather, all souls had to wait until the resurrection, and the resurrection would not occur until the Second Coming of Christ, when Jesus, sitting on his throne, would judge each soul, determining its eternal fate.

My father as a young boy would not have had much of this mystery worked out in his mind—even the adults thought it best not to try to be too precise about such things. But in his nine-year-old understanding, Dad would surely have been struck by the permanency of death. His next older brother, whom he had known all his life, was gone forever, passed into *Ewigkeit*, eternity.

This photograph comes from my dad's album. I have the intuition that the boy in the centre is Dad, in which case Johann would be the boy on the far right. I cannot identify the girls.

The next year, Dad's beloved grandmother Katharina died. She had been sickly over the years with what was called "a weak heart." In August of 1912 she became very ill and within four days she died. She was buried in the cemetery in the centre of the village, beside her grandson Johann.

#

Together with his siblings, Dad went to school, and liked it. At age ten, very likely encouraged by his teacher, he wrote a letter to a Mennonite publication based in Scottdale, Pennsylvania, called *Der Christliche Familienfreund*:

> March 22, 1913: Dear Editor and Readers: I will try to write a couple of lines. I am very well, and wish the same for you. I go to school. My teacher's name is Bernhard S. Rempel. He is a good teacher. I am ten years old. The school is half a mile from my home. There are 32 children in our school. We have very nice sleighs here. With another greeting, Peter D. Friesen.

The cheerfulness in Dad's little letter may well have been inherited from his mother, Helena. On the whole, she was very much a woman in the background, but from the few clues that do exist, a portrait emerges. She was devoted to her husband and children, and her neighbours liked her. Her nephew Isaac Plett depicts her as a steady, pleasant person:

> I lived with Uncle and Aunt Klaas Friesen for two years, and Aunt Helena treated me as one of the family. One day was like the next, and it seemed that all of us became so used to her happy, sunny nature, that we took it for granted. . . she was sometimes called *die Gutmütige* [the cheerful one] perhaps because her natural character was expressed somewhat more in the superficial.

Grandmother provided a stable, positive home environment for her children, despite all the duties of housework and child care that fell upon her. For years one day might have been like the next, but then everything changed, very suddenly. Grandmother, who had enjoyed good health most of her life, became very ill after a quiet evening at home with her husband. On May 27, 1914, they went to bed as usual, but suddenly, after midnight, Grandmother sat up, struggling for breath. She had had a similar attack a few months prior, but this one was much more severe. She told her husband that she would die this time. He got up immediately, lit the lamp, and said: "If you have to die now, do firmly hold onto Jesus who is our loving Saviour." He asked her if she could believe and hope that the Saviour had died for her. She repeated, "I believe that the beloved Saviour died for me." In less than a quarter of an hour, she was dead of heart failure. She was thirty-seven.

The children, having been awakened by their father, witnessed her passing. There were nine of them: Abraham, 18; Klaas (Nick), 16; Elisabeth, 13; Peter (my father), 11; Henry, 9; Jacob, 7; Catherine, 6; Helen, 4; and Bernhard, 2. They gathered around in silence, looking upon the source of their own being as the warmth left her still body. Probably Elisabeth held little Bernhard in her arms. Helena had died with words of faith on her lips. But how could the children understand? Even their father's faith was challenged:

> What should I now do? I could not do anything, nor could I readily comprehend what really had taken place. Our happiness now was all gone. I had to drink the cup now, whether I wanted to or not; even though it was very bitter, there was no escape. Constantly it seemed to me that it was all a dream. But it was real.

Helena had been a constant and comforting presence in the family, but now, without warning or visible cause, her life was over. It had been lived, not for herself, but for others. With her sudden absence the family was thrown into a crisis.

For me, the phrase "disorder and early sorrow" captures the state of affairs of Dad's family then. It is the title of a novella by Thomas Mann— in German, *Unordnung und frühes Leid*. Actually, the travails of Mann's fictional bourgeois family in the Weimar Republic were light compared to the suffering of my ancestors on the great Canadian plains just before the First World War. The family struggled along with the help of relatives. Elisabeth, herself still a child, tried to fill the role of mother as best she could. The two eldest, Abe and Nick, spent a lot of time with the K. W. Brandt family, their aunt Helen. Grandfather's sister Elisabeth, Mrs. John D. Goossen, also helped care for the children. Grandfather would say, later: "People sometimes say they 'cried out' to God for help, and that's what I did."

He cried out to God, and then went back to work in the machine shop, where he could escape his grief and memories. He was at home in the shop and the machine yard, and his mind was most engaged and creative when he was inventing. Accomplished as he was, there was always a part of him that was not at home in the world. Like his brothers—and like his father, I suspect—he was emotionally distant from his children, and the losses he suffered only increased that distance.

Grandfather quickly became preoccupied with the problem of raising a large family while still having to make a living. The mourning process was cut short, but that would also have been the norm for the Mennonites of the time.

Nine months after Grandmother's death, Grandfather married Katharina Thiessen, aged thirty, from a farming family near Giroux, seven miles from Steinbach. Now the family again had a mother, and Grandfather a helpmeet. As an adult writing in his diary, Dad referred to Katharina as "Ma." But as an eleven-year-old, did he accept her as his mother? The children had to accept that their mother was dead, and this woman, though different, was the mother they would have. Circumstances required that everyone had to make accommodations, and so they did.

Katharina's family was strict in observing the Mennonite traditions of humility and separation from the world. She scolded her stepchildren and grandchildren by admonishing them: "*Ye mutte nich opp ludes lache.*" (You must not laugh out loud.) She was sometimes overwhelmed with the enormity of the task she had taken on. She had several children with Grandfather; of these, all but one died in early childhood. She too took lessons in the school of sorrow.

What I did not know until I started to research family history was that Grandfather had been married before he married our grandmother. This first marriage was to Katharina Janzen of the neighbouring village of Blumenort. It ended after little more than a year in February, 1894, when Katharina died of "childbed fever," known clinically as puerperal fever. She had given birth to a girl also named Katharina, who died nineteen days after she was born. Grandfather, only in his twenties then, was brought low with grief: "Oh, how I, poor soul, then wished to be redeemed from this earth (*von dieser Erde erlöst zu werden*)". Who speaks this way today? That generation of Mennonites believed that this earth was not our home, and we should not become overly attached to it.

Dad never told us about his father's first wife. For that matter, he was also silent about his own mother. It wasn't as if he had no sense of family history; he was an active participant in the large reunions of the Reimer family (his paternal grandmother) and the Dueck family (his mother), and after his stroke he made a chart of his Friesen ancestors, and closely studied his father's memoir book from which the above account is taken.

At the age of twenty-eight, Dad made a simple entry in his diary: "On Thursday it was 17 years ago since our mother died." Did he miss her, then? In the diary he did not speak of his thoughts or feelings, or of how he was affected by this stunning loss. He never spoke of it to us, his children, either. We had no knowledge whatsoever of the life and personality of our grandmother. The pictures of the grandmother enclosed in rarely opened black photo albums were of Katharina Thiessen. For a long time I thought she was my grandmother. Of Helena, no picture exists. Did Dad, in the last years of his life, the last days, or hours, remember his mother's face?

Dad's silence, I believe, was a symptom of incomplete mourning. We children had a grandmother but in our consciousness she did not exist. Dad must have grieved her loss, privately. But it would have helped us if he had shared his experience. Our family has a history of wrenching loss. I do not think we have fully acknowledged it or come to terms with it.

#

A few months after Grandmother's death, in August, 1914, the First World War commenced. Dad, like other Steinbach children, would have been largely ignorant of the causes and events of this distant conflict, but he would certainly have known that a war was going on in Europe. He might even have been aware that English Canada regarded German-speaking communities like Steinbach with suspicion.

Dad was a pupil in Steinbach's private school, begun as a conservative alternative to the government-funded public school, and located in the house-barn of well-off farmer Franz M. Kroeker at the south end of Main Street. The school was funded by local men, mostly Kleine Gemeinde, including Grandfather.

Although the community valued basic literacy, so you could read the Bible and bills of lading; and numeracy, so you could make sure you weren't being shortchanged, it did not really trust education. Parents sent their children to school—but only to the point where the child had acquired the basics. Then he or she was pulled back into the family's labour pool.

At the private school the children sat on long wooden benches with rough desks attached, girls on one side of the classroom and boys on the other. The curriculum was close to that of the local public school, with more emphasis on German, though some instruction was in English.

At Easter, Dad and his fellow pupils received a greeting card, a "present" from their teacher Bernhard Rempel. The card is a study in contradictions. It depicts a doll-like little girl with her arm around her pug, seated on a lawn amongst cherry blossoms, smiling dreamily. A Psalm is stamped above the picture: "*Der Herr behütet alle, die ihn lieben*"—"The Lord preserveth all them that love him." The image could hardly be further removed from the gritty everyday realities of the little Mennonites in

Rempel's class; it introduces an "English" ideal, legitimized by a familiar Bible verse. By such subtle and unsuspected means, the "world" made small inroads into Steinbach.

The second part of the Psalm—"but all the wicked will he destroy"—was discreetly excluded.

Dad's friend and later ministerial colleague Peter J. B. Reimer had fond recollections of their time in primary school. Bernhard Rempel was "strict but also loving" and played ball with the boys at recess. Most of the teaching was in German and included Bible stories, Bible verses which had to be learned by heart, and the Mennonite catechism. Rempel, a good singer, taught the children hymns according to the "numbers" system, without notes. In the afternoons, instruction was given in English, and calligraphy was taught in both languages. No Low German was allowed.

Dad responded at some deep level to Rempel's music instruction. This and the training in formal German helped him later when he became a church minister.

In a class picture taken in 1915, the children stand in orderly rows on the grass outside the building, with the teacher off to the left. The older boys are in the back row, Dad the fifth from the left, distinguished from the others by being much the smallest. His features are not clearly discernible; he might be smiling or not. His blond, straight hair hangs over his forehead. He leans forward ever so slightly, as if under an invisible weight.

Credit: *Mennonite Memories: Settling in Western Canada,*
Lawrence Klippenstein and Julius G. Toews, eds (Winnipeg: Centennial Publications, 1977).

Soon after, Dad left school to help with the chores at home. Increasingly, Steinbach, now with a population approaching 500, was assuming all the characteristics of a town, but one not far removed from its rural origins. Grandfather copied out a kind of work schedule for his sons, in rhyming doggerel form, in which he instructed Dad—now fifteen—to mix the crushed grain in the hog barn, make the cow a manger for its feed, and split firewood with his brother Abraham. The boys were charged to perform such tasks with a spirit of obedience and good will, learning at the same time that their value to family and community lay in useful, practical work. Hard work was a necessity not just for survival, but also for salvation; it was part of their religion.

After he was out of school Dad maintained a friendship with his former teacher, and this connection was preserved over time. Many years later Dad visited Bernhard Rempel on a visit to Kansas.

As the war dragged on and more and more young men were slaughtered, English Canada's suspicion turned to outright anger, especially toward immigrant communities who claimed exemption from carrying arms on the grounds of religious conviction. The Dominion government required all Canadians from ages sixteen to sixty-five to sign a registration card "for the national purposes"—which, for young men, meant either military service or conscientious objection. Dad registered just after he turned sixteen in September, 1918, but the war ended two months later and so nothing was required of him. When twenty-five Canadian soldiers appeared in Steinbach, seeking to press young men into military service, Dad was presumably grateful that he had a registration card to show.

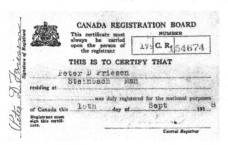

Although hardly any Steinbach Mennonites ended up serving in the military, the war nevertheless brought about changes, alerting church elders to the renewed importance of teaching the core tenet of non-resistance to young people, and also giving impetus to the use of English. For a time the *Steinbach Post* was required to publish in English, and some local citizens publicly called for more English-language teaching. Dad would become adept in the English language, but held on to his belief in non-resistance.

Meanwhile, Grandfather was elected a minister of the Manitoba Kleine Gemeinde in February, 1918—even more responsibility for a man who keenly felt that he already had too much to carry. For his children it meant that their father, who had had little time for them before, now would have even less.

In the fall of 1918 the world-wide Spanish flu pandemic reached Steinbach. Grandfather became sick and "completely confined to bed." Dad's sister Elisabeth, who volunteered in Steinbach's makeshift hospital, also got sick, and after a ten-day illness, died on November 20. She had been a little mother to the younger children; now, still just a teenager, she followed her own mother in death. Her stepmother's parents sent a letter of sympathy, quoting a number of Bible verses on the transitory nature of this life. "God tests us," they wrote, "so that we may see that we should put the world at a greater distance."

Dad's sister Elisabeth.

Grandfather agreed. More than once in his memoirs he quotes Hebrews 12:6: "For whom the Lord loveth he chasteneth, and scourgeth every son whom he receiveth." He felt that he had a tendency to become lax in his Christian walk, "and exactly for this reason the dear heavenly Father sometimes sends us a new cross to bear." On the other hand, "when one lays everything at the feet of Jesus and seeks consolation then this Jesus also has enough consolation for everyone who has surrendered himself to Him." In this way of thinking, we are scourged for our own good. If we accept our suffering as necessary correction, then everything can be borne. It is a matter of *Gelassenheit*, surrender.

How do you distinguish between attachment to the "world" and attachment to a person—especially if that person is your own child? Parents who know that the child could easily be lost to them through illness or accident might tend to hold back from expressing their love.

Grandfather, already wounded from the death of his first wife and first child (1894), his son Johann (1911), his mother (1912), his second wife (1914), and a new-born girl of his third marriage (1916), by now had plenty of practice in restraining himself from becoming overly attached. In his memoir he says nothing about his sorrow over Elisabeth's death; he is primarily concerned for himself, as he was left with no female to do the housework and child care.

Dad, growing up, continued to witness loss after loss—in 1919 his step-mother gave birth to a son who died half a year later, followed by stillborn boys in 1924 and 1926. Another boy, again named Johann, died at age

Grandfather and second wife Katharina, 1930. In the middle is their daughter Greta.

twelve in 1929. Of six children born to Katharina, only one, her daughter Margaretha, born in 1921, survived—and she had to contend with a congenital hip defect for which her parents ineffectually sought treatment all through her childhood.

Grandfather almost allowed himself to wonder about the divine plan that included all this loss and sorrow: "One could ask the question why it should happen this way?" Then he retreated behind the familiar submissive answer: "God's ways are not our ways." He went on to say: "Each time we received a child, that was in part a joy, yet in looking back, in view of the fact that the world is so seductive, we always had apprehensions, that the child would lose itself in this enticing world."

Such a tentative embrace of relationship life! Almost a rejection of it. Grandfather could more easily embrace his work world. He loved his work all his life, and his religion allowed him this attachment with very few limits. His work, even more than his religion, he could always have with him; it would not leave him nor forsake him.

How much of his father's attitude did my father inherit? He carried the legacy of childhood loss wordlessly, and perhaps did not even think about it much. Probably his religious faith helped him in that way. Nor did he ever have to contend with the loss of a spouse or children. But he seems to have replicated his father's strategy of distancing himself from his children. He too immersed himself in work.

CHAPTER 6:
TURNING FATE INTO DESTINY

There is a picture of Dad reading *Lone Scout* magazine—identifiable as such because someone, probably he himself, has penned the words on the photograph. The Lone Scouts were formed as a kind of outreach to boys in rural areas where Boy Scout troops might not exist. "Lone" would prove to be a theme in Dad's life, even though he was a member of a big family and took full part in his community.

Dad is wearing a suit and tie and a flat "newsboy" cap in the style of the time. He is perhaps fifteen or sixteen, a little old to be a Scout, but the surprise is that he even has a copy of the magazine, as his parents would certainly have viewed the Scouts as a paramilitary organization whose very existence ran counter to their pacifist beliefs.

The picture intrigued me when I came across it because it seemed to illustrate that in his youth Dad had experimented with the very activities he had forbidden to his children. When I was a boy our neighbour, Earl Kreutzer, joined the Boy Scouts. Sometimes he would wear his uniform with its nifty neckerchief and tell stories of the marvellous camping trips he went on, and I felt envious and wanted these things, too. I asked my parents, who gave me a categorical "no." The Boy Scouts wore uniforms, like the army, and in our family we did not join the army. It was a sin to kill another human being. I pointed out that Boy Scouts did not kill anyone, but this objection was brushed aside.

The prescribed reading for Dad would have been the Bible and possibly the *Steinbach Post*, but even in his late twenties he had a penchant for Zane Grey's novels of the rugged Wild West. His good friend and neighbour Henry Kreutzer—one of Earl's uncles—loved reading as well. When they were teenagers, Henry would come over to the Friesen household and on cold days the two boys would get into bed, pull the covers up to their chests, and read together. They hardly spoke. After a while Henry would go home.

I too loved reading as a young boy in grade school, especially comic books and adventure stories, which Dad tolerated even though the church frowned upon such materials. Once I accompanied him on one of his business trips to Winnipeg. It was just the two of us, a rare event. He dropped me at the Goodwill Store on Princess Street and left me to forage amongst the rows of used books. My eyes ranged along the shelves, hoping to find something by my brother Vern's literary heroes, Edgar Rice Burroughs or James Oliver Curwood. There were thousands of books, not arranged in any system that I could figure out, and I searched aimlessly for a while. Finally a title caught my eye: *The Devil to Pay*. The author was Ellery Queen. Strange name, I thought. And an intriguing title. The devil to pay . . . maybe it was a story of someone who had committed the unforgivable sin? I was a bit frightened, but drawn in. Who was the devil, and how would he be depicted? But would Dad let me keep such a book? I took it to the counter and paid my fifteen cents, figuring I would come up with something if Dad asked questions. Sure enough, when he came to pick me up he wanted to know the title of the book I'd bought. I felt a small surge of panic. He would surely disapprove. But I had no choice; the book was in my hand and the title was clearly printed in dull black on the red board cover. "*The Devil to Pay*," I said, adding quickly: "But it isn't about the devil." I didn't know that; it was a desperate ruse. Dad raised a quizzical eyebrow. "Why does it have that title, then?" he asked. I confessed that I did not know, and for some reason he decided to let that pass. The book was mine.

I felt guilty during our quiet ride home—but not guilty enough to admit that I hadn't strictly told the truth. When I got home and eagerly opened the book, I was disappointed. The devil actually did not appear in the story anywhere. It was a crime mystery; the winding plot and adult themes quickly lost me, and I never finished it.

#

Dad, on right, sitting atop giant chimney manufactured by his father for the village flour mill, circa 1922.

In other photographs of his early manhood, Dad can be seen amidst the tractors brought in for repair at Friesen Machine, wearing overalls and boots and a cap. But he was not destined for machine work, for which some of his brothers had more talent in any event. He did have a knack for carpentry; at the Boys and Girls Club fair in the fall of 1919, he won third prize in the woodworking category.

Dad, centre front, with steam engine repair crew.

Steinbach continued to grow during the First World War. By this time businesses and private households had adopted a basic electrical supply and telephone system. Previously, houses were lit with oil lamps and candles and the streets were not lit at all. Those who ventured out were guided only by kerosene lamps or the light of the moon and stars. Now people began to travel less by horse and wagon, and more by car. The streets of the village were illuminated during the long winter evenings, and communication no longer depended solely on face-to-face encounters.

After the war, hopeful villagers kept starting new businesses. A list printed in the *Steinbach Post* includes a couple of watchmakers, a few barbers, a tailor, a butcher, another lumber yard, a print shop, a dealer in gramophones (a sign of the encroachment of the "world"), and, at last, a medical doctor. The Royal Bank of Canada opened a branch in Steinbach, merging with the previously established Northern Crown Bank. The larger enterprises employed increasing numbers of local men, who formed a new class of labourers, many of them heads of households who worked for low wages. The village was thriving, but even so, not everyone could find satisfactory employment, and some left to work in Winnipeg, or moved west.

Dad decided that he wanted to become a teacher. This was not a high-status job; pragmatic Mennonites compared it unfavourably to the productive work of farming or manufacturing. Nevertheless, at the age of seventeen, he returned to school. The private school had closed, so he now attended the district school, first taking a combination of Grade 7 and 8. He finished Grade 9 in May of 1921 with an average mark of 78, scoring in the 90s for arithmetic and geography. In the first term he was second in class, behind Henry Kreutzer.

He was breaking new ground. No other sibling in his family had gone beyond grade school. The June 1921 Canadian census listed Dad as living in the Klaas Friesen household. His profession—carpenter—is crossed out and replaced by "student." His siblings are listed as Klaas, Heinrich, Jacob, Katharina, Helena, Bernhard, Johann, and baby Margaret. (His eldest brother Abe was living elsewhere.)

Between work and school there was time for play, or horsing around: pictures show him jumping from a barn roof, doing handstands, and playing horseshoes with his brothers or friends. But he took his schooling seriously, with an eye to getting a profession. By the fall of 1922 he had enrolled at the Mennonite Collegiate Institute (MCI) in Gretna, a little border town on the west side of the Red River, 125 kilometres from Steinbach. Improbably, his conservative parents supported him in this; they hoped he would become a teacher. It may have been Dad's first extended stay away from home, and he declared he "liked it very much." MCI, under the principalship of Prussian-born Heinrich H. Ewert, taught the provincial curriculum with an emphasis on Christian education.

Friesens and friends getting a new perspective on their world.

While at MCI, Dad corresponded with friends and relatives. His cousin Catherine congratulated him on his English: "Your writing has improved." Neighbourhood friend Olga Kreutzer (Henry's sister), only eleven years old at the time, wrote from Steinbach to tell him that everyone at home was well. Precociously, in her haphazard spelling, she addressed him as "sugar candy sweat heart," wished him good night and ended with a friendly warning: "Don't let the Gretnas Girls bite you." Some of the girls at MCI were, in fact, quite striking, on the evidence of a class photo. Mixing German and English, Olga referred to him as "*uns* Minstrel"—evidently he was already known for his singing ability. His sister Margaret remembers Olga as a very good-looking, outgoing girl and speculates that Dad was probably "smitten" by her—presumably at some point five or six years later. Maybe that was why he kept the letter.

MCI students. Dad is at the back, second from left.

In September 1923, Dad turned twenty-one, which meant he had become *mündig*, or "of age." Accordingly, his father paid him his share of the estate allocated when his mother had died ten years earlier—$112, about $1500 in today's currency.

After a year at MCI he applied for a teaching position at the Mitchell School near Steinbach, but the district trustee informed him that the school board was continuing the incumbent teacher's permit—and there were no other vacancies. Still, his cousin Nick wrote a letter in 1924 referring to him as a schoolteacher. Apparently Dad had pointed out that Nick had omitted the middle "D" initial in his name. Inserting a middle initial was a common practice of the Mennonites because so many carried the same first and last names. A man took the first letter of his mother's maiden name—in Dad's case, "Dueck"—and this helped distinguish him from all the other males with the same name. It also added a touch of class.

Nick, who had enlisted in the U. S. militia, took offence at being corrected. He threatened fiercely to "settle it with you on the right way," adding: "I'd sure like to be in your class once, I'd sure raise the dickens. They don't have such things as male teachers here except one or two here and there. They're mostly all woman teachers." The bellicose cousin had a certain point; teaching was one of the few professions open to women at the time. Dad, however, wasn't the type for physical confrontations or blustering man-to-man competitiveness, which was beside the point anyway, as he did not become a teacher. But he greatly valued his time as a student at MCI. A decade later he and others braved a fierce winter snowstorm to travel to his former principal H. H. Ewert's funeral in Gretna.

By 1926 Dad was back in Steinbach. At an age where most of his cohorts would have been baptized, married, and working at a steady job, he was footloose. He was still not a church member, and without a wife or regular work.

#

Dad drifted for several years in his late twenties, working at odd jobs, mostly carpentry. He was short, tending toward portly—in a booklet he listed his height as 5'5½", weight 167, and collar size 16½. He was also handsome, with an affinity for three-piece suits in the style of an urban citizen to be taken seriously. Well, not suits in the plural, really; he had one, and in pictures of the time, he is almost always wearing it.

Off and on for a few years, he lived in Winnipeg. In the summer of 1928 he earned $700—a goodly sum—working in the city at a variety of jobs, mostly carpentry. Conservative religious people in Steinbach would not have approved; for them the city embodied all the temptations and follies of the world, which was Satan's domain. A young man living there, untethered to home and church, might well go astray. Sometimes Dad would stay with his brother Nick and sister-in-law Marie, and sometimes he would socialize with cousins who were also exploring urban delights.

In 1929 Dad's earnings dropped to $365. He dated different girls, and one female admirer sent him an Easter card:

> If I could be an Easter Egg
> Of red or white or blue
> I'd roll and roll this Easter Day
> Until I rolled to YOU.

In neat handwriting on the reverse side of the card is the following: "Peter my beloved. What are your thoughts these days. Why don't you ever try to come to me so we could have an enjoyable evening 'together'? From one 'Who'll' never forget you. 'Elmwood.'" Underneath, the writer drew a branch of green holly and red berries with the greeting: "A merry Xmas. 1929." The sender apparently was economizing or did not have a Christmas card at hand.

Who was "Elmwood"? Presumably, a young woman who lived in that working class part of Winnipeg. What had happened between her and Dad, that she could be so forward in her invitation, scarcely bothering to

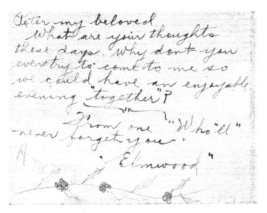

conceal her ardour? Why would she never forget Dad, and just how, exactly, had they ever been "together"? What sort of person was she, to substitute Christmas—no, Xmas—for Easter so casually, with a touch of Valentine's Day besides? Why did Dad keep the card after his marriage, so that it could be found by anyone going through his photographs and papers? All of these questions have only speculative answers, but there is something touching, even tantalizing, in the simple fact that he had some experience of romance before becoming our father. He could have made choices other than Mom.

In the sermon notes Dad wrote much later, he laments: "So often our senses are our undoing. Lust of the eye, the flesh." In our household we became accustomed to this language, this mistrust of the body and desire. But this card, with its rabbit and chick and egg, with its amorous language, from a woman who called my father "beloved," suggests an almost pagan world, not bounded by the religious rules we took so seriously.

In October, 1929, Dad's half-brother Johnny died at the age of twelve—the same age the first brother Johnny had been when he had died, also in October, seventeen years before. Again, Grandfather was grief-stricken: the second Johnny had been an intelligent and favoured son, apt in machine work. Aunt Greta remembered that "he would watch his father at the lathe and hand him the tool he needed even before he was asked for it." The following spring, Dad planted a tree on his grave.

Johnny and Barney "racing," circa 1928.

#

In 1930, at the age of twenty-seven, Dad began a diary, inspired, perhaps, by a sense of life passing him by. By way of explanation he said only, "My interest was aroused." He maintained the diary faithfully until the early1950s. Anyone who keeps a diary for that long must believe in the importance of his own quotidian life, in the noteworthiness of events and facts, in the need to structure otherwise formless experience. Maybe he even thought that he'd tell the story of his life one day. In the diary he rarely made judgements or declared his feelings. It was not a journal for personal reflections, although a few such do appear. In the later years, especially, it probably served as a reminder of church meetings or pastoral visits.

On the inside front page of the first notebook his address is listed as "Steinbach" but also as: "Winnipeg, Man., Lynwood Block – Suite 3, Norwood." An undated paragraph reads: "Sunday nite with all delight from all the merry crowd at Portage Avenue. Oh my what a life." Portage Avenue was Winnipeg's busiest street, running east-west across the breadth of the city. Sometimes Dad got together with his cousins Ed Friesen and Peter Dueck. He also lists the address of Lieutenant Kathryn Loewen, originally from Steinbach, who seems to have been a member of the Salvation Army. He wrote her in February after she had been relocated to Petersburg, Alaska, but after that the correspondence ended.

For most of 1930, however, he lived in Steinbach, taking whatever work came along. Perhaps, at the start of the Great Depression, job opportunities in Winnipeg had dried up. He carted concrete while building a house ("I never sweated as much in my life as I did in Wm Wiebe's new cellar"). He tended a friend's hot dog stand at a town picnic. For a stretch in September and October he worked as a driver—"wheeling," he called it—for a road or pipeline construction project in the Whiteshell Provincial Park area, near the Manitoba-Ontario border. The conditions were miserable. He worked a night shift some of the time, fighting sleep. Accommodations consisted of rough tents shared with rough men: "We slept on bare boards. More rain." But on days off a kind of camaraderie developed:

> Here it is Sunday, a very nice day, and we got to stay here like sailors marooned on an island. No work today. The whole camp will be moved 2 ½ miles east along the road tomorrow morning. We spent our time playing horseshoe for a while. Some boys chased squirrels, others cut down trees. We also read stories and played cards.

Not at all how Sunday would have been spent in Steinbach! Food was sub-par and the cook quit, it seemed to rain all the time and the trucks were constantly getting stuck in the gumbo, or breaking down and having to be repaired. At last he gave it up and returned to the comforts of home.

In the road construction camp, 1930. Dad crouching in front. Behind him, smiling, his friend Ben P. Toews.

In mid-April a "Galician from around Marchand" came to Friesen Machine Shop to have a saw shaft made. The Friesens gave him shelter in

Dad, October, 1929.

the stable overnight—just as their ancestors had often done with their Ukrainian peasant workers in South Russia. Drama ensued: "While we were not looking, he swiped bolts, drills, crescent wrench and 3 wrenches of my wrench set." The man disappeared and within half an hour Dad found the missing articles—except the wrenches—hidden in a manger in the stable. Henry, Jake, and Dad jumped into Jake's car and chased after the thief for thirteen miles, but found no sign of him. "Woe him," declared Dad, in a rare display of anger.

Strangely, the man returned of his own volition a couple of weeks later, with an engine that needed repair. "Bro. Henry cross-examined him and after a while he pleaded guilty." Another week passed, and the man "paid for the whole set so I gave him the rest of the wrenches." A roundabout way of making a sale, to be sure. Dad might not have had need for the tools in any case, as his future did not lie in mechanical work.

There was also time for leisure that summer—taking carsful of friends (often including his sisters Catherine and Helen) to swimming holes, singing with groups of young people, going to baseball tournaments and fairs, and playing tennis (he won two out of three sets in one match). One "beautiful and romantic" evening, with "stars shining by the millions . . . a number of neighbour kids came over at night and we had lots of fun on the lawn, told jokes, sang songs, and made music." For the son of a strict Kleine Gemeinde minister, he was definitely testing the limits of propriety.

Picnicking with sisters and friends.

But he was lonely, and beset with a great longing, a yearning that stretched beyond himself and everyday events, into the heavens, to the very moon: "You can't beat this weather for spring. Such a lovely morning, warm day, romantic evening, the moon shining, gliding through the sky. It makes one surely feel different and it affects one so much."

Chapter 7:
Movies, the secret sin

Of all of the many discoveries I made in reading through my father's diaries, the biggest, and most surprising, was this—that he had gone to the movies. The opening lines of his first booklet came as a quietly delightful shock to me: "Went to Wpg yesterday and am staying at A. D. Friesens', 26 Maralbo Ave., St. Vital. Saw *The Virginian*, a good talkie." *The Virginian*! He went to a movie?! Going to movies was a sin. Our church said so, on the grounds that movies were "worldly," meaning that they stirred unhealthy, fleshly appetites. But I was pleased at my discovery, which revealed a new dimension of my father, one I'd never suspected. He was human. Like me, he had "sinned." I didn't think of him as hypocritical, but I was surprised at the silence he had maintained about his own youthful experience. Here was another part of himself that he had hidden.

In May, 1930, while working in Winnipeg for a ten-day period, Dad went on a movie-watching spree, seeing at least five: *On with the Show*, *Show Boat*, *Montana Moon*, *The Gold Diggers of Broadway*, and an unnamed picture at the Roxy on Henderson Highway. He seemed to have an affinity for musicals, show tunes, and dancing girls. Sometimes he went with a male friend; often he went alone.

On with the Show has a thin storyline about a dance troupe in danger of going broke, but most of the movie consists of masses of dancers on-stage—women as flappers or nymphs

or ballerinas, men in tuxedos and top hats. A few black actors appear, including Ethel Waters singing a mournful solo about her absent man. At one point, astonishingly, fox hunters riding real horses bound across the stage. In *The Gold Diggers of Broadway* the format is similar, with myriad tap-dancing performances, including George Raft doing a number so blazingly fast that you think it might have been speeded up on film. Dancers doing cartwheels and backflips provide comic intervals. The male actors are commanding or foolish, while the females are fetching and flirtatious. All of this could not even have been imagined in Dad's village childhood. Movies gave him a glimpse into the sinful world in all its entertaining splendour, featuring its often-repeated myth of romantic pain and happiness.

Credit: Wikipedia Commons.

A few times, he went with his non-Mennonite friend Henry Coote to see "he-man" melodramas: *Frozen Justice* and *Dr. F.* They also saw a Western starring Hoot Gibson, and a rerun of the Jack Sharkey–Max Schmeling world heavyweight boxing championship match, won by Schmeling on a foul.

The following year, Dad was back in Steinbach, but he made a few visits to Winnipeg, including one in January when he stayed with a Doerksen family. He took their daughter Helen to two movies. One of these was *Anybody's War*, starring comedians George Moran and Charles Mack, who were known for their vaudeville act, in blackface. Earlier that day Dad and his cousin Ed Friesen had already been to a movie at the magnificent Metropolitan Theatre—*Morocco*, a romance directed by Josef von Sternberg, starring a tuxedo-wearing Marlene Dietrich and Gary Cooper as a womanizing legionnaire. Dad's assessment, "a very good picture," was borne out by the film's nomination for Oscars in four categories, including best director.

Dad also saw Charlie Chaplin's silent classic romance *City Lights*, bringing his total of Hollywood movies, as noted in the diary, to eleven. This was at a time when he was facing the stark necessities of making a living, but perhaps that was precisely the reality he wanted to escape. At the same time he sidestepped, or ignored, another reality. The movies glorified the body, told stories of passion and lust and betrayal, made light of serious matters, glamorized smoking and alcohol and sex, and in general represented everything that a good Mennonite was to avoid.

#

After finding out about Dad's movie-going, I thought of my own experience (much earlier in life than his) and wondered about my siblings' stories. I had already taken notes when listening to my eldest brother Alvin reminiscing, so I had that. I emailed Norman and talked to Don and Mary Ann on the phone. I would have loved to talk to Vern, too, if only he had still been alive, because I'm sure he would have had dramatic tales to tell.

We grew up knowing that movies were strictly off-limits, except for educational films we might be shown at school on special occasions. And even then, the teacher in charge would block out "dangerous" images such as kissing scenes. Yet all of us, individually, were drawn by the dark magical appeal of movie theatres. We all sneaked off to the movies, knowing our parents disapproved.

As a fourteen-year-old, Norman went on an all-expenses-paid trip to Minneapolis that the *Winnipeg Free Press* put on as an incentive for its carriers, and for the first time ever, went to see a real movie in an actual theatre:

> It was a Western, and one of the heroes had to bite on a stick while whiskey was poured on his gunshot wound and the bullet was extracted using little finesse with a knife. I was truly impressed by the "huge" screen and vivid colour. After that first ice-breaker, I went to a couple of other

movies. I only admitted to seeing one movie when Dad asked about it after I got home. I gave him the impression I had very little choice because we were all scheduled to go there as a group activity. That was stretching it. In my argument for the defence, I may have queried him on whether HE had ever seen a movie . . . and he admitted that he had gone to movies as a youth.

Norman did not share the news of this astonishing paternal confession at the time, so I grew up ignorant of it. In this story, Norman tells a lie. But Dad had "lied," too, by telling us nothing about his own movie-going career, while forbidding this pleasure to us. He had a dilemma, to be sure: if he had told us that he'd once gone to movies, we might have interpreted that as permission for ourselves.

Alvin had had a similar experience some years earlier. He was also a newspaper carrier, and had recruited a sufficient number of new subscribers to the *Winnipeg Free Press* to win a two-day trip to Winnipeg in March, 1947. His friend Stan Reimer also qualified. They stayed at the Marlborough Hotel and went on a tour of the airport with the rest of their group. But the most important thing was seeing a movie. Al and Stan went to the theatre and saw a murder mystery. Al was scared—but hooked. The next day he went to another one, a Western. When he got home he said nothing about it to our parents, but started to go to the newly opened Playhouse movie theatre in Steinbach. It was important to avoid detection. He would approach on the side of Main Street opposite to the theatre, look all around to see that the coast was clear, and then make a frantic dash to get in unseen. Inside, his heart pounding, he sat in the back row, trying not to be seen.

Donald also sneaked into the Playhouse as a teenager, using the same other-side-of-the-street approach as his brother. He did not have a clear conscience, and his enjoyment of the films was undermined by fear: "What if the Lord should come?" Then he would be found in a sinful place, and in danger of losing his soul in the Judgement to follow.

Mary Ann, naively, did not cross the street, and once, as a teenager on the way to the Playhouse to meet her friends, ran into Mrs. P. D. Reimer in front of our church. Mrs. Reimer wanted to know if she was coming to the revival meeting that evening. Mary Ann made some excuse and continued on to the theatre. Not surprisingly, Dad found out about this. He sat her down for a serious talk. She tried to argue that the movies she had seen were good ones, and so there was no harm in it. Dad said: "If someone looks in the garbage can for food, they might find something they can eat, but it still comes from a garbage can." She had no good answer for that.

The Playhouse had opened in 1941 despite protests from citizens, including Dad, who recorded this encounter: "The theatre manager came to see me in forenoon to talk 'friendly,' but I gave him to understand that we strictly didn't want the theatre in this town." That owner, a man named Frank Tarnopolsky—so, a Ukrainian, not a Mennonite—was found asphyxiated in his car on a cold Sunday evening in January, 1944, the car windows turned up, the garage doors locked. The new owner, a non-religious Mennonite, gamely carried on for a few more years. Then he sold the business to yet another man who also faced continued pressure from townspeople to shut down the theatre. This owner finally caved in and had the whole building moved ten miles down the Number 12 Highway to our neighbouring French village of Ste. Anne in 1956, leaving Steinbach without a theatre.

As for me . . . when I was around twelve, I accompanied my parents to Winnipeg, where Dad had some business to do. Probably Mom wanted to do some shopping. I told them they could drop me at the museum and then I would meet them at the Eaton statue in a couple of hours. When they had driven off, I made my uncertain way down Portage Avenue in the direction of Main Street, looking for a movie theatre. I'd never been to one before, but I knew they were somewhere downtown.

I spotted a place called the Rialto—exotic name with the promise of adventure—and crossed the busy street. The marquee read: *Beneath the 12-Mile Reef.* A poster showed a diver in deadly conflict with a giant octopus, with a shark lurking nearby. I walked up to the ticket vendor, a red-lipsticked lady, and stood there, uncertain of what to do next. "Yeah, whaddaya want, kid?" she said, in a bored voice. "I want to see the film," I said. "So give me the money for the ticket," she replied. Blushing, I dug into my pockets and set my quarters down on the counter. I proceeded hesitatingly into the high-ceilinged dark chamber, the theatre itself, where I found a seat and was immediately taken up into the technicolour world on the immense—as it was to me then—screen. I had come in after the movie had begun, but that almost didn't matter; what mattered was, I was in a real theatre for the first time in my life. I took no notice of how seedy and dilapidated it was, or that the movie had first been released a few years before. When the diver's air supply was cut off, I could hardly breathe myself. When the American girl kissed the handsome Greek, I imagined her lips on mine. For an hour I succeeded in blotting out the nagging of my conscience. Part of my excitement arose from the very fact that I was "sinning," and no one was stopping me. Then the titles came on, and I hurried out, blinking in the late afternoon light and hightailing my way to Eatons, nervously rehearsing lines I would tell my parents if they should ask about my time at the museum. They did ask, as our car rolled along the highway in the direction of Steinbach. Having been to the museum before, I described an exhibit or two, and that seemed to satisfy them. I did not like lying and the uneasy feeling that went with it—but this was a price I was willing to pay for the experience I'd had.

At least, I think that's how it went. Would the Rialto really have been playing a three- or four-year-old movie? Also, did a strange man come and sit in the seat beside me and put his hand on my knee? I seem to remember that, and jumping up and moving to another row of seats. Would my parents have been so trusting, or casual, as to leave me to my own devices in the big city when I was only twelve? It appears so.

The movies were lies, too, in a way—merely *ütjedochte Jeschichte*, thought-up stories. Mennonites had long condemned the productions of the imagination as "not true." Good Christians were meant to keep to the script—the Scripture, that is, and even there, to skip over the wilder stories such as Lot's daughters getting him drunk and having sex with him. We were to keep our feet on the ground, in the barnyard, or in our case the machine shop yard. Giving free rein to the imagination could only result in mischief at best, and evil at worst. Human minds and hearts were the devil's playground.

But in our household we had free access to adventure novels, which Dad stocked in the bookstore he opened in 1949. Somehow comic books, large stacks of them, also found their way into my brothers' bedroom. Vernon and Norman also brought in *Mad* magazine, which they must have discovered somewhere at a newsstand in Winnipeg, as such "trash," as the *Mad* writers happily called their own work, would not likely have been for sale in Steinbach. We only half-understood the satire and anarchic humour of the writers, most of whom were New York Jews, but we loved it. Thus we absorbed urban culture and Yiddish vocabulary (our favourite word was "furshlugginer," meaning old or junky), mystifying our parents. In general, the sway of community and church rules was weakening and our parents were helpless to stop this change.

Chapter 8:
Conversion:
Your Sins Are Forgiven

In the hyper-religious town of my childhood, we all had a pretty good idea of what salvation was supposed to be. It happened when you admitted you were a sinner, repented, and accepted Jesus as your personal saviour. This was a one-time event, accompanied by high emotion and resulting in a changed, improved life.

I had no idea that traditionalists had thought quite differently, believing in salvation bestowed through humble discipleship and loving your neighbour. This was the prevailing ethos until the 1920s and '30s, when American-style fundamentalism and evangelism started making an impact on Steinbach. Chicago evangelist George P. Schultz held a series of revival meetings in the Bruderthaler church in 1931. Schultz was known for his powerful voice and a no-holds-barred preaching style. The Bruderthaler ("brethren of the valley") were also Mennonite, but had formed a church of their own some decades earlier, more evangelical and less averse to the pitfalls of commerce than were their Kleine Gemeinde co-religionists. They later changed their name to "Evangelical Mennonite Brethren" and were known as "the EMB."

On May 27, 1931, Dad was "born again" at one of Schultz's meetings: "Quite a few sinners came to the front, Dad wrote. "My belief in the Saviour was strengthened very much tonight." Did he count himself among these

George P. Schultz. Credit: God, Working Through Us (Steinbach: 1972).

sinners? Did he actually answer the altar call and go up to the front of the church himself? He's not clear about that. In any case, he made a decision. Post-stroke, he amplified the moment: "I received a new faith in the Lord my saviour and I accepted him as my saviour too oh glory, hallelujah, praise his name." His conversion happened almost on the exact anniversary day of his mother's death on May 28th, seventeen years before.

Dad had taken his time before coming to that moment. He attended church—or churches; quite often he went to the Bruderthaler service—regularly all through 1930. Surprisingly, he was not a church member. It would have been expected that the son of a well-known minister, a descendant of a pioneer family with deep roots in the Kleine Gemeinde, would be baptized by the time he reached twenty or twenty-one, and married shortly thereafter. But Dad did not conform to this expectation. Neither, for that matter, did any of his five brothers.

Abe, the eldest, married at age 30, and he and his wife Gertrude, the daughter of *Steinbach Post* editor Jacob S. Friesen, waited two years before joining the Steinbach Bruderthaler church. Nick, the next-eldest, was 26 when he married Gertrude's sister Marie in Winnipeg, and they did not have a conversion experience until five years later, in the Dallas, Oregon Bruderthaler church. Henry, Dad's junior by two years, got married to his wife Catherine at the home of a Lutheran pastor in Winnipeg. He also was not a church member at the time. In fact, he and Catherine carried on in their daily lives in Steinbach for several years, even becoming parents before answering an altar call at a Schultz revival meeting and joining the Bruderthaler church. Next youngest brother Jake quietly married Julianna

Schmidtke at the age of 24. He had been baptized by a Bruderthaler minister in the Seine River near La Broquerie the previous year, and never joined the Kleine Gemeinde.

Dad's brother Nick with sister Catherine and wife Marie.

Abe, Nick, Henry, Jake, and sister Catherine were all married before Dad. His youngest brother Bernhard delayed getting married until age 27, in 1939, at which time he was not yet a church member. He became one only four years later, when he and his wife Katherine from the nearby village of New Bothwell attended a revival meeting at the Steinbach tabernacle and, in Dad's words, "gave themselves up to the Lord." After that they joined the Steinbach Kleine Gemeinde congregation.

Growing up in our neighbourhood, surrounded by these uncles and aunts, my siblings and I had no idea that they might ever have been anything other than their respectable church-going selves. Like our father, all our uncles had taken their time before falling into line. Could their hesitation before stepping over the threshold into formal religion have been an unconscious reaction to losing their mother when they were children? The women they married had an "outsider" quality, tending to be outspoken and even flamboyant, unlike the more sedate Friesens.

In contrast, Dad's sisters Catherine, Helen, and Greta followed the normal pattern, joining the Kleine Gemeinde as single girls before marriage.

The siblings, oldest to youngest: Abe, Nick, Peter, Henry, Jake, Catherine, Helen, Barney, Greta.

#

Except for Abe, Dad was the oldest of the siblings to become a church member and get married. He must have worried about falling behind. How would he find direction in his life? His conversion marked a turning point.

Post-stroke, he described his experience: "It was nothing extraordinary, no evangelistic campaign had preceded or any other efforts were visible." Apparently his stroke-afflicted brain had trouble with sequencing and actual events, since later in the same account Dad went on to tell of attending a revival meeting:

> I had really waited for some spectacular happening like St. Paul who was struck down in his sinful way, but nothing like that happened to me and then I argued that I wasn't so very sinful at that and now I believe old Satan kept reminding me I wasn't so bad, and so I had kept putting off this final step to openly confess that I would completely break with the world and renounce everything that was sinful. And then it happened, one day as I was listening

to a sermon in one of those evangelistic meetings, I don't remember just what his text was or what he said but this I remember very clearly, that a voice in me said: your sins are all forgiven. And I know this was clear and definite that my whole outlook was different from that day on. I timidly told some other friends but still was very shy about this, but later on I was painting with another friend in a house that was being remodelled . . . and I was singing almost continually so my friend asked me why so happy and I told him that everything was different now, even nature outside, even the birds sang more cheerfully, even the sun was shining brighter. Well, he seemed to understand and rejoiced with me.

The voice in Dad that said "your sins are all forgiven" was not an ancestral voice. Historically the Kleine Gemeinde had taught that one could not be sure of such forgiveness—certainty was a sign of pride. It was better to say that you had the "hope" of forgiveness and eternal life. That would be a sign of true Christian humility. Dad's inner voice aligned him with the new evangelicalism which would eventually overtake the Kleine Gemeinde.

He had waited for something spectacular to happen to him, as it had to Paul on the way to Damascus. Perhaps he felt that his own energy for life was insufficient and he needed the help of something or someone stronger to help him break through to living more intensely and fully. Even if not spectacular, his experience was powerful enough to put him in touch with the transcendent.

At the same time, he made his commitment to a Christian life in a community context. He did not join the Bruderthaler as might have been expected, but stayed with the Kleine Gemeinde. He and a large group of other converts attended a meeting with the bishop Peter P. Reimer, who declared that "we are just like a big family . . . and want to be quite free to talk and express ourselves." Some of those present confessed sins, some expressed doubts, others told of how happy they were to have accepted the Lord as their Saviour. All would be baptized and become church members.

The reassuring message of forgiveness of sin was the essence of the conversion experience for Dad. For some of the more sensitive Kleine Gemeinde people, the church's emphasis on working out one's salvation in fear and trembling resulted in an ever-present sense of guilt and inadequacy. To stop "working," to give over the effort of controlling your own life, letting your grip relax and truly believing that, however flawed you are, you are forgiven—there could be deep self-acceptance and peace in this. No wonder Dad sang "almost continually." Now he was secure, not only for the present, but also for the future. You may stumble, you may fall, you may even despair—but through it all, God holds you in his loving hands.

One young man in the group of baptismal candidates "told us how the Lord had saved him from certain death." Nothing so dramatic had happened to Dad, but now he made a complete break with the world. Where previously he had gone out on dates, seen movies, attended sports events, umpired a baseball game, gone "mixed bathing" at the swimming hole near La Broquerie, and on one occasion played the drum and banjo at "Barber" Peters' place—now he left all this behind. For a brief time he allowed himself a few worldly indulgences—he bought a crystal radio, went to the Johnny J. Jones circus in Winnipeg, played a few games of tennis. But even such innocent diversions would soon cease.

Steinbach tennis court, 1920s.

He told some friends of his conversion, but did he say anything to his father and stepmother? No mention of this. Grandfather was a traditionalist, so soft-spoken from the pulpit that his contemporaries noted his lack of preaching skills. He might not have responded with much warmth to his son's emotional experience. In his memoir Grandfather wrote: "Before God nothing prevails but a sincere life and faithfulness given with all one's might, exactly as the Holy Scripture teaches." In other words, salvation is not a free gift; it requires strenuous effort.

Dad would at least partially have agreed. He ruefully observed that "I didn't always have these happy feelings, and the Lord showed me in a very emphatic way that I must not build on or depend on feelings and still be secure in Him." His pursuit of an authentic Christian life was not dramatic, but persistent and persevering. He had a practical and rational mind, which in turn was what he showed to us, his children, and also to the church community.

Maybe it isn't surprising that Dad did not tell us stories of his "sinful" younger years. But he did not tell us anything about his conversion, either. This was the very thing he wished for his children, but for some reason he was completely close-mouthed about it. My mother once shared with me that he had wanted a great event, a breaking-in of the divine into his orderly and ordinary life. I did not know, then, what to make of this information, but it stayed with me. I think Mom's words opened up a possibility I had not previously thought of. That my father had yearnings, like me. That my father dared to hope for something extraordinary to happen to him, as I secretly hoped for myself. That on some level, he was drawn, as I was, to an ideal of personal heroism.

I dreamt of becoming a writer. Dad in his youth showed interest in reading novels, in going to movies, in singing and playing music. He tried his hand at photography. He had an aptitude for languages, and was bold enough to write a letter to the *Steinbach Post*, in 1931, suggesting improvements and criticizing the quality of one correspondent's German. But all of this belonged to the world of the imagination, which he now set aside for his religious calling.

The Mennonites mistrusted the arts, and individual creativity, as belonging to the sinful world, distracting the Christian from the serious worship of God. Dad fell into line with that view after his conversion. If he was to express himself creatively, he would contain that expression within religious boundaries, as in composing sermons, or leading choirs, or singing hymns.

Chapter 9:
"The greatest day
of my life"

After his conversion Dad soon made three fundamental life decisions. First, he found a profession. Second, he got baptized and joined the Kleine Gemeinde. Third, he got married.

After giving up his teaching ambitions, he had moved from one thing to another: truck-driving, taking a woodworking course, helping his father collect accounts for the Machine Shop, doing grunt work on a house-building crew, painting house interiors—whatever came to hand. But none of these jobs promised an occupation for him in the long term. Family friend and former *Steinbach Post* publisher Jacob S. Friesen died, and this death opened a door. Jacob Friesen had supplemented his newspaper income by repairing watches, and the watchmaking tools, of no use to the widow, were now available. The two Friesen families were close; Dad's older brothers Abe and Nick were married to Jacob Friesen's daughters, Gertrude and Marie.

A year earlier, Dad had considered his options: "I don't know what I shall do, go back to Winnipeg to work in spring or stay in Steinbach and start a business?" Now he had the answer. With his meagre assets and financial help from his father, he bought the watchmaking tools. Grandfather, himself a proficient watch-repairer, gave him some training. Dad set up his office in the building that had previously housed Jacob Friesen's print shop on Main Street. Customers were advised to "come to K. R. Friesen across the street" if they found the door locked. He took his place as a fledgling member of the village's vigorous business community and now had something to offer to a prospective bride.

At first the demand was sparse, and Dad supplemented his income by taking on a time-keeping job for crews working on a government-sponsored road-building project near Kleefeld, the village of his Dueck relatives.

On Sunday, July 12, 1931, Dad was baptized along with twenty-nine others in the Steinbach Kleine Gemeinde church, and became a member. "May the Lord help in my struggle in this world," he wrote in his diary. Thirty years later, post-stroke and following decades of religious service, he amended his prayer: "May the Lord help me to commit my life and dedicate my all to Him." In hindsight, struggle, with its implied uncertainty, had been transformed into commitment, with its direction and purpose. At whatever point the commitment became firm, it did in fact shape Dad's life in the form of a lasting partnership with his wife, fatherhood to his children, entrepreneurship in business, and, finally and always most importantly to him, leadership in the church.

Present at the baptism were visitors from Kansas, young George Rempel and his wife, and unmarried sisters Helen, nineteen, and Margaret, twenty-six. They were the children of Peter F. Rempel, a farmer and mechanic living near the small town of Meade. In his diary Dad, with an uncharacteristic superlative, declared, "Today is the greatest day of my life." He was referring to his baptism, but as it happened, it was also a prophetic acknowledgement of his first encounter with the woman he would marry. After the service, the Kansans came to the Friesen home: "George Rempels from Meade came to our place for dinner & lunch. With them were his sister and her sister."

Of the two sisters, it was Margaret who attracted Dad's eye. She recorded her version of events in her diary: "We went to Klaas R. Friesens, had a fine time, many people. In the eve we went to Peter B. Kroekers. A nice bunch was there—K. R. Friesen children" . . . she goes on with a list of names. So Mom and Dad spent that midsummer afternoon and evening together, albeit in the company of many others. In Dad, Mom would have seen a handsome man, short but still taller than she was, with penetrating blue eyes. He would likely have worn his three-piece suit. He took himself seriously, and she may have sensed that this sobriety would provide a balance for her sometimes ungoverned expressiveness. She may also have intuited that his personal integrity would help build a solid foundation for their relationship. Both of them were at a point in their lives where they felt some urgency to find a partner.

The next day Mom and Helen, who had stayed overnight in Kleefeld, visited at various households, talking and enjoying themselves immensely ("remember the kisses," Mom wrote, without naming names). Dad, presumably, spent his time dreaming of ways he could see Mom again.

Margaret Rempel, left, visiting the K. R. Friesen family, July, 1931.
She stands beside her future sister-in-law Helen Friesen.

#

Mom was not a conventional beauty. As prescribed for Mennonite farm girls of the time, she wore her hair flattened with a mesh net, parted in the middle and covering her forehead, emphasizing plainness. Yet she had a spontaneous smile, a ready laugh, and deep brown eyes. And she was a free spirit.

Dad took a holiday from work, borrowed his parents' car, and drove to Winnipeg, "taking along sisters Tin & Helen, & Marg. Rempel." In the city, they met up with three of Dad's Kleefeld cousins. Dad had the chance to impress the country girls with his experience of the city, and he took full advantage of it: "We went to City Park, then to Eatons and then to River Park where we went on roller coaster & dodger cars. Got home at 11 o'clock. We also went through Free Press building."

For Mom these same events rated a much more effusive description:

> July 14 – We went to Winnipeg. Went along with our precious friends Pete, Kath. & Helen D. Friesen. We saw so many things, interesting—words fail me—Free Press, Parliament Building, Garden of Eden, I mean green house, animals, and I just can't remember what we didn't see. A beautiful hot day. We need sleep more than anything. What a thrill it gave me to ride on the roller coaster and so forth. Words fail. We were at K. R. Friesens for night.

On a downward plunge of the roller coaster her hair came free of its confinement—it flew straight up and she lost all her hair pins. The "Parliament Building" was actually the legislative provincial building. Dad took a picture of her and the others smilingly posed on a limestone ledge, the lawn far below.

On the ledge of the the Legislative Buildings.
Mom in the centre, Aunt Helen left, Aunt Catherine, right.

The "Garden of Eden" was the Assiniboine Park Conservatory, a lush interior green space in brilliant contrast to the semi-arid plains of either Manitoba or Kansas. A part of Mom was awakened to what must have looked like a far richer and more promising experience than she had known in her everyday life on the dusty homestead, working hard each day cooking, cleaning, and generally being of service.

Mom's mother Sara had died at the age of forty-seven from complications of an abscess in her teeth, when Mom was eighteen. All of her older siblings except George were married and out of the house by then. Her father remarried only months after Sara's death, but the remaining children did not readily accept this new mother. Mom was left to fill that role, caring for five younger brothers and sisters ranging downward in age from sixteen to seven. At the time of her Manitoba visit, all of the younger children were still at home, and Mom was dreaming of breaking away.

It was the mode, back then, to exchange poems and proverbs with friends in autograph books. Dad and Mom sent each other coded messages. On the first day they met Dad very nearly declared his undying love:

> Steinbach, Man. July 12, 1931
> Dear friend Margareth
> When the golden sun is sinking
> And your mind from care is free
> When of absent friends you're thinking
> Won't you sometimes think of me?
> Your friend till Kahnsas grows hairless wheat, Peter
> D. Friesen

Steinbach Man
July 12, 1931

Dear friend Margareth

When the golden sun is sinking.
And your mind from care is free.
When of absent friends you're thinking
Won't you sometimes think of me?

Yours friend till Kahnsas
grows hairless wheat,

Peter. D. Friesen

A week later Mom seemed to accept his offer:

> Meade, Kansas, July 19, 1931
> Dear Friend,
> Everybody thinks you're great when your luck is going
> fine. Folks all slap you on the back, hard enough to break
> your spine. But it's only honest friends that will show how
> much they care, when misfortune comes to you, and the
> load is hard to bear.
> Your hairless Wheat friend, Margaret Rempel

He asks to be kept in her thoughts; she suggests the possibility of being at his side when misfortune comes—an unwitting prophecy of events that were to occur much later.

"Till Kahnsas grows hairless wheat," with its intentional misspelling, seems like a comical way to pledge one's love; the light tone protects the writer from the possible pain of rejection. For her part, Mom played along, but coyly. On the eve of her departure Dad resorted to straightforward prose, concluding with an insistent string of question marks:

> Margareth, when you look at this page, and see the lines of this scrawl, you can read between the lines and read to your heart's desire. Now I'm asking you, how did you like it here, and also these people? We sure are sorry to see you go home and hope your next visit will be much longer. Your eyes always give you away, so also now we can read it in them, that you have liked it here. As you have said a few times yourself so we quote: forget our weakness and God bless you.
> ? ? ? ? ? ? ? ? ? ?

For a week Mom had kept up a frenetic pace of visiting, getting together with large groups of young people, and twice staying overnight at K. R. Friesens'. She also paid a morning call to Dad's watch repair shop. One day she "landed in Steinbach with the buggy and two white horses," and "laughed till I was all weak." At another place she and her friends were so rambunctious they broke the bench they were sitting on, and here she also prompted herself to "remember the big boy." While she may have been interested in Dad she was also attracted to others, keeping her options open. Dad, meanwhile, had thoughts for no one other than Margaret Rempel.

On July 23rd, the Kansas party left for home. "Good bye, boo hoo," Mom comically lamented. By comparison, Dad's tone was almost religious:

> Thursday. Lovely weather continuing and such romantic moonlit nights. One is apt to go wild over it, or something or other makes one's feelings run amok. God has created man and everything. He has made it so that one can enjoy living in his creation. Oh what a peace seems to be settled all over the universe on nights like these.

Peace settled over the universe but his feelings ran amok. A correspondence between them ensued. By August 3rd he had a letter from Mom, whom he called "my sweetheart." This term of endearment does not exist in his original diary, but was interpolated many years later, after decades of marriage, and after his stroke, when his altered brain allowed freer expression of tender feeling.

Whatever other options Mom might have considered during her visit, she seems to have set those aside, strengthening her commitment to Dad in regular letters. He deeply appreciated and admired the writing ability of his brown-eyed Kansas farm girl with the Grade 7 education. For him she was an equal to Shakespeare:

> September 12: Got a letter from M. R. last night, boy but can't she write letters, every word with a big meaning.

> September 24: Got a letter again from M. R. what a soul uplifter she is in her letters, oh my!

> October 8: Got a letter again from Margaret Rempel, and boy, what did she write; it's quite astounding.

> October 16: Got a letter again from M. R. and oh what a letter that is. Boy oh boy!

Among Dad's papers there are a few cards and letters from young women, some frank in their romantic intent. But none of my mother's "astounding" early letters can be found. Why were these not kept, when they gave Dad so much joy? But Mom survived Dad, and perhaps she was the one who decided that her words would not be read by anyone for whom they were not intended.

#

Four of Dad's brothers were already married, while his younger sister Catherine had announced her wedding date as November 1st. Now it was

Dad's turn. Encouraged by Mom's letters, he decided on a trip to Kansas. By October he had quit his time-keeper's job, arranged for a friend to fill in for him in his watchmaking business, and exchanged Canadian for U. S. currency. He borrowed his brother Jake's Ford coupe and was all set to leave, when, to his surprise, if not dismay, "Ma declared that Dad would go along with me."

Dad's parents had already met Mom that summer, but for some reason they judged it right that Grandfather should travel with him now. Perhaps church business was a pretext, or visiting relatives. The trip took four days, with overnight stays with relatives in Nebraska and Kansas. Father and son had never had that much unbroken time with each other before, but neither one was by nature talkative—one imagines long stretches of silence. When they reached Meade they embarked on a program of intensive visiting, Mennonite style.

K. R. Friesen surveying Kansas fields from the vantage point of his son Jake's Ford coupe.

Strangely, Dad did not seem to know for sure that he would be getting married even when he was already in Kansas. Visiting in the Rempel household, he was nervous and overwrought: "What a feeling . . . can hardly eat these days, food seems to choke me. . . . My thoughts seem to be in a turmoil (mess)." Only when he had been in Kansas for several days did he "pop the important question." And even after Mom said "yes," his heart beat fast on the following day when he asked for her parents' blessing. They gave their assent. They were probably happy with their daughter's sensible choice, although Mom's stepmother might have been disappointed at losing a valued housekeeper. Mom's younger sisters also were sad to see her leave. A wedding date was set for November 27.

The Friesens and Rempels were related. Two sets of great-grandparents from both sides were siblings. Far from being seen as an obstacle, such connections were preferred; the known was better than the unknown.

Another round of visiting ensued as Dad met his future wife's extended family: "They were all very nice and met me almost with open arms." Dad borrowed a typewriter and laboriously tapped out the wedding invitations, in German, attempting a touch of elegance by centre-spacing the lines. The temperamental keys tended to skip and leave unintended gaps. The day before the wedding, American Thanksgiving Day, a fairly heavy snow fell. Dad and his soon-to-be-brother-in-law Ben Rempel fetched extra benches and chairs from people's houses and brought them to the church.

The next afternoon, a Friday, Grandfather made the opening remarks, after which Mom's uncle Jacob F. Isaac conducted the ceremony. With a

watchmaker's precision, Dad noted: "The time was exactly 3 p.m. central standard time." The ceremony over, the newlyweds had some difficulty leaving the church as "we got into the milling & pushing stream of young fry." The Rempel family held the reception in their home, featuring a Depression-era Mennonite lunch of "moos and potatoes and baloney." Next day, unceremoniously, was devoted to cleanup: "we literally shoveled and scraped the caked mud from the floor & stairs but it was worth it for what I got."

Visitors' cars on Peter F. Rempel's yard.

On the return trip to Manitoba one person had to sit in the back seat of the coupe, and sometimes this was Mom. She did not care for this arrangement at all, and was not pleased to spend her "honeymoon" chaperoned by her dour new father-in-law, but in this matter she had no say. She parted tearfully from her family, knowing that she was going to be living more than 1,000 miles distant from them. She came to Dad's home territory, to the town where he had been born and where he had staked his future.

#

Mom in K. R. Friesens' front yard.

marg.
Now doesn't look as if she feels quite at home. She does too. On east side of our folks' house

Mom deeply missed her siblings, and began a chatty correspondence with them which was to last for the rest of her life. She sometimes wrote of *bangen*—homesickness. Maybe some sense of displacement always remained with her. In a studio photograph taken at a sibling reunion in Kansas fifteen years later, her eyes are soft with a deep and wordless sadness.

A little while after that, when Donald, turning fifteen, experienced intense loneliness, he threatened to run away —not speaking to his father, but his mother. She called his bluff: "Go ahead," she said. He stayed, but was wounded. Perhaps she wanted to teach him that he had to deal with his pain as she had to deal with hers. There was nowhere to run to. Dad was away a lot, attending meetings, preaching. Mom herself might have fantasized running away, but such a traitorous notion could not be entertained.

One summer afternoon in 1932, "Margaret didn't feel so good . . . when all at once at about 3 p.m. a car drove up, and upon looking we saw our expected folks from Kansas"—Mom's parents, her brother Jake and her younger sister Marie. "What a joy that was, and what a happy reunion," said Dad. Mom was especially close to Marie, and when the visitors left after a stay of three weeks, "Tears flowed freely. And what a pain it is if two loving sisters are torn apart by the fate of long distance. We are trying to smile again."

Mom, left, with her brother Jake and sister Marie in front of the Dodge City Depot, Kansas.

But even smiling might be risky. Mom once related that she and Dad, shortly after they were married, were sitting in Grandfather's living room on a sleepy Sunday afternoon, and Dad had placed his arm around her. Her mother-in-law happened to walk through, and casting a disapproving glance at the couple, said, "*Schaem jie junt nich?*" [aren't you ashamed?] Public displays of affection, or even semi-private ones in living rooms, were reminders of lust, the most dangerous of sins for a Mennonite.

Even so, marriage was sacred and, as the Psalm says, children were the "heritage of the Lord." Mom got pregnant within the first few months of marriage. At half-past one on Easter morning, 1932, she had what Dad called "some trouble with her lower abdomen." Dad phoned the doctor, who said the problem was quite serious. That night Mom "had some terrible pain and passed some blood"—evidently a miscarriage, though Dad never uses this word in his diary. The doctor ordered her to keep to her bed, and she soon began to feel better.

In mid-April, after the roads had improved sufficiently, Dad took her to St. Boniface Hospital, where she had an operation under general anaesthetic, but requiring no incision. Presumably, the procedure was to remove any tissue that might have remained in the womb after the miscarriage. Dad returned to Steinbach to find "a pile of watches" waiting for him. After two weeks he finally got the word that Mom could come home. He took his father's car and rushed to Winnipeg in an hour and ten minutes—record time.

Before going to the hospital Mom got a very bad headache, eased by "a few white tablets from the doc." She would suffer from frequent, severe headaches—often migraines—for the rest of her life. She and Dad learned to accommodate this condition, as nothing could be done to cure it. Perhaps the headaches were her body's way of forcing her to rest periodically from her never-ending responsibilities, a kind of indirect but almost violent protest against servitude.

Mom soon became pregnant again and gave birth to her first child, Alvin Peter, on May 10, 1933, in Steinbach Hospital. It was an all-night labour, and later that morning Dad returned to his shop to fix watches. While his wife was in hospital, he went over to his parents' house for meals.

After nine days Dad brought Mom and little Alvin home, and was relieved to discover that "the babe is fairly decent."

That same year Dad and Mom made an extended visit to Kansas. During their five-month stay there, Mom had the chance to show off her new baby while Dad brought in some money by repairing watches. The young couple harvested corn, butchered pigs, "inspected" the post office in

In Kansas with little Alvin, 1934.

Dodge—whatever caught their interest. They also attended worship services, and Dad began leading singing practice in the Kansas Kleine Gemeinde church, helping to establish their first choir.

They made two more Kansas trips that decade, while Kansas family members also came to Steinbach. Mom's sister Marie came to live with our family for a twenty-month period beginning in March of 1938, helping with child care and household tasks. Eventually Marie would marry Jake Thiessen and move to Canada permanently. The sisters remained close friends all their lives.

Altogether Mom and Dad made about ten trips to the U. S., later ones including Colorado and Oregon after some of Mom's siblings moved to the west coast in the 1940s. The whole family was too big to all go together, and for each trip some children were left behind in Manitoba in the care of relatives.

Mom, highly sociable, made many friends soon after arriving in Steinbach. She joined the sewing circle of church women, and also a large all-female "cousin circle" made up of Dad's cousins and in-laws. She and Dad seemed able to resolve their conflicts; we as children never heard them so much as raise their voices against each other. Their compatibility made everything, even the frigid Manitoba winters, easier: "If you are happily married I guess you can adjust to the cold," she noted many years later.

The Friesen cousin circle (all in a row). Mom second from left.

But what of Mom's headaches? She lived in a male-dominated culture and a male-dominated house. Perhaps the headaches were her body's way of forcing her to rest periodically from her never-ending responsibilities, a kind of indirect but almost violent protest against servitude.

Dad, the former Lone Scout, did not tolerate solitude well. Once Mom went to Morris, taking the children with her, and he complained: "I'm all alone and it sure gets lonesome at times without the wife and boys. Now one can feel the real family ties or the attachments to the dear ones if they are absent."

One of Dad's sermons after becoming a minister was on the theme "Choosing Life's Partner." One should not marry too young. Those seeking partners should not give up too soon, should pray, and never should a Christian marry a non-Christian. Don't think you can change your partner. "Women," he added, "should know how to save." Presumably, men would automatically possess this virtue. The notes say nothing about women and modesty, but in his bookstore Dad sold John R. Rice's *Bobbed Hair, Bossy Wives, and Women Preachers*. Rice was against all three. Mom, for her part, would cut her hair and freely express her opinions. As to women preach-ers—that was not even a notion that the Mennonite mind in Steinbach could entertain.

CHAPTER 10:
WATCHMAKER AND FATHER

The beginning of the Great Depression was hardly an ideal time to start a business. Farmers, on whom Steinbach merchants relied, were especially hard-hit—wheat prices, which stood at $1.13 a bushel in 1929, plummeted to 19 cents in 1932. Households did not have extra money, and what little there was might not be spent on a watch or clock, or even having a time-piece repaired. But Dad had made his choice, and he stayed with it.

When he returned to Steinbach with his bride, he took up his watch repair tools and added a component to the enterprise—selling new watches. Men's watchbands had to be of leather and ladies' of black cord, in keeping with the church's prohibitions against ornamentation. Obediently, Dad sacrificed profit and did not sell metal watchbands, wedding rings or jewellery of any kind.

On the shop walls, pendulum clocks competed with each other in their loud ticking, and customers would often comment on the noise level. Dad became so accustomed to it that he didn't notice.

Mom in front of watchmaker's shop. Home was the back part of the ground floor.

His introduction to his trade had been surprisingly casual—he bought tools, received some pointers from his father, and set out. Had he lived in Europe, he would have had to spend years in apprenticeship, learning the craft. But this was the new world, where no such rules applied. Dad had an aptitude for this small-scale labour involving little metal gears and polished jewels which functioned as bearings for the moving parts. Physically, it was demanding work, requiring him to lean forward and keep a steady hand. Mentally, he had to draw on his reserves of patience and curiosity and problem-solving skills. He took satisfaction in bringing a "dead" watch or clock back to life and then restoring it to its owner. In one newspaper ad he reminded prospective customers that "your watch is a very delicate and exact instrument, so be careful to whom you entrust it." He began to build a reputation for reliability and trustworthiness.

#

Steinbach was a time-conscious community where punctuality was highly valued and wasting time was a sin. There was always work to be done, and idleness or unproductive activities were fertile ground for the Devil to sow mischief. Most households would have had a clock or two, and watches, once the ornaments of the rich, were becoming more popular among common folk. To be on time, to save time, and to spend time wisely were all important virtues of farm and town folk alike, and vital to commerce.

And then there was time everlasting. In Dad's diary the oft-repeated word "eternity" seems infused with dread. His entry for March 1, 1932 reads: "Another month gone into eternity, and another 29 days closer to the judgement day." On his birthday that year, he asks himself: "Have I improved? Have I failed to make good?" Warming to the subject, the entry for July 17, 1933 reads:

> Oh, how time flies! And every day, every hour, yes every second we are coming nearer to eternity. Where will we spend our eternal life? Through the blood of our saviour it has been made possible to have everlasting life. God, be merciful to us! We thank thee, that we too are cleansed through the blood of Christ. Amen.

"Where will you spend eternity?" As a child I had that menacing question imprinted on my mind by the revival preachers who held annual campaigns in Steinbach. The reassurance that Christ had died for me so that I could have eternal life was never quite as strong as the cold fear of being turned back at the pearly gates. To be sent down to an eternity of suffering.

I was not alone in my fear. All Mennonites more or less subscribed to the view that time marched along in a straight line, ending in the grave. After which would come the great Judgement Day, and eternity—time stretching endlessly, either in the company of tortured sinners in hell or blissful saints in heaven. While everyone naturally hoped to find themselves with the saints, many were nagged by doubts, wondering whether they had lived purely enough to earn that reward.

Even time past had an eternal or absolute quality—it could not be retrieved, could not be lived again; if you had wasted it you could not do anything to redeem it. Thoughts and actions took on an earnest, anxious quality. For Dad, eternity always lurked somewhere in his awareness; more so, perhaps, because he made a living by "keeping time." Every moment was a gift from God, not to be wasted in frivolity.

Time could also be benevolent:

May 21, 1933: Sunday. Very nice day. When one takes a
walk on Sunday morning, when peace & rest seem to be
settled all over God's universe, birds singing, giving praise
to their creator, then one is likely to have deep feelings of
humble thankfulness stirred up and one also is ashamed
about not being more thankful.

He was newly a father when he wrote this. His romantic sentiment,
finding God in nature, is countered with a Christian self-admonishment
to show more gratitude. This despite an economic environment so pinched
that some local farmers had reverted to pulling their wagons with oxen on
their visits to town.

#

Dad seemed to be taken off guard by the arrival of babies in his household.
His earnest prayer betrays his uncertainty: "Yes, it is a great responsibility
to bring up children in the way of God. Oh Lord, give us wisdom to do
what's right to these children that thou hast intrusted unto us."

Dad and Mom sent $10 to the Chicago Mail Order for a little overcoat
for Alvin. The order included a "premium" of six silver teaspoons—as close
as any of us would get to being born with a silver spoon in our mouths. Very
likely the slightly extravagant purchase would have been Mom's idea, but
on the other hand Dad might have been hooked by the hint of wealth and
status in the midst of his struggles to make a living during the Depression.

Dad even took two-year-old Alvin to "Toyland" in the Eatons store in
Winnipeg at Christmastime. It turned out that Alvin "was scared of the
Santa Claus." What is surprising is that Dad would have exposed his child
to a myth that most Mennonites regarded as an idolatrous distraction from
the true meaning of the holiday. Ironically, as an adult Al would for many
years play Santa Claus at his neighbourhood Royal Canadian Legion.

There are more pictures of Alvin as a baby than of any of the rest of us.
He was the first, and he occupied that special place in our parents' hearts.

He would grow up to be a tall and handsome young man who would challenge the hallowed Mennonite value of "obedience to parents." This was not so much a matter of willful rebellion as it was instinctual, a boy following his wishes and desires.

Another boy, Donald, was born in 1934. Dad, perhaps remembering stories of children in the community dying of whooping cough at the turn of the century, had his boys vaccinated against the disease. In those early years, Dad would sometimes babysit while Mom went to church or "cousin circle." But as they got older, the boys were more than a handful for him. He declared them to be "mischief makers, as all lively boys are." "And," he added with a note of exasperation, "they take up much time in being watched." The boys ran away when called; in church they would not sit still. On the sidewalks of Steinbach they not only failed to step aside for adults, they actually took a running start and tried to butt their heads into the ample belly of "Bosch Reima," one of the town's heftier citizens. One Sunday when Dad was preaching, the boys sneaked out of the church and took some valve caps from the engines of cars in the parking lot.

Donald and Alvin on Main Street in front of Dad's shop.

Dad did what he felt was his parental duty in punishing his sons. He would take them to the barn and hit them on the buttocks with a length of rubber heater hose, his face reddening with anger. He perceived a telling character difference in the boys when they were just two and three: "When Donald gets a spanking he'll try very hard not to cry, in which Alvin is different." Donald's refusal to cry—did Dad think of this as rebellion? Rebellion was not to be tolerated. Had not Satan led the angels in rebellion against God? But it was Alvin who stole the hose and chopped the offending strap into little pieces with an axe. He got another licking for doing this, with a new length of hose.

As a boy Dad also had been spanked, by his grandfather or his father. Mennonites of the time thought that physical punishment of their children was a parental and even a religious obligation; without such measures children would become headstrong and go astray.

The boys were on their best behaviour on a family trip to Winnipeg on Victoria Day, 1939, to see the visiting British Royals, King George VI and Queen Elizabeth. W. Finkel, a business counterpart, invited Dad to watch the parade from his downtown jeweller's show window. Alvin thought that his father must be an important man, to be accorded this honour. Dad documented the occasion:

> Wednesday. The big Day. At 4 A.M. parents & we arose, got ready, left at ¼ to 6, at Winnipeg at 7:10 but rather early yet. Went to W. Finkels, got breakfast yet. Went to Finkels office, sat in show window, saw the Royal couple, drizzling all forenoon. Went to Finkels for dinner [i.e., lunch]. In afternoon, saw King & Queen twice & twice in eve. Big crowds roaring welcome. Everybody likes the King & Queen, God save them.

Dad's praise for the monarchy corresponds with the belief of his ancestors, that God had ordained these rulers. In contrast, democratic governments were suspect because they were human institutions established by the grace of the people, not God.

Finkel's name suggests he was Jewish. His warm and generous invitation to a small-town Mennonite family implies a kind of friendship—and also, the ability on both sides to transcend religious and ethnic differences.

Dad tried to help his sons channel their energy in positive ways. On a few occasions he made them toys. Once when they got the measles, he built toy steam engine tractors for each of them, using a short log for the body, wooden wheels, and strings for a steering mechanism. Don remembers: "We were proud of our new toys. I could tell my friends, 'Look what my dad did.' He was my hero."

#

Soon after establishing his business, Dad got involved in community affairs, becoming assistant secretary of the Steinbach Board of Trade and successfully campaigning against the planned opening of a beer parlour.

The routine of everyday life was broken one summer day when Dad's brother Jake's little niece fell head first into a full rain barrel. The girl's sister cried out and Dad quickly ran over to the rescue. No medals were handed out for this small act of heroism. Dad is completely self-effacing in telling the story; even the words "I pulled her out" were added to the diary only after his stroke.

In 1935 Dad bought the Steinbach Hall, next door to his parents' house on Main Street. The vendor was Loewen Garage but the hall had previously been owned by one Harry Schwartz, who put in a maple hardwood floor and held dances. This enterprise failed for lack of participation in a community where dancing was seen as a sinful expression of carnal lust. Seventh Day Adventists and Jehovah's Witnesses had also used the hall for their meetings, but neither of these sects was able to get much of a toehold in the solidly Mennonite village. Dad borrowed $200 from his future brother-in-law, mink rancher Jake Thiessen, for the down payment on the total price of $615. His father signed a promissory note on the loan, to be repaid within three years. Thus Dad entered the ranks of property owners, gaining status and more ability to influence local affairs.

After they moved into the building, Mom painted the hardwood floor. Grandfather asked Dad: "*Wua'romm latzt ar daut foawe . . . en dann noch greiw?*" [Why do you let her paint it . . . and then grey?] Dad shrugged; when it came to their living space he wanted to please his wife. He made a few basic renovations; the front part of the building became his shop while the rear served as a residence. He installed a glass counter. On the front sidewalk, he placed a penny scale for citizens worried about the poundage they might have added from their latest over-indulgence in farmer sausage

and *Vereneki*. Dad noted that "the scale is doing fairly good business, about 35¢ a day. Some boys are also trying monkey shines on it."

By the end of the year he had a telephone connected. He got more customers. "I believe business is decidedly better than last year or the three or four last years," he declared. Soon, an old, leaky-roofed wood-frame building was moved to the lot behind the shop and attached, becoming the family's living quarters.

The village's library, a collection of morally uplifting and religious material, all in German, was moved into Dad's office. He ran the library purely as a community service for ten years or more, in accord with his life-long love of books and his belief that the German language provided a spiritual vocabulary for the Mennonite people.

Later, in the early 1950s, Dad would become part of a community movement called "*Die Erhaltung der deutschen Muttersprache*" [preserving our mother tongue]. Perhaps he loved the language because it had become a part of Mennonite identity and represented a proud heritage of great German philosophers and poets. But Canada was an English-speaking country, and two world wars had been fought against a German-speaking enemy. During the 1930s, the *Steinbach Post* and German-language newspapers in Winnipeg published articles sympathetic to Adolf Hitler, promoting Mennonite identification with the German *Volk*. To some extent the German language itself was tainted because of this. Also, more than one Steinbach citizen had to answer in civil court for sympathizing with the Nazis.

My brother Al says that he once found a book in this library with Hitler's picture in it. Dad immediately took the book away and tore up the picture, without explanation. Al thought he had stumbled upon a secret, and the evidence had to be destroyed.

When the horrors of the Nazi legacy became widely known, the future of the German language among the Mennonites was also imperilled. In any case, the assimilative power of English was already overwhelming the *Muttersprache* advocates, in both the church and the community at large.

The watchmaking business was steady but the profit margin was always nerve-rackingly small. In the middle of a long cold spell when temperatures sank deep below zero, Dad noted, half-comically, that "many a citizen is vainly looking for milder weather, at the same time watching with horror the rapid vanishing of his woodpile." In his own place, "we didn't put more wood into the stove during the night & the water froze in the wash basin, also a flower plant that Margaret had planted a few days ago, froze." One morning he got up after a frigid night to find three goldfish lying at the bottom of their bowl. "One revived though."

Yet it was a time when citizens could rely on each other. Dad was distraught when he somehow lost or misplaced $13—a very significant amount of money at that time. When the money was found and returned, his great relief found expression in Biblical language: "Rejoice with me because the $13 are found." One Christmas he had the opportunity to help a fellow Steinbacher. Someone had stolen a parcel from Abram R. Toews' sleigh ("about as mean a thief as you can think of") and a man named Frank Dueck collected $20 from sympathetic townspeople. The money "was later brought to A. R. Toews by me & Frank in Dad's car. A real Christmas joy."

In July of 1936 the weather was again extreme—except now it was unbearably hot. Temperatures climbed to 104 degrees Fahrenheit, and twenty Manitobans died. The sun seared the crops in the fields. People could hardly work, but Dad carried on, getting some relief at his repair bench from an electric fan. "Sweat everybody, sweat," he exclaimed. But ultimately he cultivated an attitude of acceptance: "There is an almighty Creator, he knows what's best for us."

Like all the businesses fronting onto Main Street, Dad's shop had to contend with dust kicked up by the wind or passing vehicles. The street was improved in 1937 with a fresh coat of gravel. A *Steinbach Post* correspondent commented: "We used to dream about having gravel when we were deep in the mud of Main Street. What should we dream now, when every car that goes along the street raises a cloud of thick dust? What should we do with our eyes, ears, and last but not least, our lungs?" Merchants were obliged to clean their shop windows regularly. The street would not be paved until 1947.

Steinbach Main Street, 1930s.

Dad scraped together sufficient funds to do a major renovation of his shop in the summer of 1938. He contracted a local builder to tear down the old wood-frame structure and replace it with one boasting a fresh white stucco exterior and new display windows. He kept the dance hall flooring from the old building and reused it in the new one. He also had local painter Bill Wiebe make a sign declaring "P. D. Friesen, watches, clocks," in sans serif wooden letters slanting to the right as if blown by the winds of progress. He was happy with the results: "The office sure stands out beautiful & looks better as I had expected as a whole." A special business bulletin in the *Steinbach Post* boasted that "our people were at no time in the grip of the Depression 'fear' that was so much in evidence in many localities," and Dad's expansion project was one example of the village's progress that year.

Renovated shop on Main Street, with Mom in front.

Where he could, Dad made economies: "I bought some index folders and made a crude letter file from a pear box." He was more extravagant in buying a safe for $125, with payments of $5 per month.

INSPECTORS

That's what we all like to be. So come and inspect our new

WATCH & CLOCK REPAIR SHOP.

We have also inlarged our stock, and added some other lines.

NOTICE — We have many articles that are very suitable for gifts like watches, clocks, chains, change purses, key cases, lamps etc.

FINE WATCH REPAIRING.

P. D. FRIESEN Phone 56-1 STEINBACH

Ad in Steinbach Post, 1938.

No repairs were done to the leaky-roofed shack which served as a home. Alvin and Donald started school and were shocked to discover that they were expected to speak English. On his first day, Alvin went home at noon and told Mom he wasn't going back because he couldn't understand anything. At home everyone spoke Low German. Meanwhile, church services and even Sunday school were held in High German, which the boys did not understand either. The languages of school and church were not the language of home, and the boys struggled because of this disconnect.

By the time I was born, our household was speaking both English and Low German. I had no need to adapt to a new language at school but I did pay a price, never learning our mother tongue properly. And neither my nor my siblings' children learned it at all.

Mom was relieved and glad when Mary Ann was born in April of 1937. Now she had a daughter, offsetting the overwhelming energy of her boys. Dad was also excited; he passed by the offices of the *Steinbach Post* that morning and announced: "A girl! Just arrived!"

Mennonite girls and women were expected to fit into the traditional female role, learning the tasks of running a household and garden, and showing modesty and submissiveness in their overall comportment. Mary Ann, friendly and outgoing, did not conform to this role and occasionally came into conflict with Dad because of it.

Mary Ann was born with the soul of a rambler. As a young girl she demonstrated a love of *rommdriewe*, of drifting, exploring the neighbourhood and beyond. She would go out without telling anyone. She was curious to the point of nosiness, knocking on random doors and asking the inhabitants if she could see the house. In the close community that Steinbach was at that time she was probably quite safe, but still, her parents did not care for this unauthorized wanderlust, and Dad warned her that she was not to go out without permission. She persisted, until one day he tied her to a chair to show her that he meant business. Also, he put pepper onto her tongue to cure her of lying about her whereabouts, or perhaps as a reminder that she was to tell the parents before gallivanting off.

Donald, Mary Ann and Alvin, circa 1940, at the back of house behind the watchmaker shop.

One Christmas Eve when she was perhaps six or seven, Mary Ann got into trouble for violating an unwritten dress code for girls. Mom had made her a charcoal grey dress with red flowers embroidered on the hem, and Aunt Greta was inspired to make a red crocheted coil which accented the dress beautifully at the neck. Mary Ann proudly wore her new dress and the coil, feeling ready for the church program, where she would sing or say a Bible verse along with other children. When everyone was seated at the table to eat before going, Dad noticed the "necklace." "You are not wearing that!" he said, and tore it off her neck. In his mind it should have been understood, even by the child herself, that such a worldly ornament was not befitting a daughter of a Kleine Gemeinde minister.

I think of Dad's reaction as harsh and unjustifiable. Yet I, like him, have acted toward my children in ways I later regretted—hitting, yelling. Dad might have been in pain from the sores on his legs, which bothered him all during the Christmas program in 1943, or he might have been feeling the stress of keeping the store open right until 5:00 p.m. that day for shoppers still wanting greeting cards. Or he might simply have been carried away by a fear that he would lose control of his daughter if he did not take swift action. What he forgot, or did not know, was that a show of tenderness would have created a stronger bond with her, and a greater desire on her part to please him.

The business got a boost when a scrawny red-haired young fellow named Peter Bergen, also a watchmaker, arrived in Steinbach on a visit from Morden. He dropped in to the shop to say hello and instantly struck up a friendship with Dad, who hired him for $40 a month, including room and board in the Klaas R. Friesen house. Dad knew right away he had a good thing: "He's a good worker and knows his job. He'll be quite a help to me." Bergen, true to this prediction, proved to be a reliable and skilful assistant, and Dad was chagrined when he left in May of 1941.

Aunt Marie, Mary Ann and Peter Bergen, 1939.

A parade of assistants followed. None stayed for very long. Dad noted that "my work in the office just simply won't get less, usually I'm working till 12 midnight or even later." He suffered from eyestrain but carried on: "My eyes are still affected & I have to work slow & take it easy. But it's so busy that it can't be helped overloading them."

The town's physician, Dr. Whetter, vaguely diagnosed the sores on Dad's legs as "skin disease." These sores would sometimes weep, and he wrapped them in clean rags concealed under his trouser legs and went about that way. He also suffered severe gall bladder attacks and spoke of a steady gut pain so harsh that "I can hardly work, or sleep during the night." The doctor advised "dieting, avoid fat & fried food." But fat and fried foods were staples of the typical Mennonite meal, and the diet fell by the wayside.

One of Dad's most promising helpers, eighteen-year-old Alvin Reimer, had business ability and a flair for promotion. He assisted with watch repair and helped do the books until enlisting with the Canadian military and shipping out overseas in 1944. Dad would surely have tried to persuade his young protégé to honour the centuries-old Mennonite teaching of not carrying arms, but the lure of adventure was stronger than any religious argument. Reimer became an instrument technician with the Royal Canadian Air Force.

Like others in the village, Dad eyed the possibility of expanding his business during wartime. He was one of sixteen men who gathered in a school classroom in 1941 with the intention of organizing a credit union. The manager of the single small bank in town had a reputation for parsimony, and would-be borrowers were frustrated at their inability to get loans. Very soon the Steinbach Credit Union became a going concern with a steadily growing membership. It was one of the few cooperative endeavours in the village's intensely competitive business environment. Dad was appointed to the "supervisory committee" but does not seem to have availed himself of any significant amount of money in the years that followed. However, he introduced his children to the concept of savings at an early age, helping each open an account of their own. Money management always mattered to him.

**Alvin Reimer
R. C. A. F.**

*Credit: Steinbach Collegiate
Yearbook, 1944.*

In 1942 Dad allowed himself the luxury of buying a new suit and hat from the tailor Sebastian Rieger—"for the first time in 25 years." Photographs show that, even as a young man, he had a penchant for three-piece suits, however shiny with wear they became. He wore the uniform which befitted a respected businessman and church leader even before assuming those roles. Dad's youngest sister Greta told me that sometime after his election as minister he received a new suit each year with the help of businessmen in the church, but none of us children remembers this generosity.

#

On Easter Sunday, April 5, 1942, the Friesen family world was shaken. That morning, just before Dad was to leave for the Blumenort church, Grandfather collapsed on the bathroom floor of his house, "dazed & unable to move." Dad and Barney dragged their father to his bed. The doctor came and determined that the old man had had a stroke. Grandfather lay in bed all that day, getting steadily weaker. At around 9:30 that night, sensing the end, he said: "Now God has put a wall around me, and Satan can tempt me no longer." At 10:10 p.m. he died.

K. R. Friesen's wife, children and in-laws around his coffin.

After the family recovered from their shock—"now we are dazed, can hardly believe that it has actually happened that father is no more with us"—Uncle Henry, who had long demonstrated a talent for machine work, took over the operation of Friesen Machine Shop. Other brothers were also interested in becoming partners. Grandfather, anticipating the possibility of jealousies and bad feelings, had written a note a few years earlier enjoining his children to "work together so that no person would cause disharmony." By and large, they succeeded in this. Dad served as executor of the estate. Grandmother, as spouse, received a settlement according to the guidelines of the traditional *Waisenamt*, a church agency tasked with ensuring fairness in matters of inheritance for women and children especially. Some years later, Barney became Henry's business partner.

Until this point Dad and Mom had not had a car of their own. For more than ten years they had managed by borrowing or hiring other people's vehicles or getting rides. Dad often accompanied his friend, the merchant Peter D. Reimer, to Winnipeg on business trips. Now Dad bought sign-painter Bill Wiebe's 1929 Model A Ford, for $250.

Dad built a wooden trunk for the Model A and installed it at the back of the car. For long trips he placed a length of 1" x 6" board inside along the doors, as a shelf or table for food. The car's cruising speed on the highway was only 45 mph. But now Dad had much more freedom to travel when and where it suited him.

Reckoning sheet for items purchased by K. R. Friesen's children after his death.

The family car, a 1929 Model A Ford. The picture was probably taken in 1945; the baby on Mom's lap is me. Mary Ann peers out of the side window from the back seat.

Grandmother lived on for another year and then died of cancer. Dad, who was again an executor of the estate, had previously declared his hope of buying the family house and lot, and the deal went through on August 1, 1943, for a price of $2150. His sister Greta, still single, took two small upstairs bedrooms. He now had a more spacious house for his family, which by that time had grown to five children. And he still had his watchmaking shop a few steps to the north on Main Street, and more work than he could handle alone. That October he sold a portion of the lot he had acquired when he bought the Steinbach Hall. The buyer was Peter K. Penner, owner of Penner's Transfer, and the price was $1400.

Our house, with barn at left rear.

In their new home Dad assigned Alvin and Donald responsibility for bringing in wood for the kitchen stove and coal for the living room Booker stove. The wood and coal were stored in the backyard barn which, by the 1940s, no longer sheltered any animals, although we kept chickens in an adjacent coop. The boys had to haul out ashes—always, it seemed, over-flowing—and dump them behind the barn. They also had to carry out the heavy *Kjietamma*—the slop pail stored underneath the kitchen sink—and empty the contents. In summer this smelly ash and slop heap was over-grown with tall weeds through which the chickens made pathways. When the chickens were no longer good for laying, Alvin slaughtered them with an axe. I watched in fascinated horror when Al let them run and jump about, their life-blood geyser-spouting out of their headless bodies.

Mom kept canned goods and pots and pans in the pantry adjacent to the kitchen. In the pantry was a long trap door which you could pull up with a thin rope and secure with a metal hook. Steep, worn stairs led down to the damp, earth-walled cellar. Mom sent the boys down there sometimes to fetch a jar of preserves from the shelves. They usually came back up very fast.

In that dimly lit cellar, on a shelf holding rows of canned pickles and tomatoes, was a jar containing something that was not food—a tapeworm, a long, pale, flat, segmented monster, preserved for no-one-knew how many years. This thing had once lived inside our father, and that was all we knew. It was a wonder, and we did not know whether to be proud or ashamed of it. You can get a tapeworm by eating undercooked meat from infected animals—in Dad's case that would likely have been pork, the main meat in the Mennonite diet. He does not mention this problem in any of his writings.

In the northwest corner of the cellar a small electric engine with a large drive wheel periodically burst into life to pump water from our artesian well. Grandfather had been one of the first citizens in the village to hook up an indoor plumbing system with running water and a flush toilet, and we children still took pride in this fact even after every other house in town was similarly equipped. Friends who might be hanging around the kitchen were surprised when the pump would abruptly start up with a trip-hammering clamour from below.

#

Had Dad been talented and ambitious enough in business, he might now have been positioned to prosper. But he had never been interested in making money for its own sake; his true ambition was to find a way of making a living sufficient for his family's needs while giving priority to what he called "the Lord's work." He was already pursuing the Lord's work as a minister, having been elected as such by the Steinbach Kleine Gemeinde in December of 1936. He preached on Sunday mornings, made visitations to parishioners, and attended ministerial and brotherhood meetings. As was customary among most Mennonite congregations, the church did not pay a salary.

In 1944 he made a ten-foot addition to the shop, providing more storage space. He hired other watchmaking assistants, and had to pay one of them $34.40 in arrears for a cost-of-living bonus after a visit from the government tax man. Always he struggled to keep up: "Usually work late in evenings, but still way behind." Other evenings he would be away on church business. Time pressures only increased when he was elected as the pastor of the Steinbach church in January, 1945.

Dad risked church disapproval by advertising fifteen-jewel watches, both men's and women's, with fancy-looking bracelets. One was called "Goddess of Time"—a name Dad must have thought blasphemous, but that's what the company called it, and that's how he advertised it. By this time his former employee Peter Bergen had set up "Bergen Jeweller" next door, promising "quality work and snappy service." Bergen sold jewellery as well as repairing watches, and was able to attract customers who were drawn to worldly ornamentation. The town was gradually giving way to the forces of assimilation and business owners were under pressure to keep up, or set the pace.

Dad made a non-business investment in the winter of 1945–6 when he hired a local man to tear down a small barn once used as a pigsty, and build

a wooden slide out of the scrap lumber "for the boys." The slide was located on part of the garden land he had acquired when he bought his parents' property. The neighbourhood children had fun zipping down the iced wooden chute for many winters after that

We children were told to frequent certain businesses because of family or church ties. Isaac Thiessen, our uncle Jake Thiessen's brother, had a shoe repair shop down Main Street, and we never went anywhere else. As a young boy Donald used to go to Thiessen's shop with his friend

Neighbourhood kids on the slide.

Floyd Hiebert to watch the "uncle" at work. They noticed that Thiessen made little trumpeting sounds with his mouth while he worked, and this they found funny and delightful, so they started to mimic him. Thiessen, not amused, phoned Dad to complain. Dad, in turn, told Donald that he had to go back to the shop and apologize. Slowly, heavy-hearted, Don traversed the section of Main Street between our house and the shoe repair shop. For a long while he stood in the shop doorway, not saying anything. At last he blurted, "I'm sorry," spun around, and ran back home at top speed. Perhaps it wasn't the full apology Dad had in mind, but that's where the matter ended. Growing up in Steinbach, one learned that every business transaction was also a personal one.

Select families in the town pulled ahead of the common people in building elaborate houses, driving big cars built in Detroit, and travelling to exotic destinations. Well-off businessmen said that God was blessing them because of their hard work and talent and willingness to take risks. Our feeling, growing up, was that we were not poor, but not well-off either; there was little money for "extras." We were taught to be *spoasaum*, thrifty, and not waste anything. Dad was close friends with one of the wealthiest men in Steinbach, C. T. Loewen—he even calls Loewen "my Dad" in one early diary entry—and maintained friendships as well with C. T.'s sons Edward and Cornie, who were driving forces behind the steady growth of the family lumberyard business.

Dad believed in the free enterprise system that Steinbach embraced so ardently, but he also was mindful of Jesus' sympathy for the poor. Always at mealtime prayers he would include a plea for "the poor and the needy."

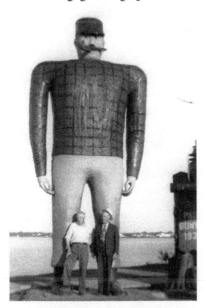

Dad and C. T. Loewen with legendary lumberjack Paul Bunyan, Bemidji, Minnesota, on a 1950 trip.

CHAPTER 11:
EVANGEL BOOK SHOP

Dad found a way of bringing his material and spiritual ambitions closer together. When his former employee and war veteran Alvin Reimer offered to buy his business in 1946, it seemed that the opportunity had come. Dad sold everything—the lot, building, stock, and most of the tools—for a total of $7000. The sale was made official on September 13th, with Reimer making a down payment of $2500, which he had borrowed from the bank. By this time Dad had clear title to the property he had purchased from his parents' estate three years before, and this gave the bank sufficient reassurance. It was a high-risk transaction, but necessary for the next part of Dad's plan.

He took out an ad in the *Steinbach Post* thanking customers for support over the last fifteen years and stating that "the reason for making this change is to devote more time to the Ministry." Ministry with a capital "M."

Together with his church colleagues Archie Penner and Ben D. Reimer, Dad now started negotiations to buy the local bookstore in Steinbach, owned by P. W. Friesen. Penner was an ambitious young Bible scholar from nearby Landmark and Reimer was a teacher at the Steinbach Bible Academy. The trio intended to stock the new store with Bibles and religious material. Dad was to run the business while Penner and Reimer were to be silent partners. In the meantime, Dad continued to repair watches, working for Alvin Reimer on a "60-40" basis for a few months until the deal could go through.

The store opened for business on January 2, 1947, as Christian Publications Service. The official purchase price was $3267.95.

That summer the small consortium paid $240 to buy out the complete stock of another shop, John R. Unger's small book and stationery sales business. They also bought an enterprise called the Variety Store. Theirs was now the only bookstore in Steinbach, and, although its mission was religious, they anticipated making profits from selling school books and supplies. When school started at the end of August, the new store was "busy as never before." Dad travelled to Winnipeg and returned with car-loads of school texts and supplies. In frustration he complained that "it's just impossible to know just what books are needed as there are quite a few options on some topics."

All of Dad's watchmaking assistants had been male, but for helpers in the bookstore he hired young single women from Kleine Gemeinde church families, like Tina Doerksen and Marianne Loewen, and then Wilma Toews of the Johann R. Toews family. Wilma recalls that "I was young; I couldn't do the same job that Tina and Marianne did, but your dad was always patient. He never said, 'You have to'; he was always gentle in his instructions."

Alvin Reimer, meanwhile, lost no time in transforming the humble watchmaking shop, renaming it "A. F. Reimer, Jeweller." Now custom-ers could buy not just watches, but diamonds, costume jewellery, and silverware.

#

Reimer misjudged the local market, however, and soon ran into finan-cial difficulties. By April, 1948, he had skipped town, leaving a large amount of inventory—and a host of unpaid creditors, including National Revenue Canada—behind.

Dad was the principal creditor. Reimer fled to Los Angeles, where he found employment in a jewellery shop while staying with his uncle and aunt. Severely pressed, Dad sold the school textbooks and supplies part of the enterprise to A. A. Toews for $1900, leaving himself with a mixed business of Christian books, religious supplies, and, once again, watch repair. This last he named Main Watch Clinic.

Dad held onto the inventory Reimer had left behind, but much of it could not be sold, as dealing in jewellery, in particular, would have been unacceptable to him and to the church. Whatever anger he might have felt toward Reimer, or distress about lost money, go unmentioned in his diary. In fact, there are no entries at all from January 1 to mid-May of 1948, possibly because Dad was scrambling desperately to keep afloat financially.

Eno Reimer was now listed as the watchmaker at Main Watch Clinic, and P. D. Friesen as proprietor. Dad also recruited his own son Alvin, just turning fifteen, as a helper. Dad looked after the Clinic's paperwork while also running the bookstore. Ben D. Reimer withdrew from the bookstore partnership and Dad bought out Archie Penner's share. He was now sole owner of both the watch repair and the bookstore enterprises.

Perhaps thinking that he needed to step up his marketing efforts, Dad got carried away with a *Carillon News* ad:

> Come in and see our complete display of Bibles. Large Bibles, small Bibles, illustrated children's Bibles, Bibles in German, English, Ukrainian, French, Catholic, School Bibles, Bibles for the older folks, for pulpit use, teachers Bibles, pocket or purse Bibles, white, red, black and blue colors, with soft or stiff, leather or cloth binding, and then you should see all the different types of New Testaments! Christian workers' Testaments, Testaments showing the wonderful promises, the sayings of Jesus in red. A Bible and Testament for every need, pocket or purse.

Evidently Dad wanted to support mission work among the surrounding French and Ukrainian communities. But he also risked offending them by selling an anti-Catholic booklet called *I was a Priest*, written by a former cleric from St. Pierre and published by the Canadian Protestant League.

Eugene Derksen, editor of the *Carillon News*, refused to carry advertising for it, but the book still sold out.

A new buyer for the watch repair business now stepped up. In April, 1949, Dad's former employee Peter Bergen purchased the Main Watch Clinic, giving Dad the wherewithal to expand the bookstore operation. He bought the Royal Bank building on Friesen Avenue from his uncle John D. Goossen for $1500, intending to move it onto his own property in front of the family residence. First he had to remove the row of freshly budding maple trees lining the street—the same trees which had been planted by his grandfather in the first years of settlement. He sent sixteen-year-old Alvin up with a bucksaw to cut away branches, and then he pulled down the trunks with a block and tackle rig. By June, Loewen Brothers Moving had settled the old bank structure firmly on its new concrete foundation.

The former bank building being moved in front of our house.

#

Dad wanted his sons to have a good education, perhaps follow in his foot-steps running the bookstore and doing church work. The Steinbach Bible Academy had introduced a high school program and Dad persuaded Alvin to attend. The teenager didn't care for Bible study but was enticed by the shorter school year at the Academy. He liked one teacher especially—John

Peters, a Russian Mennonite who had transferred his church allegiance from the Mennonite Brethren when he married his Kleine Gemeinde sweetheart. Peters brought personal warmth, artistic flair, and bottomless enthusiasm to his work. Alvin was astonished to see his teacher shedding a tear when reading a poem—it had never occurred to him that poetry could have such an effect, and besides, he was completely unaccustomed to seeing soft emotions in a man.

Alvin had a penchant for skipping school and hitchhiking to Winnipeg to watch movies with a friend. One day a number of male teachers formed a circle around him and pressured him, strenuously, to get "saved." He put a hard shell of silence around himself and simply withdrew. This event marked a kind of turning point for him, away from the school and from religion, and in that sense away from Dad as well. Before long, he quit school and started work at Friesen Machine Shop, now owned and operated by his uncles Henry and Barney. So he stayed connected to the extended family business, but it was clear that he would not be succeeding Dad in the bookstore, or any kind of religious vocation.

Donald and Alvin with cinder-block wall of Penner's Transfer as backdrop.

Donald earned spending money with a paper route. One day he bought a radio, a crystal set. He brought it home and tried to conceal it, believing that the set would not be allowed in our household. Inevitably, Dad discovered it, and Donald was sure it would be taken away. Instead, Dad would even sit down with him to listen to the occasional hockey game. Sometimes it was hard to know what Dad would really think of as sinful, or how seriously he would take misdemeanours.

Dad's tolerance may have had something to do with memories of himself as a younger man going to Loewen Garage to listen to the Schmeling-Sharkey boxing match on the wireless. As a twenty-eight-year-old, he had even traded in his car for a radio. It must have been a great radio, or not a very good car. Even after his conversion experience, he installed an aerial on the roof of his first watchmaker's shop "for my crystal set."

When Donald was in Grade 9, Dad told him that if he passed his grade, however marginally, he would continue in high school. If he did not pass, he could go to work. Going to work was exactly what the boy wanted, so his response was predictable. He ignored his studies and failed his grade. He went to work as a labourer with C. T. Loewen Lumber, at sixty cents an hour. Most of his earnings had to go back to our parents for room and board, but he didn't care; he was working and making money, and had left school behind at last.

I think Dad, when he was a boy, would have stayed in school if he could have, and I think that's why he tried to encourage Donald to continue. The elementary schools of the time held an official visitors' day every March and Dad would usually drop in to classrooms. One year he was nominated for a school trustee position, though not elected. He even thought his sons might pursue a profession, which would have been a leap into new territory in our family. But nothing like this materialized for the older children.

In the early '50s Dad was helping a branch of the Kleine Gemeinde to get established in Winnipeg, and Donald, who was taking accordion lessons, accompanied him on his weekly trips. One day Dad, driving back to Steinbach, got a severe gallstone attack and began to writhe in pain. He told Donald to take the wheel. "*Jung, nu foah,*" (son, now drive), Dad commanded, and Donald pressed the accelerator to the floor and got the Model A up to 60 mph. He could see that Dad could hardly contain himself. He was proud that he could help him.

As an eighteen-year-old, Donald made the decision his parents hoped he would make. In her diary Mom wrote: "We cry for joy because the Lord is so merciful, and in this day saves sinners, and that He saved Donald today." And driving, it happened, would be his profession; he became a long-haul trucker.

#

I was four when Dad had the bank building moved in front of our house. I wanted to be part of the goings-on. On a late June afternoon, when the adults were preoccupied with organizing things, I was there, too, big-eyed and curious. An impressive glass and oak counter was brought in to stand behind the show windows facing Main Street. On one wall a white wooden bookcase, reaching almost to the ceiling, stood empty, the horizontal boards making a kind of natural ladder. I was inspired by a desire to climb it. Intent on my purpose, I grasped the shelf above my head, placing my feet on a lower shelf. I thought I noticed a slight movement but told myself it wasn't a problem; this thing must surely be nailed to the wall. I hoisted myself up another level and looked back excitedly; I could look at the place

With Mom in June, 1949; I'm clingy but apparently okay after the shelf fell on me.

now from almost an adult height. Emboldened, I reached for the next higher shelf . . . and then I felt myself tipping backward with the whole unit rushing swiftly down toward me, while I clung on with my little hands as if my clinging would save me.

I woke up on the chesterfield in the living room. My mother's worried face gazed down at me. Norman remembers her sitting in a chair, shaking. Was my father there? "*Etj well Gjrett,*" I said. I want porridge. Perhaps I was under the impression that it was morning time, breakfast time. No harm had come to me, as my head had fortuitously been positioned in the space between shelves. "God protected," wrote Dad in his diary.

#

Dad equipped the store with a coal-burning furnace and put up a new sign in wooden lettering above the show window, in the same style previously used for the watchmaker shop: "P. D. Friesen, Evangel Book Shop." He rented one side of the building to the barber John Kehler, and rooms at the back and on the second level as apartments.

Alvin and Donald had to transport coal for the furnace from the barn behind our house. It was hard and dirty work, loading the big chunks onto a sleigh and then trudging through the deep snow past the house and up to the store. Later Dad connected the house and store with an unheated passageway and had a bin constructed for the coal. An electrically powered augur moved the coal directly to the furnace. That worked well, although the boys still had to take the *Kjlietasch* (lumps of unburned material) from the furnace and carry them to the dump behind the barn. Also, it was not a safe system.

In the store, Bibles formed the backbone of the inventory, but Dad also filled the shelves with Christian literature, including the polemics of American fundamentalist John R. Rice and the moralistic fiction of Bernard Palmer, whose protagonist Danny Orlis was well-known to most Steinbach young people from the *Back to the Bible* radio broadcast of Theodore H. Epp, out of Lincoln, Nebraska. Young female readers, especially, were drawn to the works of Grace Livingston Hill.

Dad also stocked secular fiction. Sometimes he allowed himself to be influenced by Vern and Norm, who lobbied successfully for animal titles (*Frog, the Horse That Knew No Master*, or *Big Red*, a boy-and-his-dog story). Dad even stocked the full series of Franklin W. Dixon's crime-solving Hardy Boys.

The store was a kind of haven for bookish and sensitive young girls in Steinbach. Iris Reimer Nowakowski remembers, as a girl in the early 1950s, heading down the left aisle where the popular books were stocked and wishing she could make a purchase. One time she did have money, and bought *Bambi*, the novel by Felix Salten on which the Disney film was based. Most of the time she just looked, poring over books that she found interesting. Dad never asked her to leave, and didn't even watch very carefully to see what she was up to. He let her be.

Marianne Kroeker Moll, daughter of church members Ben D. and Marie Kroeker, recalls that the store carried all the Grace Livingston Hill and Emily Loring books. Dad carried more than thirty titles by Hill, whose "story books," selling at $1.59 each, he advertised as "wholesome, refreshing, with a good Christian message." Marianne was a customer of some means, and reckons that she must have bought every new book in these series as they came in. She remembers Dad as a soft-spoken, gentle man, sitting on his high stool behind the counter—again, letting her be. On one occasion, however, her purchase elicited a comment. She bought a diary with a lock. "It's important to have a lock," she said, "so nobody can read it." "Well," he said, "you should make sure that you write about things that, if others read it, you wouldn't be ashamed you had written it."

Dad's own diary would probably withstand the "unashamed" test.

Marianne's younger sister Phyllis also remembers Dad "actually noticing me as he descended the steps coming out of his store with a book under his arm: very blue eyes behind his glasses, with a lovely smile as he greeted me. It was extremely unusual for me to be noticed by an adult, and I was warmed by the interchange."

I remember one constant in the front show window display. For years, an eighteen-inch ceramic slinking black panther stood there, incongruous with the "evangel" name of the store. I loved that piece and would have liked to have it in the house. When Vern led a neighbourhood group of boys on various escapades, he called them "the panther gang," possibly inspired by this figurine.

Was the panther an avatar from the ancestral past? When Dad's aunt Helena was nine she accompanied her father to Winnipeg, and, while visiting the home of his acquaintances, gazed with longing admiration at a plaster figure of a lion fighting a snake. Touched by this innocent covetousness, the people said she could have the statuette, and to her delight her father let her take it home. These figures—the lion, the snake, the panther—pointing silently to an exotic, animal world, were almost pagan in their power to excite a child's imagination.

Even more improbably, Dad displayed a large balsa wood model of an F-86 Sabre jet fighter, painted silver, with U. S. Air Force decals on the fuselage and wings. Vern had a passion for model-building and was meticulously faithful to authentic detail—perhaps Dad admired that. He certainly opposed the glorification of warfare, but somehow overlooked the blatant contradiction.

After hours we could access the rear of the store by a flimsy wooden door which opened with a skeleton key, whose very name evoked the possibility of mystery. Sometimes the last person in the store forgot to lock the door. But we never had a theft. Once Norman tied one end of a string to the metal doorknob and the other end to my loose tooth. I was dubious but also curious, and consented to the operation. Norm slammed the door but the tooth stayed in my mouth. That hurt, so I called off the experiment.

In the furnace room in back of the store, a dusty zither sat on a shelf, and we boys, passing through, would sometimes strum its strings. We never asked how it came to be there, or who had played it, but it was mute evidence of transgression against the church's "no instruments" rule in an earlier time. Mary Ann recalls that we used to have a ukulele in the house, apparently belonging to Dad, although she does not remember him playing it.

Besides books, Dad sold 78 rpm records of religious music, Sheaffer fountain pens, office supplies, wall plaques, Bulova watches, leather watch fobs, and even plastic Mountie figures. Mary Ann remembers a toy "car of tomorrow." We boys rejoiced in the metal kazoos, pretending to be saxophone players doing spittle-infused renditions of "When the Saints Go Marching In." We gave no thought to customers who might then buy these "instruments." The records included titles by southern gospel quartets like the Blackwood Brothers and the Stamps, some of which found their way into our household, accidentally creating a platform for "jungle music." Elvis Presley, a favourite of Vern's, was rooted in southern gospel.

In time Dad added a film processing service and even sold a few cameras and typewriters. Even prior to owning the bookstore he had bought a portable typewriter from Eatons for $74.75. He rationalized the expense to his diary: "Quite a price, but they are very scarce." He probably used it in his duties as secretary at ministerial meetings. Mary Ann taught herself to type on this machine during slow hours when she was clerking in the store. The typewriter also provided us younger boys with hours of diversion on Sunday afternoons when the store was closed, as we took turns tapping out sentences of a story whose plot unfolded as we wrote.

My cousin Grace, now deceased, recalled a moment not long after her father's death, when she and her mother and two small brothers were in the living room of our house. Baby Leroy was being *schlemm*, or irritable, and could not be calmed. Suddenly Dad got up, took the child into his arms, and went with him into the rear section of the bookstore. Grace was horrified because she thought Leroy was going to get a spanking. But she was much relieved, a little while later, when Dad returned with a now-smiling Leroy, having diverted his attention.

When the hired clerks had their days off and Dad was away, it was mostly Mom who minded the store, even though she already had more than she could handle with the housework. All of us children helped out as the years progressed, but no one wanted to get involved with the store in any serious way.

Even I, at twelve and thirteen, learned to ring in sales on the old mechanical cash register and to make proper change. It must have been Dad who taught me. Occasionally I was on my own, and then I hoped that customers would stay away, leaving me to read. I never asked anyone whether I could help them, and avoided eye contact. I did participate in the annual, laborious task of taking stock, recording all items on the shelves, from Bible concordances to shoelaces. I was given responsibility for the small stuff.

The store was a training ground for Norman, who had an aptitude for numbers. He actually liked taking stock, adding up figures on a clunky metal adding machine which spilled out long curling spools of paper. When Norman got a paper route, Dad noticed that the boy was spending his gains on ice cream and comics, and sat him down to teach him how to set up bookkeeping entries. Norman started recording his income and expenses in a notebook and before long saved up enough money to buy a new bicycle. After high school, he got a job at Barkman Hardware as a bookkeeper.

#

Mary Ann, the only girl, felt imprisoned by her situation. After Mom had done all her Saturday cooking and baking—and it was a lot—Mary Ann had to wash the kitchen floor. She hated this job, and decided she had to get away from it somehow. Perhaps it was her suppressed anger which came out so awkwardly once when Dad asked her to "phone ahead" and tell some people that he and Mom were coming for a visit. Impulsively, she shouted, "No!" and threw the comb she happened to have in her hand to the floor. Dad lost his temper, took her to the parental bedroom, and strapped her with his belt. She was fifteen.

Mary Ann tells this story calmly and without rancour. Of the strapping, she says, "I was too old for that," but adds: "I deserved it."

Soon Mary Ann started wearing earrings, in direct opposition to the church's teachings which Dad was committed to uphold. He objected, she insisted—and he let the matter drop. As a teenager, she attended church and Young People's meetings but wasn't overly interested in religious life.

She had a plan. The store became the means by which she would purchase her freedom. Like Donald, she disliked school, and when she finished Grade 9, she quit. Dad would have liked to see her go on, but her mind was made up. So he employed her as a full-time clerk in the bookstore, paying her $15 a week, with free room and board at home. She saved enough money to buy a bedroom suite, which then became part of her "dowry." By the time she was eighteen, Dad made one dramatic gesture toward pleasing her, buying the piano she had long begged for. But it came too late; by then her interests had shifted to romance and courtship. When she wasn't around I would sometimes sneak into her room to read her love comics, but was disappointed to find that nothing interesting ever happened in them.

The family, November, 1953. I have the same kind of jacket as Vern.

In 1956 she got married. Dad would not conduct the wedding, since neither she nor her husband, Dave Goertzen, were church members. He also refused to "give her away," as that would have broken church rules.

Mary Ann and Dave made their home in Winnipeg, as did Don and his wife Anne when they married the following year. Don and Anne were church members, and Dad did officiate at their wedding. He raised no objections to his children leaving Steinbach, although he probably would have preferred them to stay. He respected their autonomy and by this time had also come to believe that the Mennonite faith could be practised in an urban landscape. When a branch of the EMC opened in Winnipeg in 1957, he gave his active support.

Only after some years of marriage did Mary Ann become converted, at a revival meeting of the Janz Team. Dave followed her example, and subsequently they both faithfully attended an EMC church in Winnipeg. Mary Ann, like Don, became a life-long member of choirs and other singing groups.

CHAPTER 12:
THE YOUNGER BROTHERS

Photographs of the house from the 1950s show sagging eaves troughs, storm windows leaning against the wall, and a missing plank in the low platform on which Mom stood to hang out the laundry. Dad, although he certainly had the skills to do repairs himself, was too busy; he could not afford to pay others, and we, his sons, either did not know how to do the work or did not care to learn.

Mom tried planting flowers beside the house but had little time or energy for nurturing them and eventually gave up. A patch of *Brennkrüt*, or stinging nettles, grew tall at the side of the driveway and Dad handed me a "grass whip" to cut it down. I didn't mind this job because I felt kind of powerful wielding this scythe-like tool.

In the summer kitchen at the back of the house, Mom did the laundry using a wringer washer, passing the soaked shirts and sheets through tight rollers and into a metal tub. Then she'd take the tub out to the umbrella-style clothes dryer outside and pin up the wrung wash. Her stepmother before her had always taken pains to hang underwear on the inside lines and sheets on the outside, but I don't know whether Mom followed this extra-modest method.

When I was little, we had meals in the summer kitchen on hot days. Mom cooked on a rusting old wood stove squatting at one end of the long room. The summer kitchen got an intensive cleaning from Mom and Aunt Marie every spring but inevitably accumulated junk, and after a while the shelves and cupboards and tables were again covered with dust and mouse shit and cardboard boxes. Somewhere along the line, the place slipped from my parents' grasp and become a holding area for stuff we weren't ready to throw out. Once Mom unexpectedly fired up the stove and the toy cars and trucks that Vern, for reasons nobody understood, had stored in a box underneath, melted into a multi-coloured mass of plastic. Vern was enraged, Mom was apologetic, but there was no undoing what had happened.

Mom outside the summer kitchen.

At my friend Allan Toews' house on Mill Street, his mother kept a flower garden alongside their house. She grew tiger lilies, which appeared each summer, flagrant in their brown-spotted orange display of curving petals and proudly erect stamens. I liked how the tiger lilies looked, and I liked their fierce-sounding name. I thought that my own parents would not have dared to plant such an extravagant flower.

As a child I was a little embarrassed by the messiness of our place, in comparison with some of our neighbours' well-kept houses and yards. Our place, and perhaps we children too, suffered from a kind of benign neglect. Our parents did take care of the basics; they made sure that we went to Sunday school and church, and had food and clothing. They took us on trips both large and small. They tried to keep us out of harm's way, and taught us to take responsibility for our actions. Mom faithfully nursed us through every childhood sickness imaginable. At the same time, our parents gave us our freedom. There is a Low German expression, a kind of admonishment parents give attention-seeking children: "*Weet jüselfst*"—meaning, essentially, figure it out yourselves. Once we had exited the house on a summer's afternoon, we happily roamed the neighbourhood at will.

There was nothing terribly unusual, when I was young, in having a father who was often absent, or reserved in emotional expression toward his children. Such fathers were commonplace in our culture and in the mainstream culture too. We children did not think of ourselves as deprived. We accepted family patterns as they were, and did not dream of having the ability to change them.

In learning how to figure things out for ourselves we both gained and lost. We gained because we learned how to be comfortable with our own company, reading or inventing games or drawing. We lost because at least some part of ourselves might have been unsure of our parents' love for us—were we valued for ourselves, and not just as performers of never-ending chores? We knew what our religion instructed. We were to respect and obey our parents. We did not expect hugs or words of endearment from them. In Sunday school we were told that Jesus loved us, and we believed that, but our everyday experience of this love was somehow disembodied.

"Neglect" is a word I had not considered in relation to my upbringing until I went to therapy as an adult. My counsellor suggested to me that my parents, in leaving us children to our own devices, had been neglectful. I was taken aback. I did not agree with this suggestion then, though I now concede there is something to it.

If there was neglect, then religion was part of it. Dad didn't seem confident in his own example but thought he needed to hand his children over to the designated soul-savers—Bible camp counsellors, revival meeting speakers, even local businessmen and church ladies—who would bring us to a conversion experience. But none of these could take the place of a human, personal connection with our father. I think Dad knew that, but also forgot it.

Norman, attending Daily Vacation Bible School in our church one summer, felt suddenly compelled to be *bekjeat*, converted. He was perhaps twelve. His teacher instructed him to kneel and pray. Norman was reluctant, and put off by the man's bad breath, but he obeyed, and then felt happy:

I thought, well I know Mom and Dad would be ecstatic. (But would I?) Feeling very light hearted after "the process" I ran home to bring Mom the news. Dad was somewhere else, I know not where. She casually replied, while doing dishes, "That's nice" or something to that effect. I expected a much more profound reaction. Disillusionment! My "saved" status lasted all of a few hours. Might it have been otherwise if there had been weeping acknowledgements?

The young boy, thinking he has pleased his parents, comes to them holding his soul extended in front of him, having made the sacrifice that will mean so much to them—and finds a casual, even indifferent response from his mother, and none at all from his father, who "was somewhere else." Did Mom even speak to Dad about the great news her son had brought home? Neither of them mentions the event in their diaries. Dad didn't come to Norman with tears of rejoicing. He didn't come to him at all.

And so Norman was "saved" for a few hours only before returning to

Norman and Vern, my role models.

his previous outlook. Had he been older, he might have understood that our spiritual experiences are not meant to be offerings to our parents. But he was only a boy.

Dad surely wished that his children would experience the same joy he had in the knowledge that his sins were forgiven. In general, though, we hung onto the same notion he'd had of himself before his conversion: "I wasn't so bad." Dad believed that such a self-forgiving idea was one of "old Satan's" wiles. But what if old Satan was fairly accurate in this assessment?

Vernon, two-and-a-half years older than Norm, was a sensitive and creative child, closer to Mom than to Dad. All of the boys were given second names, usually the names of uncles, and Vernon's was "Jacob." He had nothing against Uncle Jake but took an intense dislike to this name, as, for him, it carried the association of traditional, rural Mennonitism. His strong reaction naturally provided others with teasing material. Alvin delighted in calling him "Jakie," and, even worse, the Low German "Jasch." As soon as he was old enough Vernon legally changed his second name to "James."

From early on, Vern experienced Dad as quietly but insistently demanding—whenever Dad saw the boy, he wanted him to do some task. Once Vern and Norman shovelled coal until they were as black as Welsh miners, and this heroic effort earned . . . nothing. Not an extra dime or even a word of thanks. Vern would not have known, or cared, that Dad was probably treated the same way by his own father. Carrying wood or hoeing the garden or picking striped beetles off potato plants had no appeal for the imaginative boy. So he learned to hide, avoiding his father.

Vern created a kind of alternative world more to his liking, borrowed from Tarzan comic books and the frontier romances of James Oliver Curwood. As leader of "the panther gang" he made neighbourhood boys follow him in various feats of derring-do, such as jumping from the barn roof to an adjacent outbuilding, or climbing high into the neighbourhood trees. I was too small to be a member but would tag along sometimes just to watch the older boys do stuff I would never dare.

In his imagination Vern was the brave warrior, the hero, a misunderstood yet well-born protector of the innocent, like Tarzan, or a cleanhearted bringer of justice such as Sergeant Preston of the Yukon. I followed in Vern's footsteps and practised Tarzan's spine-tingling victory cry or shouts of "Kreegah! Bundolo!" in the presence of bemused neighbourhood girls.

The fantasy of being a protector of the innocent might have emerged from Vern's own lack of such protection. As a young boy Vern, with some friends, climbed onto tractors standing in A. D. Penner's car lot and began to play, pressing the starter buttons just to make a noise. They were seen by a local businessman who phoned Dad to tell him that his boy had been caught "illegally" playing on the tractors. When Vern got home, Dad told him he would have to go and apologize to Mr. Penner. Vern protested his innocence, pointing out that no damage had been done. But there was no way out, only an apology would do. Reluctant and scared, Vern went to Penner's home. A. D. himself answered the door. Seeing the young culprit in front of him, he said: "You know what I should do? I should go and get a rubber hose and teach you a lesson." Vern was terrified. Penner did not carry out his threat, but the next day he requested that Vern come to his office at the garage. When Vern got there, Penner read a Bible verse to him and let him go, but Vern did not let go of the memory.

On the other hand, when it came to a direct offence against himself, Dad responded graciously. When Vern accidentally broke Dad's electric shaver and went to tell him, the response was: "That's okay, we wouldn't worry about that." There could be "forgiveness of sins"!

And then again there could be shame. During a family vacation at Clear Lake, five-year-old Vernon became curious as to what it would be like to undress completely. Not for a bath, but just to be naked. He was wearing an old-style swimsuit with shoulder straps, and enclosed himself in an outdoor toilet to take it off. But then, to his horror, he couldn't get it back on properly; the straps got all twisted. The adults must have commented. He was mortified.

A year or so later he had just started school, and was walking home when he felt a strong urge to urinate. He had wrongly estimated his ability to hold back and there was no place to go to the toilet, so he decided just to go in his pants. When he got home, Dad became very angry and made him wear a diaper for the night. For Vern, the lasting lesson was: your body is shameful, loss of control is shameful.

As an adolescent, Vern wanted to ask Dad some questions about sex and started to come at the subject indirectly, when Dad interrupted him and said: "You needn't talk about having a girlfriend." Something shameful here, too, something off-limits, a fear of the power of sex and desire. This was a wordless lesson we learned from our father, who must have had his own shame-body experiences.

Hanging in the second-floor hallway of our house was a facsimile of the *Mona Lisa*. We boys probably had some idea that the original was a famous painting, but no idea how the picture happened to be in our house, which otherwise did not have paintings. One day Vern and Norm discovered that Mona Lisa's barely discernible cleavage had been completely covered with the dark blue ink of a ballpoint pen. Now she was covered right up to her neck. The boys concluded that this was Dad's work, though they never worked up the nerve to ask him.

Of all of us children, Vern was most able to push our father toward bending the many rules which governed our actions. Guns were taboo, but somehow Vern was able to buy an air rifle. His sensitive nature apparently had a dark side; he proceeded to pick off large numbers of unsuspecting sparrows perching on the branches of our maple trees. Vern was also a talented artist, and it is a testimony to his powers of persuasion, or to Dad's desire to support his son, that Dad actually agreed to subsidize the cost of a "Famous Artists" correspondence course.

Vern did not take to Sunday school and church very well. Church services especially were boring to him, and so instead of listening to the sermon he and his friend Jim Reimer would make up new words for hymns, trying to contain their laughter and not attract attention. When the congregation sang "sometimes it causes me to tremble," he used the back of a church bulletin to draw a choir of finger-pointing ghosts in a cemetery.

He felt that the church demanded a decision of him with eternal consequences, either heaven or hell, and as a teenager considered himself too young to have to deal with such heavy questions. He wanted to be left alone. As a young adult, however, he did get baptized and joined the EMB church before getting married. He made his living as a parts man for different car dealerships in Steinbach, and kept late nights like our father had, only he built model airplanes as a hobby instead of repairing watches for a living.

Dad wore sunglasses on this trip to the U. S., but Vern was the coolest of us.

#

We also did connect with Dad at times.

It amused us boys to see him position his back against the lintel of the doorway between the kitchen and the living room and move rhythmically from side to side, like a papa bear at a tree scratching an itch. It did not occur to me then that he might have put on this display partly for our benefit.

On weekdays, the noon meal finished, he would retire to the living room chesterfield and have *Meddachschlop* (afternoon nap) for fifteen minutes or half an hour. Seeing him that way—snoring softly, in stocking feet, the pink skin of his skull visible through the strands of his thin grey hair, I felt faintly ill at ease. When he sat in the overstuffed blue rocking chair decorated with the white doilies Mom had crocheted, reading the *Winnipeg Tribune*—that seemed more like the right order of life. On the floor, we boys spread out the funny papers and I strained to understand the humour of Pogo.

When our parents weren't around, though, Vernon and Norman fought. Of all of us, they played out the age-old theme of sibling rivalry most dramatically and noisily. As teenagers they shared an upstairs bedroom. Our parents' bedroom was on the main floor. For Vernon and Norman, this meant they would hear Dad when he came up the stairs, which gave them time to hide whatever illicit comic book or toy gun they might have in their hands.

They slept in a double bunk bed, Vern occupying the top and Norman the bottom. At night, when they should have been readying themselves for sleep, they began squabbles about one thing or another, usually sparked by Vern's annoyance with Norman's behaviour earlier in the day, such as opening a new milk bottle when there was already an open one in the fridge. A ruckus would start, when all of a sudden the boys would hear the ominous sound of Dad's footsteps on the stairs. They knew he was a no-nonsense disciplinarian. Quickly Vern would pull the ceiling cord and switch off the light. A tense, preternatural silence ensued. Dad would come in, switch on the light, glance at the "sleeping" boys, pick up a Donald Duck comic and stand there reading until the fight energy had dissipated and the silence became heavy with genuine weariness. Then he would switch off the light and leave, without reprimands or scolding. What he had offered, though, was his calming presence.

Who knows what Dad remembered of his own experience with his own brothers, long before, perhaps in that same room?

We often visited relatives. Dad got along well with all of his eight siblings, and we children in turn enjoyed playing with our numerous cousins. We especially liked going to visit Aunt Catherine, who was married to Uncle Peter Loewen. The Loewens lived on a farm in the Rosenhof area across the Red River, and getting there required that we take the small ferry at Ste. Agathe.

Norman tells the story of one of these trips, when our Model A got horrendously stuck in the gumbo on the uphill slope from the ferry:

> Several guys from nearby vehicles came over to assist, and one of them, cigarette in mouth, exclaimed, "Jesus Christ!" when he saw how deep our rear tire was mired

in the guck. My first reaction, as a small child, was: "What will Dad say about such blasphemy?" As I recall, Dad chose not to comment or rebuke. These guys were helping us push the car out, after all.

Ste. Agathe ferry.

We always looked forward to the ferry ride. It was the only time that we didn't have solid ground underneath us, and we stared down into the opaque brown water as if it might teach us something important. Mother would call us away from the guardrails.

Cousin Eileen Loewen Dueck recalls:

> I have very fond memories of your parents and your family. I think back to the many times they came to visit us on the farm, and your dad would shake my hand and always make a comment about my ring finger not being

healed because I wore a ring. I guess I never really thought about it, but maybe he didn't think I should be wearing jewelry?! Other times all the aunts would come for my mom's delicious chicken noodle soup, and boy, the cackling was louder in the house than out in the chicken barn! Another time I remember going to the sand pit to swim, and I can still see your dad swimming underwater as his hat floated along atop the water. I remember the old barn next to your house, and all the comic books you and your brothers stowed away.

Eileen's intuition is probably right; most likely Dad would have disapproved of jewellery of any kind, including "finger rings" as we called them. It was typical of him, though, to be indirect in his admonition, not wanting to hurt his young niece's feelings. On these visits it was the women who laughed, as Eileen describes so well, while the men were more reserved. And then again, Dad's hat floating on the surface of the sandpit pool is a mute joke itself.

We had large family gatherings at the sandpits or at Dugard Park near Beausejour in the summer months. Usually we would eat watermelon and *Rollkuchen*, and if at all possible Dad would avoid picking up the melon slices and having the sticky juices run over his hands. Instead he would fastidiously put the slices on a plate and cut them into cubes which he ate with a fork. He even ate cinnamon buns that way, with a knife and fork.

We often made these Beausejour trips on Dominion Day, July 1st. Only later did I find out that this timing was intentional, to keep us boys away from the Steinbach Fair Grounds and the amusement rides and games of chance. "I don't know if a Christian can let his light shine there," said Dad. But he did get us home in time to see the evening fireworks.

Our family at Dugard beach, with my cousin Bob Friesen on the left. The woman holding the baby (me) is my aunt Marie, wife of Mom's brother George.

#

As a family, we came together at lunchtime especially. This afforded Dad the opportunity to teach Christian practices. We all sat around the long, rectangular, oilcloth-covered table, eating the "chop suey"—it was actually a macaroni and hamburger mix—or *Vereneki* cooked by Mom. But before we could eat, Dad would say grace, praying for "the sick and the needy," remembering people we hardly knew or cared about who might be in the hospital. Or he would lead us in singing "Praise God from Whom All Blessings Flow," Al joining in from the opposite end of the table in his deep bass. Sometimes we passed around a little box full of rectangular cards, each printed with a Bible verse, and took turns reading aloud. This did not seem to have the desired devotional effect, however. Our minds were elsewhere. Once, when Dad read a passage including the words "wake up!" we younger boys chimed in, singing—"little Susie," from the Everly Brothers song popular at the time. Dad looked startled, but carried on.

We did not have discussions at table, except for taunts we siblings might throw at each other. And Dad did not talk about others in front of us. Although he knew a great many people, and probably a great many secrets, he refused to criticize anyone. Accordingly, we, his children, felt psychologically safe; we assumed that he would not complain about us to others. We did not necessarily stay until the meal was declared over; if you were finished eating you could leave, make your escape.

The older siblings learned the German *Tischgebete*, or table prayers, such as *Segne, Vater, diese Speise*, or *Komm, Herr Jesus, sei unser Gast*, and were called upon to recite them. I never properly learned even these simple prayers and had only a general idea of their meaning. My mother did teach me this classic bedtime prayer, in English:

> Now I lay me down to sleep
> I pray the Lord my soul to keep
> If I should die before I wake
> I pray the Lord my soul to take.

Once I knew the words, I repeated them at night, on my own. Although the implications of "if I should die" were unsettling, I ignored that part and took comfort in the notion that my soul (whatever that was) would be kept by the Lord.

Dad was schooled in the Stoic style of Mennonite males. Most of the time we had very little information about his feelings. But we boys could get screamingly, murderously angry with each other, and physically violent when our parents were not around. We did not know what these feelings were about, or what it was about our family system that gave rise to them. Maybe we didn't think there was enough love to go around.

When Wilma Doerksen, who once worked for Dad in the bookstore, told me, "He really loved his children," tears sprang to my eyes. I had never heard that.

A friend's mother told me that she had heard Dad say: "If I had my life to live over again, I'd spend more time with my family." This was before his stroke. She went on to describe the overwhelming demands on my father's time. He did what was expected of him.

Overall, our father was kind to us, and we now see his sometimes misguided attempts at discipline as essentially well-intentioned. He did not mean us harm, and none of us today will speak of him with rancour. We've all lived long enough to know that we have faults and omissions of our own. Except for Vern, who died at sixty-one, we are aged now, all of us older than Dad got to be. We give hugs and speak of our love for each other.

Dream
August 29, 2012 *"He Loved Us"*
I'm in a gathering in what might be the basement of the EMC church. I don't specifically know anyone there; I think of them as members of the church. I start to speak to them about Dad, and I feel like crying. I stop myself, collect my feelings, and start again: "My dad was pastor of this church in the 1950s. He loved us." This is what I want them to know.

Dream
August 17, 2010 *"I Only Have One Dad"*
Dad sits in his wheelchair. He holds something back from me; he's not quite happy with me. I say: "You have many sons, but I only have one dad." He softens. I hug him, feel some love from him.

Chapter 13:
The record player

The record player, like the Trojan horse,
was a present that concealed
an invasion
given by my older brothers
to my parents at Christmas

It stood in a corner of the living room
a polished mahogany box
with brass-handled cabinet doors
enclosing a secret:
the only piece of furniture
in the house
whose use was not
immediately evident

It made my parents nervous
Dad thought it too worldly
Mom said it was very nice
but she preferred the kitchen mantel radio

for listening to *Back to the Bible*
and the funeral announcements

They seemed not to notice
when my brothers
started smuggling in records
gleaming black 78s
to be handled only on the edges
and not at all by me
the youngest

Only they, the self-appointed,
were allowed to lower the tone arm so lightly
and fit the diamond needle so precisely
into the vinyl grooves
producing, through the scientific mystery
of electronic transubstantiation,
forbidden harmonies:

Kiss of Fire,
The Naughty Lady of Shady Lane,
Don't Let the Stars Get in Your Eyes
Songs that rhymed desire
and conjured up the mystical "you . . .
the only one I'll ever love."

#

One drowsy Sunday afternoon
while our parents were away visiting relatives
eating *Platz* and criticizing the Catholics
my brother put on a new record
for the curious boys from the neighbourhood
and turned up the volume

Bill Haley and the Comets
burst into our living room
from outer space:
"One, two, three o'clock, four o'clock rock!"
My brother metamorphosed into a gazelle
bounding around the room

I too leaped to my feet
like a joyful cripple cured
by a miracle

In the very heart of the religious town
we enacted a profane ritual
pounding across the linoleum floor

wayward sons of the Mennonite pastor
abandoning our bodies
to outlawed rhythms
that thumped all biblical prohibitions
right out of our brains

jumping and gyrating so
our white Sunday shirts
stuck to our torsos with sweat
drunk with forgetting
we pursued the chant of saxophones
around the buckling room

born again
through rock and roll.

#

Childhood friend Earl Kreutzer recalls sitting in our living room, listening to Fats Domino on the record player, and my dad walking through, saying, "That's not good, boys." But he did not tell us to turn the music off.

CHAPTER 14:
PETER RALPH:
"TOO BIG OR TOO LITTLE?"

May 21, 1945, Monday. Pentecostal holiday. Getting nicer, but windy. At 6:40 a.m. I took wife to Hospital & at 8:34 a.m. a nice 6 lbs baby boy was born unto us. Everything O. K., praise the Lord! Of course we wanted a girl, especially Mary Ann, but this boy is a darling. (P. D. Friesen diary)

"A baby boy was born unto us," says Dad, his phrasing Biblical. If not the Prince of Peace of Isaiah, I was nevertheless born into a hopeful world newly at peace. Germany had surrendered to Allied forces. The Japanese defeat was imminent.

I sit regally, if a bit sulkily, in the trailer of a wooden truck, perhaps built by my dad. Behind me is Vern, flanked to the left and right by cousins Leroy and Elvera Friesen. Mary Ann, who thought I looked cut in a bonnet, coyly hides in the background.

Unlike so many Canadian men of his generation my father had hardly been touched by the war. Or rather, he had been touched, as a peacemaker. He had worked hard on behalf of the Mennonite church to prevent young men from enlisting, and also to support conscientious objectors in alternative service. I have sometimes wondered: if military action in World War II was nation-building for Canada, were my father's peace efforts a drag on that development? Or did peace-building also contribute to our identity?

Certainly, we children never found any medals in the drawers of Dad's roll-top desk. Oddly, we did find a Canadian Army helmet in our barn, and it became an authentic prop in our neighbourhood war games. Dozens of young Steinbach men did enlist, and presumably the helmet had been brought back by one of them. We had no idea where it had come from, and there was no one to ask.

Steinbach in 1945 had grown to a population exceeding 2000. It still had the feel of a place where everyone knew everyone else, but that was actually not the case. Descendants of the original settlers were still easily the majority, but Ukrainians, Lutheran Germans, English Canadians, and even French Canadians made up a significant part of the population. Improbably for a conservative Mennonite location, car dealerships flourished. Before long, Steinbach would audaciously label itself "the Automobile City."

Churches also had multiplied, and by this time there were a dozen of them, mostly Mennonites of different stripes. Such differences would hardly have been discernible to the outsider's eye, but to us town children they mattered, and formed a part of the subtle gradations of who was "in" and who was "out." Unspoken assumptions of being "better than," "holier than," underlay our social interactions.

Altogether, Dad was absent for extended periods in 1945—not just on these local missions, but also to a conference in Winkler and another in Indiana. Astonishingly, at the end of the year he reflected: "Ashamed, we cast our eyes down & deplore the fact of having done so little."

After his stroke, Dad went back to the diary entry for May 21, 1945, and softened his comment about Mary Ann's disappointment in my gender: "but later she expressed that this would be OK too it was such a lovely baby cute, blue eyes blond hair." He says my eyes are blue. Perhaps they were, at birth, but in fact they are brown. Did he not know that? Or maybe the colour changed as I grew older; that happens. His own eyes were blue. I was called Peter Ralph—after my father, I've always thought, though where the "Ralph" came from is harder to figure.

The largest age gap between siblings, four years, is between Norman and me. I think that Mom would not exactly have been thrilled to have this last pregnancy at age forty. And if there had to be a baby, a girl would have been much preferred. Mary Ann so badly wanted a sister that she dressed me up in girls' clothing. Sometimes Dad, with a smile or chuckle, would say of me: "He is our caboose." Which might have been code for: "We definitely did not want any more." I did not hear that, though, and felt a kind of pride. I was the end of the train. There would be no more "cars" after me.

The Friesen boys, eldest to youngest. I do not look happy, even though I'm wearing a charming overcoat and beret.

Hoisted high by the strong arm of my big brother Alvin, I survey the kingdom of our backyard.

I also felt some responsibility to fulfill a role, even though I wasn't sure what it should be.

With a kind of innocent arrogance I took for granted that others looked upon me with favour. If someone mistreated me, it was all the more an insult; my spirit was sacred. I did not learn to walk until I was a year and nine months old. My older brothers like to tell of me, as a baby, dragging my bum along the linoleum, my wet diaper gradually blackening with dirt. But I could talk, and would issue princely baby commands from my perch on the worn, rounded arm of the brown chesterfield in the living room.

"Darling," Dad called me in his diary, and "lovely baby." He could write such words, which means he was thinking them. But such language was never heard in our house. In fact, words of endearment would probably not have been heard in any typical Mennonite household of the time—my people feared that praise and adoration would inflate the child's ego, engendering pride and endangering the soul.

Yet the soul also yearns for just such praise and adoration. When I was ten, a lipstick-wearing waitress in an Omaha department store café called me "sweetheart." The word penetrated me; I felt warmth expanding in my chest. She didn't even know me! Yet she acted as if there was something dear about me. My heart was intrigued by this possibility.

On some of his trips, Dad sent postcards meant for the children. Mostly he signed off with "God bless you" from "Daddy" or "Dad." The "God bless you" pushed us away, I think now, because it was our father's own blessing we wanted, not one from an abstract sky father. His use of the diminutive "Daddy" is touching, and now, so many years later, brings him closer. We never called him that; to us he was always "Dad."

Dad on a trip to the Mennonite World Conference in 1948, stopped to have his picture taken on a Case steam tractor in Wisconsin.

Growing up, I missed my father, but was not bursting with enthusiasm to get to know him. Getting to know him was not in the scheme of things. I had learned not to have that need because I knew it was not going to be met. By the time I was born, his reputation in Steinbach was firmly established. Equally established was the family pattern of his being away much of the time. We children organized our lives around this absence, and left to our own devices, we could play the sports we liked, go to movies, read comics, form unapproved friendships, daydream our private lives. His absence was a kind of gift, then. So we did not let ourselves understand that we also desired his blessing.

Most of my memories of Dad are clustered around just a few years when I was between ten and twelve. Then he had his stroke, which marked a sharp turning, and a different set of memories.

The house of my childhood was the same as the one my father grew up in, and very likely not much had changed over time except for the surrounding neighbourhood. When Dad was a child, open fields stretched out to the west behind the machine shop. By the time I came along, streets and houses had been built. Three of Dad's brothers and their families lived close to our place, their garden plots adjoining ours. This was Friesen territory, our home.

Behind the house a long-handled pump, set in concrete, no longer brought up well water, despite my childish efforts. A rough-barked cottonwood spread its fluff around the yard every spring. Its great branches hung over the summer kitchen roof and its trunk was too thick for me to climb. Thirty metres from our house, the back of Friesen Machine Shop butted up against our property. Sometimes I would visit the shop, with its complex system of belts and pulleys suspended from the ceiling, to watch my brother operating a lathe or drill, silvery metal strings peeling away and dropping on the oily wood floor.

Grandfather inspecting a tub for leaks, before my time, with the pump on the left.

Early on, my mother trained me to be independent. Overwhelmed with her household responsibilities, she sent me off to play on my own, or with friends. I made up stories and conversations with dolls and teddy bears. I could do this happily for long periods of time. I created my own world and took pleasure in it.

When I got older, in winter I would strap on Huron-style snowshoes and head out to the fields west of town with my friend Earl Kreutzer. We pretended to be coureurs-de-bois on some important mission. Earl taught me how to identify wrens and nuthatches, and how to find the best branches for making slingshots.

I mostly saw Dad at the dinner table, at lunchtime and at supper. He sat at one end, near the pantry door— the head of the household at the head of the table. These were brief appearances, after which he returned to his work, or went out somewhere on church business. I sat off to his left, beside Mom. I learned not to expect his individual attention, and was unaware that I even wanted it.

I watched him carefully, seeking clues that would reveal him to me. Once I heard him singing, more or less to himself: "Oh it ain't gonna rain no more no more, it ain't gonna rain no more; how didi-de-do-didi-do-didi-do, if it ain't gonna rain no more?" I'd heard that verse before, sung by one of my brothers—Vern, probably. I knew that all those didi-do's were a censored version of the actual words: "How in the heck can I wash my neck?" I liked the rhyme, heck and neck; it sounded authoritative somehow, sharp and defined, and I liked the question itself, which posed a problem both practical and nonsensical.

We were not supposed to say "heck." It was a substitute word for "hell." Just like in the comics when Tubby and Little Lulu said "gee" and "golly," and Albert Alligator exclaimed "by Jingo," these were really swear words, said Dad, milder versions of "Jesus" and "God" and "by Jesus." Somewhere in his head Dad must have had that unspoken word, "heck." And if it existed there in his head, wasn't he capable of swearing himself? And if so, might I do it too? But no, I decided. The "English" children in our neighbourhood might use those words, and maybe that was okay for them, but not for us Mennonites. Consequently, in my heart I carried the secret notion that I was a purer Christian than the Lutherans and United Churchers. The Catholics weren't even in the running.

Of course, I wanted to please Mom and Dad. Without them ever saying, "We want you to be a good Christian," I knew that this was what they wanted, and tried to comply.

In 1952, when I was seven, we travelled to Oregon in the new Dodge the church had provided Dad in lieu of paying him a salary. We stopped in Yellowstone Park. Dad promised that we were in for a surprise. At first we only saw some bubbling mudholes. I wondered why we had stopped here. "Just wait," said Dad. "Something's going to happen." And it did, steam jetting spectacularly high into the air, like nothing I'd ever seen or dreamed of seeing on the inert farmlands of Manitoba. "Old Faithful," said Dad, explaining that the geyser had that name because it spouted at regular intervals. I was in awe, and impressed with my father, who had brought us to this amazing place.

After what seemed an eternity (Mom: "Peter Ralph thought we were going 1000 miles through the desert"), we arrived at last on the west coast. Mom's relatives lived in the small town of Dallas, Oregon. On a Sunday evening the Dallas Evangelical Mennonite Brethren church held a Christian Endeavour service, and we went. My mother wanted me to sing a solo. I liked the idea of performing, but I was scared, too, and told Mom I didn't want to do it. "Why not?" she said. "They're strangers," I said.

"When you look at them," she advised, "pretend their heads are cabbages." I smiled. I guessed I could do it. I knew the words to "I Have Decided to Follow Jesus." Once up on the platform I was still nervous, but launched into the song unhesitatingly: "I have decided to follow Jesus, I have decided to follow Jesus. . . ." The key was too high for me, and I got kind of girly-sounding in the second line. I had a vague suspicion that the smiles on those cabbage heads were of people laughing at me. But I persevered to the end: "Though none go with me, still I will follow / No turning back, no turning back." Afterwards, a couple of old ladies gave me approving words. One even gave me a dime—unexpected treasure! For a few minutes, I'd been a star.

On a warm October Thursday after we'd returned home, we younger boys went with our parents to Winnipeg. Our teachers were holding a convention, so there was no school that day. Dad thought it would be educational for us to tour the Canadian Institute for the Blind building on Portage Avenue. Our guide, a pleasant man in his thirties, showed us the straw brooms being manufactured at the Institute, and we were properly impressed, unable to imagine how blind people could do such work. He explained that he had limited vision himself, and Dad asked him if he was able to read. "I can read a little, if I hold the book very close and the print is big enough," said the man. "Can you read this?" said Dad, pushing out his suit jacket lapel to show a white metal button with a message on it. He moved nearer to the man, who at first didn't seem to know what he meant. "Here, this button." The man leaned comically close to Dad's suit jacket. "Christ," he read slowly, "is . . . the answer."

There was a pause. I was suddenly embarrassed. I considered myself saved, but I didn't want my dad to be witnessing to a total stranger who might take offence, maybe thinking that his own religious belief was being disrespected. The man said: "That's so true, isn't it?" I was impressed by his quick-thinking diplomacy, but suspected him of lying; if he was a real born-again Christian he wouldn't have hesitated. I didn't think my father was quite satisfied with this answer, but to my relief, he didn't pursue the subject.

Wanting to be a good son, I felt that I should carry my share of Dad's burden for lost souls. Once I found myself in the back seat of Mr. Smith's new Ford, travelling along a country road just outside of Steinbach. The Ford had cherrywood panelling inside and out, and leather upholstery with a good smell, not like the plain cloth seats of our Dodge. T. G. Smith was the town banker and our neighbour, and I was friends with his son Bobby. I also played Little League baseball, which Mr. Smith organized in Steinbach. Bobby was in the front seat beside his dad. Somehow the conversation turned to religion, and I felt compelled to declare that you had to believe in Jesus Christ to be saved. Mr. Smith asked if I was suggesting that he wasn't saved. I hesitated. I knew he was "English," and promoted sports, and as far as I knew he didn't go to church on Sunday mornings but stayed at home in the apartment above the bank with his makeup-wearing wife and their black-and-white Boston terrier. It didn't seem like a "saved" way of living, from what I'd been taught.

He said, "Because if you think that, then maybe you'd like to walk to town from here." Blushing, I quickly recanted. I had a sense of abusing the hospitality of one of the most important men in our town. I was shocked that he was so harsh with me when all I was doing was trying to help him, and I was also a little ashamed of myself for not standing up for my faith— and, indirectly, for my father.

In Sunday school I learned choruses, and sang them with all the sincerity of my childish heart: "Jesus Bids Us Shine with a Clear Pure Light," "Standing on the Promises," "Deep and Wide" (accompanied by hand gestures), "Jesus Wants Me for a Sunbeam," "Into My Heart," and many more. The last of this list somehow stirred me with the melancholy of its slow pace, and the words: "Come into my heart, Lord Jesus, come in today, come in to stay." I didn't know how this worked, exactly, having Jesus come into your heart, but I felt that I was doing the right thing, making myself into a good Christian.

Not always so good, though. In our house we all learned the importance of honesty. Telling lies was un-Christian and sinful, and an unrepentant liar was a candidate for hell. What possessed me then, one April 1st, to try an April fool's trick on my dad? Maybe I was trying to imitate Norman. I had learned a little about fooling from him. He would ask me, out of the blue, "*Weets waut?*" And when I answered, sincerely, "*Nä, waut?*" he would shout the triumphant rhyme, "*Wota es naut!*" ("Do you know what?" "No, what?" "Water is wet!")

For my part, I'd never been able to fool anyone, partly because I never remembered when April 1ˢᵗ came around, and partly because I was *trüh-oatijch*, true-hearted, taking things at face value. That day I entered our store as usual by the back entrance and came around to the front where Dad was leaning on the glass counter, reading the newspaper.

"Dad," I said. "Hmm?" he said, not looking up. I did not ordinarily initiate a conversation with him and I felt I was entering unfamiliar territory.

"Dad, I got a licking in school today." This of course was not true, and the moment I uttered the words, I started to feel slightly sick. Dad looked up from his newspaper with sharper attention than he usually gave me. "For what?" he said. But I hadn't thought that far ahead, and didn't know what to say. I hesitated, then came up with another inspired falsehood: "For lying."

His pale blue watery eyes were fixed on me now. "Then I think you should get the same treatment at home," he said. Now I *really* felt sick. Another factor I hadn't reckoned on was the old Mennonite code that the school has authority, and the parents will support that authority, not bothering with subtleties or nuances of right and wrong. If you were punished at school it meant the teacher thought you had transgressed, and so you had to be punished again at home. Then you might understand that adult authority was indivisible, and one part could not be played against another.

"April fool!" I cried desperately, realizing I had to make my leap before everything truly went to hell. "I didn't get a licking at school."

A look of annoyance clouded my father's face, and I realized that I might actually have fooled him. "Are you sure?" he said. "I'm sure," I said. "Then I think you deserve a strapping anyway, for lying to me just now," he replied. "But I wasn't lying!" I protested. "I was just playing April fool!"

"The truth is not a toy that you can play with," he said. "I should punish you for that."

"But I didn't mean to lie," I pleaded, still hopeful that I could save my skin. I calculated the distance to the front door behind me; if I ran he would never be able to get his bulk from behind the counter to catch me.

Though this was all sheer nonsense; sooner or later I'd have to come home and face the music, and be punished all the more for running away.

"Are you sorry, then?" he said. Immediately I could see the shut door of my predicament open just a crack. I didn't want to apologize, but the alternative was worse.

"Yes," I said, though a part of me silently muttered "no" at the same time. In my heart I felt that I had meant no harm.

"Do you ask God to forgive you?" God! Why did God have to come into this? Why couldn't I just say I was sorry and be done with it? And actually I *was* sorry—sorry that I had ever opened my mouth and landed myself in this mess.

"Yes," I said.

"Yes—what?"

"Yes, I'm sorry and I ask God to forgive me." The words tasted bitter in my mouth. Dad let me go. But I remembered the humourless God who couldn't take a joke, and decided I didn't much like him.

Words mattered. The truth mattered. In Sunday school we sang a chorus, a Bible verse turned into a round song: "Study to show thyself approved unto God, a workman that needeth not to be ashamed, rightly dividing the word of truth." The word "dividing" spoke to me somehow, implying a careful, rational examination. Truth was a word that could be spoken, written, heard, read, parsed.

Later I learned to be a playful storyteller, saying outrageous things as though they were true, testing others' responses. The truth was also a toy I played with.

And then I did get in trouble at school, for real. On a warm day in June, 1955, I heard Miss Kornelsen ringing the brass bell that signalled the end of recess, and raced over to the front of the school to line up. Girls formed a line on one side of the entrance and boys on the other, waiting to march up the worn wooden steps in orderly fashion. I pulled up behind David Wiebe, a tall, amiable boy. For some reason there was a delay in moving forward. I poked David's back so he would turn around. I distended my stomach muscles under my tee-shirt and said, "Look! I have a baby." David giggled appreciatively. Just as I opened my mouth to say something more, a bony hand with an irresistible grip closed around my bicep and yanked me out of the line. Miss Kornelsen stood over me, her sharp features pulled into a glower. "Are you too big or too little to behave?" she demanded.

I considered the question, knowing that my fate hung in the balance. My mind raced around blindly, like a mouse in a maze. But I could not imagine which of these choices would allow me to escape punishment. I held silence, hoping that Miss Kornelsen might relent and let me get back into line. She took hold of my shoulders and shook me, forcefully. "Answer me!"

Haplessly I blurted, "Too big."

She slapped me hard on the cheek. Then she released me.

My face stinging from the blow and the humiliation, I mounted the steps to the Grade 4 room with my classmates. We took our seats. Right away, one of the girls shot up her hand, waving her arm to get the teacher's attention. "Yes?" said Miss Warkentin, a tall, gentle woman whom I was always eager to please. "Miss Kornelsen slapped Peter!" announced the girl triumphantly. She lived on the other side of Main Street and went to a different church. I did not know her well, and I did not know what she might have against me. Maybe she just wanted to be on the "right" side of authority. "I know," said Miss Warkentin quietly. And that was that; we carried on. Remembering the "double punishment" protocol, I did not tell my parents what had happened.

Grade 4 class, Number One School. I am in the third row, middle, with glasses and a bad brushcut. My friend Earl Kreutzer on my right.

So I learned about either/or choices. I developed a tendency to resist them, and I still have that. Whenever I hear someone say, "It's either this or that," a part of me mutters, "Or there could be more options."

As the youngest at home, I escaped the full brunt of household work demands. In the summertime, after school and again after supper, I would rush out to play with the cousins and neighbour children who lived just across the garden from us, on Mill Street a block west. Still, I had to share after-meals cleanup with Norman—a never-ending task in a family of eight. Because my mother's prodigious cooking generated so many encrusted pots, drying was preferable to washing dishes, and, like our older siblings before us, Norman and I kept a chart on the inside of the cupboard door to keep track. Only, sometimes we'd forget to post who had done what the previous time, resulting in passionate, fruitless arguments and delays, while the day's precious light ebbed from the sky and our friends played freely outside.

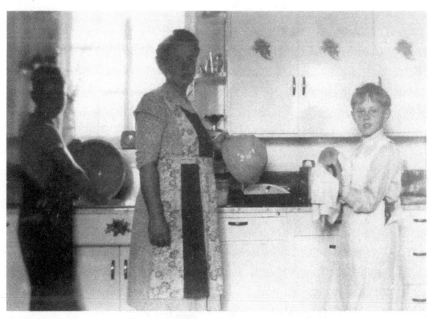

Mom supervising Alvin and Donald in the kitchen.

One afternoon Dad heard me muttering some mild complaint and interjected, "Stop feeling sorry for yourself." It was unusual for him to have

145

been in the kitchen while I was doing a chore; usually he was in the bookstore or away somewhere. I was stunned by his reprimand. Immediately I recognized the truth, that I *was* feeling sorry for myself, but that seemed pathetic, and I didn't want to admit my pettiness. I felt ashamed. I had persuaded myself that my complaints were justified; now my father was telling me that they were not. I wanted him to support me! I was stung into silence, tears welling up in my eyes. I had no way of letting him know what I felt, or why.

I especially admired Vern, and, although he was almost seven years my senior, I sought to imitate him. I heard him complain about doing the dishes, so I thought I could, too. But, ever inventive, he could also make the work lighter, singing songs he'd learned at school. Perhaps a round song like "Row, row, row your boat"—he'd have Norman and me singing too—concluding with a Low German pun; instead of "life is but a dream" he sang "life is *Bottabroot*" (butter bread). So we had to laugh and forget about feeling sorry for ourselves.

Well, not forget, exactly. My self-pity went underground, but there it still lived, like an invalid child hidden away in a darkened room. Perhaps I'd learned to feel sorry for myself from Vern. I happened to be in the kitchen one day when Vern, irritated by some chore my mother wanted him to do, blurted: "I never asked to be born." This received a half-amused common-sense adult reply, and I, too, thought it was a crazy thing to say. But it stuck in my mind after that. It was true. He hadn't asked to be born. And neither had I. So what did that mean? We hadn't participated in the decision of our own being, and apparently we had the option of disagreeing with it somehow. Vern's statement revealed a choice I had not known was possible: radical questioning of our given situation, even the fact of our own existence. A strange freedom, both dangerous and enticing.

The body remembers the insults it has suffered. Once Dad strapped me. He had used to strap Alvin and Donald when they were little, but I think he came to understand that this form of discipline, practised by his father and his father's father and so on up the line for centuries, might not be the way forward. Times had changed. But still, there was this one occasion.

Dad grew up with a traditional Mennonite view: that children, from the beginning, had a propensity to sin, selfishness, and rebellion. Adults were responsible to teach the child obedience and respect and compliance with the rules. Rebellion had to be beaten out of the child, if necessary—after all, his very soul was at stake. Besides, a rebellious child brought shame upon the parents and raised questions about the quality of their faith.

I had been out playing with the neighbourhood children on a late summer afternoon. We hid behind bushes or garden sheds or tall stalks of corn and waited for our chance to dash across an open space to home base before the person who was "it" could get there. In the growing dusk mothers called "suppertime" and soon only a few of us were left. I thought I'd better get home, too. I ran through Uncle Barney's garden and our own, flung open the back screen door, and entered the kitchen where I found that everyone was already seated at the table, eating. They all looked up.

Dad, from his place at the head of the table, said, "Peter, stand by the door." I stood, frozen. "You are late again. You were told last time already to be on time." He pushed back his chair and stood up. "I think a strapping will help you learn to listen."

My voice trembling, I said, "You don't need to. I promise, I'll remember from now on. I'll never be late again!" I felt this very sincerely. He had never strapped me before, and to have it happen now seemed entirely unnecessary and unfair. But Dad would not be moved.

So I was compelled to follow him to the parental bedroom and lie across the white chenille bedspread, whose ridges suddenly came into extraordinarily clear focus a few inches from my eyes. He removed his leather belt and hit me across the buttocks. Part of me could not believe this was even happening. The sharpness of the pain surprised me, even though he had not made me take down my pants. I cried out, and then, when he stopped after a few strokes, I wept.

"Kneel down with me," he said, not unkindly. I knelt beside him at the bed. He said that I should pray to God and ask for forgiveness, and then all would be well again. I did as he said. He prayed, too. A part of me hovered above the scene and watched all this and wondered about this God who coldly insisted on punishment, regardless of my pleas. I knew I was technically guilty, but I felt I knew, also, that I was essentially innocent. Dad might have wanted me to learn submission, and I suppose I did, but not in the way he would have wished.

I'm sure that he meant well, but even if his intentions were positive, physical punishment did not align me with them. The opposite, really. It might have been different had there been a stronger attachment between us. My response now was to comply with his rules on the outside, but to go further underground on the inside. I was afraid to be open and apparently carefree in my disobedience, like Al seemed to be. In my heart, where Jesus was supposed to live, the worm of rebellion attached itself.

For Norman at about the same age the story was different. The town had a public ice rink, but also one built and maintained by a group of young men who smoked and drank. This was known as the "sinners'" rink, and that's where Norman had been one afternoon, watching a hockey game. After supper, Dad called his son into the back of the bookstore for a private conference. He demanded to know why Norman had gone to the game, when he knew it was not permitted:

> He allowed me to express what I thought was a reasoned reply, without him responding in anger. All my friends go there and we just watch the hockey. We don't listen to bad language, and the smoking doesn't entice us. I would be lying if I said I didn't enjoy watching the Steinbach team play. Why can't I do what I enjoy? Dad admitted my feelings were true to my heart, or something of that nature, but pointed out that I was not obeying *his* wishes either. True. Whether anything was resolved, I can't say. I did, however, continue to sneak away to watch hockey games at the "sinners'" rink.

Dad treated his young son much as he would an adult, reasoning with him, and ultimately acknowledging, if only implicitly, that Norman already was a free agent who would make his own decisions about his life and actions, and who could be trusted to develop his own sense of right and wrong. Still, there's that key word at the end of the story: "sneak." It didn't feel safe for us to let our parents know what we were up to, lest they, and the entire earnest cloud of church witnesses behind them, would disapprove, forbid, condemn.

Being the youngest and most in need of parental care, I probably went on more than my fair share of family trips, including one to the U. S. in the summer of 1955. Only Vern and I went along that time—he was sixteen and I was ten. On our way back home we made a stop in the Black Hills of South Dakota, where "we sang for some Indians yet," as Mom put it. Quite possibly the two men and a dark little boy all in feathers were descendants of Sitting Bull, now living in a reduced condition. They did a song-and-dance routine for us tourists, no doubt expecting money. Instead, Dad made Vern and me sing "Jesus Loves Me," and that was the trade-off. On the picture that Dad took, my deep embarrassment is disguised as slight self-consciousness. Thinking about it now, though—perhaps the "song trade" was a more honourable transaction than a financial one would have been.

Other encounters were complicated in a similar way. Steinbach's Main Street was alive on summer Saturday evenings, when rural folks came in to do their shopping and have a look at the town. Farmers' trucks parked diagonally in front of the Tourist Hotel, often with a woman and children in the cab, waiting for their man who was in the beer parlour, drinking and trading stories. On one such evening I was strolling past the Tourist Hotel, where a visiting Salvation Army band, impressive in their crisp uniforms and shining brass instruments, countered the decadence of the beer parlour with rousing hymns. I walked quickly, a little afraid that I would be stopped and someone would want to question me about the state of my soul. And wouldn't you know it, just as I reached the J. & A. Restaurant, a clean-cut young man came forward and extended a pale green, rectangular piece of paper toward me. A tract. I did not take it. Smiling kindly, I said: "I don't need that; my father is a minister in the church." Also smiling, the polite but insistent young man continued to extend the tract. "That's good," he said, "but do you know that you are saved?"

I took the tract. It was entitled "The Four Steps to Salvation," in bold print. I shoved it into my jacket pocket and walked on, rankled. I didn't want to be lumped in with all those lost souls in need of salvation. I was aware that I hadn't handled the situation according to the expected script; I hadn't said, for example, "I'm saved already, thank God, but I'll pass this on to someone else." No, instead, I had tried to claim a kind of ecclesiastical diplomatic immunity. I considered myself saved but couldn't identify the time and place when Jesus had come into my heart, and the whole question had begun to make me nervous. Maybe I wasn't really saved? Was I really a sinner? I didn't feel like one. I didn't want to make a big public confession when it wasn't even called for.

At one point, like Norman before me, I decided to resolve my uncertainty about the status of my soul. I was eleven or twelve. Meetings were being held at the tabernacle, not far from the centre of town, and I walked there with my friends one evening. The tabernacle was a Quonset hut structure which had been built in the early 1940s expressly to accommodate large religious gatherings of up to 1000 people.

Dad's colleague Ben D. Reimer was speaking. Like the protagonist in a Franz Kafka story, I hadn't been paying close attention, but suddenly I saw how emotional Reimer had become, with tears running down his cheeks. He was calling for commitment. Now I resolved that I would get rid of my uncertainty once and for all, and go up. When I stood up, some of my friends in my row told me not to go, which I found puzzling because I knew them to be Christians. But I decided they were somehow being influenced by the Devil, and determinedly strode past them and up the wood-chip-covered aisle.

Steinbach tabernacle.

Almost immediately I saw that something was wrong. Everyone else standing up there was a young adult, while I was only a kid. Reimer explained that he had been issuing a challenge to young people interested in going to the mission field. Chagrin! With downcast eyes I slunk back to my seat. As I was leaving after the service, my uncle Jake Thiessen happened to be standing at the exit. He chuckled and made a wry comment about me wanting to be a missionary. I blushed. Afterwards, no one spoke to me about what had happened, but I made a resolution—never to answer another altar call.

I won an award for "perfect attendance" at Sunday school (not missing more than two Sundays in any given year, over a period of years). As a reward, Dad allowed me to pick a new Bible from our store. I would rather have got a Daisy Red Ryder air rifle, but that was just a silly thing to wish for, so I contented myself with the Bible. One with a cover you could zip closed, and a zipper tab in the shape of a gold cross, caught my fancy. Dad seemed to hesitate, but let me have it. I felt guilty. I knew, at some level, that I wanted the zipper Bible because of its snazzy look, not because of what was in it. I suspected that Dad knew that, too, but he never called me on my duplicity.

Did Dad notice when, around the age of twelve, I began to act uncooperatively and disobediently in Sunday school? Perhaps my behaviour was an unconscious strategy to get the attention I had been missing while punishing my parents at the same time. Once—not for the first time—I had not done my Sunday school lesson, and when the teacher asked me about it, I replied in an offhand, insolent manner. Seized by frustration, he pulled me from my bench and awkwardly swatted me a few times on the rear. It didn't hurt, but I was surprised and offended. My classmates were also surprised, and entertained. As well, we were all to memorize a Bible verse. Just one. I refused. I was threatened with "failing" my Sunday school class, and I said that was fine. Some of my friends teased me and I felt a little embarrassed, but I laughed, embracing the absurdity.I could not point to a particular time and place when I had been saved, but there was a particular moment when the smouldering fire of my doubt burst into flame. This might have happened during the time that Dad was in hospital after his stroke. My Sunday school teacher was telling us what a great responsibility we had, as Christians, to evangelize the lost world. A question popped into my mind: "Are people lost even if they've never heard about Jesus?"

"Yes," said the teacher. "Those who have heard and rejected Christ are lost, but those who have not heard also."

"That's not fair," I objected. The teacher admitted that, to our human understanding, it might not seem fair. But God's ways were right, all the same.

"So they're going to hell, then?" I said.

"Yes," he said.

"That doesn't make sense," I said, surprising myself with my certainty and my willingness to challenge an adult in the house of God. Inside me a switch went on, or off. My disbelief took hold. A just God could not punish—much less torture eternally—people for not accepting Jesus as their saviour when they had no knowledge of this Jesus. It couldn't be clearer. And if God did punish such "unbelievers"—then God was unjust, a vengeful tyrant undeserving of credence, much less devotion. I parted ways with my father's God, and embarked on a program to discredit this false deity.

During these same years my name changed. I was "Peter," and since this was Dad's name, I thought it conferred special status upon me. Yes, it was annoying when others would quote "Peter, Peter, pumpkin eater" at me, but I learned to dismiss that. But my name, a Biblical name in a Mennonite community, was far from unique. In Grade 5, it happened that three or four other boys in the class also were called Peter. The teacher, trying to simplify her life, wanted to know which of us had a second name that she could call us by. I readily raised my hand. "Ralph," I said. Even at home I was sometimes called by both names, "Peter Ralph." So "Ralph" it was from then on, and my parents fell into line and also called me that.

Only much later would it occur to me that my father might have felt some sadness, perhaps even a mild sense of betrayal, at my name change. I feel, myself, that I was unwittingly drawn into a kind of trap, without being prepared for the consequences. A part of me is still "Peter," and always will be.

Dream: January 18, 2010 *I Am Crying*
I am crying. This has something to do with my father . . . something he says about not giving me much attention when I was a child. His words are sincere, honest. He doesn't apologize but he clearly feels regret.

CHAPTER 15:
THE LIVING WORD

A couple of voice recordings of my father survive, both from the 1950s. In one, he officiates at a wedding; in another, he makes closing remarks at a missionary conference. He speaks good English, in measured tones with a light Low German accent. He seems clear about the message he wants to convey.

I was disappointed when I first listened to the recordings. I knew it was my father's voice, but I did not recognize it. My siblings had the same experience; they also did not feel that the recordings corresponded with his voice as they remembered it. Why can't we make the connection? Maybe because he spoke differently at home than in church? We want to reach back through the decades and have this bond, but it is tenuous. Even here, Dad keeps his distance.

I wonder if I would remember his singing voice. As a boy in the pews, I watched as Dad led the congregational singing in our church. By that time much of the service was in English. I remember his favourite Gospel choruses and songs—"Wonderful Words of Life," "Showers of Blessing," "What a Friend We Have in Jesus." To this day, I am put in mind of my father when I hear the Doxology, "Praise God from Whom All Blessings Flow." At family gatherings he would lead us in this iconic song, in place of spoken grace, before we feasted on the potato salad and *Rollkuchen* and watermelon, and the words and melody still recall him to me, or even embody him, somehow. Also, at family gatherings or at mealtimes he would sometimes lead with "Break Thou the Bread of Life." One line especially stays with me: "Beyond the sacred page, I seek thee, Lord / My spirit pants for thee, O living Word." I was intrigued with the idea that a page could be sacred, and lead us beyond itself somehow, to find the divine source. Which was a word, a living word. And we would be panting, like an animal, for the Word that was God. This did not happen to me when I read the Bible.

Religious music was an essential part of Dad's life and ministry. He was grounded in the old Mennonite *Gesangbuch* (songbook) which the Mennonite pioneers had brought with them from South Russia, but as a young man also learned some of the popular songs of his day from the forbidden sources of radio and movie musicals. Of course he stopped listening to worldly music after his conversion, but it must still have taken up space in his memory bank. Maybe it sharpened his appreciation for melody and rhythm.

Even before his conversion, Dad sang in the Steinbach church choir. When "choir singing was attacked, and also prohibited" at a 1932 brethren meeting, the Steinbach church, more liberal than its rural counterparts, ignored this ruling. Conservative elements in the Manitoba Kleine Gemeinde believed that beautiful harmonies attracted undue attention to the talent of the singers. Listeners and the singers themselves would then be in danger of forgetting the only proper object of admiration—God. I almost admire these traditionalists for their implicit recognition of the mystical power of harmony, strong enough to compete with the divine.

In 1934, Dad was elected *Vorsänger* (congregational song leader) of the Steinbach church, just as his grandfather, Abraham S. Friesen, had been in the previous century. He was in Kansas at the time, having been asked to go and help deal with the growing traditionalist–modernist conflict amongst the Meade-area Kleine Gemeinde. Apparently church leaders perceived that he had a gift for mediation. The modernists were pushing hard for more personal and expressive forms of worship. All congregational hymns were sung in German, probably still in unison, from the old *Gesangbuch*.

Younger people wanted to adopt the two-volume *Evangeliums-Lieder*, containing chorales and translated versions of nineteenth-century American and English Gospel songs, as the Bruderthaler had done years before. Old-timers resisted, fearing a departure from the roots of their faith. Youth won out, and the new songbooks soon came into use in Steinbach and Meade.

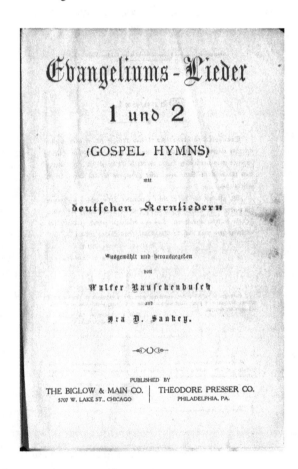

Through the 1930s and '40s, more liberal Mennonite conferences sent their choir leaders to Steinbach, and Dad attended their training sessions. Even after becoming a minister, he sang in the choir, or conducted it, with skill. As late as 1948 he led the choir at the wedding of Harry Neufeld and Tina Doerksen. The reporter of this event noted that the song was impressive and uplifting, with the right tempo and tone, "just as a song should be rendered at such an occasion."

Quartet singing would also not have met with approval from the traditionalists, but by the 1940s Dad made up the baritone part of a group informally called "The Four Peters," along with fellow churchmen Peter D. Kroeker, Peter D. Reimer, and Peter J. B. Reimer. Occasionally he would also sing in a quartet with his brothers.

In the late 1940s Dad unintentionally created a stir, especially in the rural congregations, by being part of a duet at *Jugendverein* (youth worship evening). The other singer was his watch-repair employee Peter Bergen, who added to the controversy by playing a guitar. Bergen's tenor voice blended well with Dad's baritone. They played and sang at a few other venues and were criticized by the old guard who wanted to keep instruments out of the church. Otherwise, they were very well received.

#

On December 27, 1936, three months before the birth of Mary Ann, Dad was elected a minister of the Steinbach Kleine Gemeinde. He believed that the election was a calling from God, and he was deeply honoured.

> The Lord's ways are ungraspable. As he saw it fit, the person to be chosen as his servant for the church fell upon me, full of mistakes, talents wanting. No, we can't always see what the Lord wants of us. Oh! if we only could be fit as his servants . . . it seems like a dream that I have to be a preacher, and still that is often what I have thought about . . . even I, poor sinner, have been called to work for him as a fisher of men.

Mom, for her part, was not so pleased. Later, reflecting on her life, she wrote:

> God blessed us with 6 children, 5 sons & one daughter, how happy we were that we had at least one daughter.

> Before she was born my husband was elected as Pastor of
> the E. M. Church, which I found very hard, I felt I didn't
> qualify to be a Pastor's wife—but they didn't ask me.

Actually, Dad would become pastor some eight years after his election
as a minister, but in Mom's eyes the ministerial assignment in itself was
burden enough. Now she had to share her husband with the church community, who expected her to be serious and composed, befitting her husband's position. Also, he would not be able to tell her everything that went
on in ministerial meetings or counselling sessions. He would be obliged
to keep parts of his experience to himself. As a woman, she would have
no vote and no formal role in church government, but she did not aspire
to such things, either. She would, however, be called upon to prepare food
for church ministers and visiting evangelists, on short notice, on countless occasions.

A family friend, Mrs. Peter D. Reimer, observed a kind of balance in
the relationship between Dad and Mom. That he had gone all the way to
Kansas to find a wife was considered unusual, and bold. But on the whole,
Dad was reserved, and "he took very seriously the idea that someone in his
position would serve as an example to the community." He was known to
be equitable, listening to all sides. Mom, meanwhile, did not bother to hide
her likes and dislikes. She was inclined to joke and laugh, and when she
would say something funny or perhaps indiscreet, Dad would smile, but
hold his tongue. According to Mrs. Reimer, he was "the solid one," and his
attitude conveyed a quiet, steadfast love for his wife. He didn't immediately
blurt things out, so that he sometimes caused others to wonder: "What did
he think, but not say?"

In Mennonite tradition it was expected that, upon being elected for the
ministry, the chosen man (and only men were eligible) would protest and
declare himself unfit for the position. That was what Grandfather had done,
back in 1918. Such protests were received as a display of a suitably humble
attitude in light of the high calling and serious responsibility involved.

Dad talked that way too but also allowed himself a quiet satisfaction:
"That is often what I have thought about." He had a small business, he had
a growing family, and he had a church community, but this was different.

Here was destiny, his true vocation, and he gladly said "yes" to it. He was aware, of course, that his own father was a minister, and that his maternal grandfather had been a Kleine Gemeinde *Aeltester*, or bishop. He may or may not have known that his maternal great-grandfather, and his paternal great-grandfather and great-great-grandfather had also served as ministers in South Russia.

Dad, in the mid-1930s in North America, had challenges his forebears had not faced. They had to deal with doctrinal and personal divisions within their communities as well as external demands from the czarist government to do some form of military service. They also held a lot of power, as their judgements could determine whether individuals might be disciplined or even excommunicated. But now, especially in Steinbach, the religious status quo was under great pressure. A faction of the most conservative Manitoba Mennonites, not wanting to yield up the privilege of educating their children in German in their own schools, had left to resettle in Mexico in the 1920s, weakening the conservatives who remained. In the name of spiritual renewal, American-influenced evangelical forces were promoting a more individualistic Christianity emphasizing an emotional conversion experience, child evangelism, Bible schools, and missionary work. Still, the traditionalists held fast to their usual refrain: "Why change? This is how we've always done it." At the same time, dissenting individuals now had more options if rejected by the church, and ministerial authority could only go so far.

Dad would have to find his personal way of living his vocation, and the ancestral model could not give him that.

Historian Royden Loewen characterizes the Manitoba Kleine Gemeinde during the time of Dad's ministry as engaged in "a contest between town and country," with Steinbach ministers advocating evangelical church methods and rural ministers holding out for older communitarian approaches. This tension was also at the centre of the discussions at a *Diener-Konferenz*, or ministerial conference, which Dad attended in Meade in 1937.

Dad at the Diener-Konferenz, washing what looks like our car, but was someone else's.

Dad favoured the "town" evangelical movement but also respected the tradition from which he came. He was born and raised in Steinbach but had many relatives in Blumenort, Kleefeld, and Rosenort. From the very beginning, and throughout his tenure as a minister, he played an in-between role, trying to build bridges between traditionalists and progressives.

Surprisingly, Dad was personally in violation of one of the points endorsed by the Kleine Gemeinde at the Meade *Diener-Konferenz*. In 1935 he had taken out a life insurance policy for $2000. In previous generations, the church-run *Waisenamt* (orphans' bureau) assisted widows and their children, but this support structure was gradually weakening. Maybe Dad saw that, and resorted to life insurance because he wanted to be sure that his family would be taken care of. At the *Diener-Konferenz*, however, the ministers specifically opposed life insurance as a worldly institution. Perhaps it was then that Dad let his policy run out. No trace of it was found when he died.

The ministers' efforts to satisfy both the evangelical and communitarian groups were unsuccessful. The Meade Kleine Gemeinde dissolved by the mid-1940s, and an unaffiliated Emmanuel Mennonite Church took its place. In Steinbach the church absorbed evangelical influences and flourished.

#

Once elected to the ministry, Dad immediately immersed himself in a hectic schedule of meetings of all kinds—brotherhood, evening *Verein* (a regular church program featuring singing, poetry, and speeches), ministerial consultations, church conferences, and the like.

Historically, the church had been the dominant institution in Mennonite communities, and even in the 1930s and '40s, ministers were expected to act as arbiters in social and economic relations. Dad made visitations to families and individuals. He mediated in business and estate disputes involving Steinbach's leading families, counselled baptismal candidates, and presided at weddings and funerals.

Doing God's work did not exempt him from involvement with the unglamorous details of everyday life, as is apparent in this diary entry from April 29, 1946:

> Monday. Fairly nice day. C. Wall is taking away the rubbish on our back yard. We had our last revival service in eve. Fair attendance & some sinners repented. Our septic tank is still frozen.

Rubbish, repentant sinners, and septic tanks: the profane and the sacred, all mixed together. If Dad was ever tempted to get lofty, he could be brought to earth by the demands of the ordinary.

The remodeled Kleine Gemeinde church, also known as the Southend Church, on a Sunday in the late 1940s.

Church interior, showing entrance and balcony.

Church life also had its practical aspects. Dad oversaw an extensive renovation of the Steinbach church building in 1942, which included a new basement and interior balcony, a new entrance, and an improved heating and public address system. He was involved in the decision to buy the Invalids' Home from Steinbach merchant Abram Vogt in 1946. The

Home operated under the auspices of the church, as would the Rest Haven, which was built to replace it thirteen years later.

Sunday school attendance grew exponentially in the 1940s under the leadership of John Peters, who had married a Kleine Gemeinde girl and switched church allegiances from his home Mennonite Brethren denomination. The language of instruction changed from German to English. The general congregation also grew steadily; in 1949 there were 321 members, and more joined each subsequent year.

Sometimes Dad spoke at "openings" in Sunday school, giving a little talk before we children would go to our classes. Once he said that his faith could be summed up in a line from a Sunday school chorus: "Jesus loves me, this I know / For the Bible tells me so." I felt embarrassed. Could my father only express himself in children's language? I was somehow disturbed by the words "Jesus loves me," even though I had sung them myself, over and over again.

I do not remember his sermons, though I do remember sitting in a pew close to the front and feeling a sense of quiet pride—that was *my* dad behind the pulpit, to whom all the adults were listening. He was called *Reverend* P. D. Friesen; he was someone others revered, and I was his son. In response to his public persona, I swung between the poles of embarrassment and pride.

Dad was of the first generation of ministers who did not write out entire sermons, to be read (in a monotonous, sing-song fashion) at a service and then read again at another location or in another year. Probably the majority of his preaching through the years was in German, as the church only moved slowly toward English-language services from the mid-1940s onward.

A variety of themes emerges in his sermons: love in marriage, women and modesty, the dangers of carnality, the importance of church discipline and personal surrender, the function of baptism, the lives of believers versus those of unbelievers, backsliding, the Beatitudes, the parables of the beggar Lazarus and the rich man and of the Good Samaritan, the nature of Jesus Christ, the Christian and death. The themes and their interpretations reflect mainstream evangelical Protestant theology, sometimes dipping into fundamentalist preoccupations such as the "end times," and sometimes into traditional Mennonite wellsprings like obedience and non-resistance.

"Busy" is the operative word in Dad's diary, appearing more than 700 times. His eyesight weakened under the strain of watch repairing and reading: "My eyes are . . . affected & I have to work slow & take it easy. But it's so busy that it can't be helped overloading them." After he switched from watchmaking to bookselling, his workload did not ease. When Art Neufeld, grader operator for Steinbach, drove down Main Street late in the evening, he would sometimes see the lights on in the bookstore. There was P. D. Friesen at the counter, bent over his account ledgers or perhaps the pages of a sermon. "Few people were aware of how much he gave."

Dad thought he didn't really have a choice in how busy he was, and was often overwhelmed with all there was for him to do. I think his busy-ness will have given him a sense of personal importance—and, at the same time, a sense of not being in control. For me as his son, it was also a kind of "do not trespass" sign.

#

The Kleine Gemeinde discouraged participation in political life on the grounds that politics belonged to the world from which they were to keep separate. It was best not to vote at all. The original Kleine Gemeinde set-tlers of Steinbach were at first content to let their Bergthaler co-religionists run municipal affairs. The Bergthaler had immigrated from South Russia at the same time, but from a different colony whose attitudes were not quite so strict.

By the time that Dad was a young man, however, even Kleine Gemeinde members were not unanimous in following the "no-voting" rule. Only once does Dad put himself on record in his diary—in the provincial elec-tion of 1930, he "voted for Mr. Beaubien." Arthur-Lucien Beaubien was a member of the Liberal-Progressives coalition. In the years that followed, Dad may not always have voted, particularly after becoming a minister. But it seems that his political sympathies stayed with the Liberal Party, both provincially and federally.

Through the 1930s he attended the occasional political meeting, including one in the neighbouring French village of St. Pierre after a pro-vincial election. He accompanied his uncle J. R. Friesen to congratulate the victorious incumbent Liberal, Albert Prefontaine. Numerous times he recorded provincial and federal election results in his diary.

Briefly, before World War II, Dad, along with many other Steinbach citizens, was curious about developments in Germany. In 1936 he went to a "very interesting" lecture in the basement of the new high school delivered by "Herr Goertz," an emissary from the Nazi regime who was promoting the ideal of a global "Deutsches Volk." But, listening to Hitler speak on a world-wide radio broadcast in 1938, Dad distanced himself, saying that the "speech aroused the Germans to fighting madness, but other countries to hatred." He was definitely opposed to war and war talk. He could not see a political solution to the problem, only a divine one: "There seems to be no way out but God. God can change hearts."

At one point Dad reverted to a traditional position, declaring that "we would be better off as Mennonites if we kept out of politics as much as possible." That was in 1940, but the next year he admitted to attending a local meeting where Premier Bracken spoke. Bracken maintained that party politics were getting in the way of a united war effort, as "Social Credit egotists" were speaking half-truths.

Dad had a genuine interest in political life but toned this down as he became ever more involved with church affairs.

#

In matters of evangelism Dad was on the side of modernists, but in matters of peace he was firmly a traditionalist. Probably more than any other Steinbach Kleine Gemeinde minister, Dad committed himself to preventing Mennonite young men from carrying arms during World War II. He attended many meetings of "the Committee of Elders" representing conservative Mennonite churches in southern Manitoba. He took extensive notes—seemingly acting as the informal secretary for the Kleine Gemeinde. At these meetings, ministers organized delegations to Ottawa to lobby on behalf of conscientious objectors (COs), arranged for COs to get regular ministerial visits, and generally tried their best to maintain a credible peace witness.

Dad gave evidence for Steinbach and district young men who claimed CO status, appearing before judges John Adamson and J. L. Bowman in the nearby village of Ste. Anne on December 16, 1940. He would have been asked whether these boys were really church members and sincere in their convictions. If the judges saw fit to uphold the testimony, the young men went into alternative service, working on road building, forestry, and fire-fighting projects, usually living in bush camps. Dad faced a test of nerves with Judge Adamson, who did not pretend to be impartial and was determined to bring as many young men into the military as possible.

> At hearings in Steinbach the following May, Adamson demanded to know:

> Are Mennonites going to help, or are you going to fail your country in her hour of trial and need? Every man and every woman in this country is either for Canada or for Hitler. Every man and woman, whether he or she intends it or not, is either helping Canada or helping Hitler. If there is something which you can do to help Canada that you do not do, you are helping Hitler.

Judge John Adamson.
Credit: Manitoba Historical Society.

Evading the either/or logic, the Mennonites simply reasserted the historical peace position of their religion. The teaching and life of Jesus do not permit Christians to wage war or use force against their enemies. The government had promised exemption from military service to Mennonites when they first came to Canada. Despite such arguments, up to forty percent of Mennonite young men in Canada enlisted in the armed forces.

In 1944 Dad was asked to minister to the COs in Riding Mountain National

Park at Clear Lake, some 350 kilometres west of Steinbach. He rented a cabin for his family and stayed for almost the entire month of August. The church reimbursed him for at least some of the expenses.

The children fished, swam, and played, while Dad met with the COs most days or evenings, holding singsongs and Bible quizzes. One day only twelve of the forty-five young men attended, and this number turned out to be the norm, even though Dad prayed for better attendance and "had a serious talk with some boys on their staying away." He had a point; the men were performing alternative service on the basis of their religious beliefs—if they failed to practise their religion, they would give credibility to the many critics of the Mennonites who accused them of being cowards who didn't want to risk their lives in war.

All of my siblings (I was not yet born) recall the vacation at Riding Mountain with fondness. It was the first time the whole family had gone on vacation together, and it was to be the only time. On August 1st they left Steinbach, having packed the car with "food, blankets, bicycle & all." They stopped at Neepawa en route and the children were thrilled to stay in a hotel. Reaching Clear Lake, they rented a small one-room cabin outside the park gate from a Calder family. The children went swimming and boat riding at every opportunity, Mom wrote letters and crocheted, and Dad read books.

Swimming in Clear Lake.
Left to right: Don, Al, Vern, Norm and Mary Ann, Mom at the back.

The boys got "swimmer's itch" from the lake water, and had to be "bathed & treated" every evening for a while. One of the Calder girls had a birthday and, to the children's delight, Mrs. Calder invited the whole Friesen family for sandwiches, ice cream, and cake. But the next day the happy mood was destroyed: "the tragic news came to S. Calders that the husband of Agnes, their daughter, was killed in action overseas."

On a day trip to nearby Lake Audy, Alvin found an abandoned bamboo pole and caught his first fish in a nearby creek. Dad took a picture of his smiling son hoisting a northern pike, still twisting on its line. The family also stopped to gaze at the park's resident buffalo herd, a reminder of a pre-settler era of which they knew almost nothing. On another, drizzly day, Donald, climbing up to the cabin roof, fell and sprained his arm, necessitating a trip to the local doctor. By the end of the month everyone was ready to go home.

Alvin with his first fish.

The Dominion government exempted Mennonites from military service, but still wanted them to help with the war effort. Dad served as an agent selling War Savings Certificates or Victory Bonds to assist those "suffering from the horrors and miseries of war." The money was intended "for soldiers' widows and orphans, refugees, food for civilians in England." If that was where the money was going, the Mennonites could justify participating.

Dad's sermon notes contain this zinger: "If we are to be non-resistant *at all*, we must be non-resistant *in* all." But not everyone was. From about the age of ten, a young boy named Billy Esau lived in the K. R. Friesen household. Billy's father was absent and his mother, who lived in Winnipeg, was unable to care for him adequately. His mother had some contact with Grandfather, but Billy was really part of the Friesen family. Dad was old enough to be his father, and did take a fatherly interest in him. But during the war, Billy, now a young man, left the family home one day without notice to anyone. A few days later he showed up at home wearing a Royal Canadian Air Force uniform. Dad scolded him for causing such worry to the parents, and not long after, Billy left home and did not return, dropping the name "Friesen," which he'd used for many years, in favour of his actual family name. He married, became a teacher, and sometimes communicated with the Friesen family, but it seemed that he and Dad never cleared away the tension between them.

Aunt Greta with Billy Esau (Friesen).

The Kleine Gemeinde, like most other Mennonite conferences, held to a policy of excommunication for anyone who enlisted for active military service. Billy, who had never joined the church, was immune from this discipline. Church members, however, could be excommunicated for a variety of offences, such as smoking or getting involved in shady financial deals or having extramarital sex. Those whose sins had been found out were confronted and compelled to repent. In 1940 one person was excommunicated for an unnamed offence when the *Bruderschaft* "couldn't find that he repented out of his own free will."

Excommunication in twentieth-century Canada did not have the force it had in nineteenth-century South Russia, where an individual had few choices for fellowship other than in his or her own community. But it was still a severe measure, reinforcing the importance of an attitude of submission. As a practice, it might have run contrary to Dad's general approach to life, but he felt duty-bound to implement it, and he did so with fellow ministers on several occasions.

#

At one point Dad moved decisively into the evangelical-fundamentalist camp. In July of 1945, he and fellow Steinbach ministers Ben D. Reimer and Archie Penner made a pilgrimage to Winona Lake, Indiana, home of the Billy Sunday conference centre. Sunday, a former major league baseball player known for his pugnacious style, had been the most celebrated and influential American evangelist in the first two decades of the twentieth century. He would run from one end of the revival meeting platform to the other and dive across the stage, pretending to slide into home plate. The conference centre was his legacy.

Dad and his companions boarded a Greyhound bus in Winnipeg. After an uncomfortable two-day journey, they reached Chicago, where they got off at the Union Bus Depot: "and there stood three lonesome, sleepy-eyed, dirty (not so very), forlorn, lost, inquisitive people."

They were impressed by Chicago, the second-largest city in the U. S. at the time with a population of around 3.5 million, including many immigrants from Europe as well as internal migrants from the American South. "Boy, this is a town," declared Dad. In a postcard to his family, he wrote: "We ate our meals, breakfast and dinner at a small cafeteria served mostly by Negroes, but it was clean, the eats were swell, and it didn't cost so much at that." They walked "many blocks until our feet were quite sore," dropped in at the Moody Bible Institute, and visited the art museum, whose exhibits Dad described in a tone of boyish wonder adopted for his children's benefit: "My, my but what all can't you see here. Indian hand craft, totem poles (they look very dangerous), cliff dwellers pots & other articles, even some articles taken from Pompeii."

Dad scanned the phone book looking for someone familiar and actually got hold of former Steinbacher K. B. Reimer and had the homey pleasure of talking with him in Low German: "It sure felt fine and I was thrilled." He and Ben D. Reimer and Archie Penner also tacked on a brief visit with evangelist George Schultz, who conducted the meetings in Steinbach in 1931 when Dad was converted.

Another postcard featured the imposing Palmer House Hotel in downtown Chicago. Dad couldn't afford to stay there, but wanted to illustrate the wonders of the big city. "The whole town of Steinbach, Winkler, Altona, and Sarto to boot, could all come here at the same time & sleep in these rooms and they would still have some empty rooms left yet."

Palmer House Hotel, Chicago.

Arriving at Winona Lake, Dad and his companions spent five days listening to presentations by dynamic speakers, taking in as many as six messages each day, beginning at 7:00 a.m. The speeches were interspersed with "heart stirring songs" rendered by "the coloured Negro couple the 'Findleys.'" In the heated atmosphere (both metaphorically and literally; temperatures were in the 90s Fahrenheit), Dad surrendered to evangelistic enthusiasm: "we were just melted in yielding to the spirit."

Together with Ben D. Reimer, Dad continued on to visit Meade, Kansas. "The Lord is blessing immensely & we're all 'fired up' to work more earnestly, and eagerly & consciously for the Lord, our Master," he declared. He and Reimer conducted a series of evangelistic meetings among the Meade-area Mennonites.

In a letter to Mom, Dad shared news about relatives and chatted about the food served in the Rempel household: "Ma right away put up lunch, consisting of thin pancakes & watermelons, and we ate that the juice flowed." He wrote of his walk in the evening moonlight following a 104-degree day:

> Well, Margaret, you know what this will do to me, a full moon, clear sky, soft breeze, sweet memories of long ago. . . . Yes, memories and longings, the lonely soul yearning for the companionship of its mate; oh sweet heart, look up into the sky to the stately moon hanging there in the soft sky, don't you hear whispers, sweet whispers,

coming down to your sweet ears. Oh, I was so thankful to our good Lord that He had given you, <u>yes you</u>, unto me. Yes, He had seen it fit (it's 14 years ago now almost to the day) that you should come into my life, lonely life, to stay there forever until death doeth us part here on earth, but then to go on in eternity forever and ever.

Linear time vanishes; he is back to his first falling-in-love moment with Mom. In the afterglow of Winona Lake, he becomes mystical, almost ecstatic; romantic and religious feelings flow together. "The lonely soul yearning for its mate" could be a spiritual seeker in quest of unity with the Eternal. When I first read this letter I was embarrassed to intrude on such an intimate communication, and astonished that my father was capable of such flowery language, which I had never before heard him use.

Sad-eyed Mom in the 1940s.

In the same letter Dad tells Mom that he prayed that God would give him "a larger burden for lost souls," and it was with this burden that he returned to Manitoba. Reaching home at 6:00 p.m. on August 10, he did not miss a beat, but was off the same evening to attend singing practice at the church.

He had been away for a month. Before he left he'd noted: "Our little baby Peter Ralph is still quite restless." I was now two-and-a-half months old. I would not have recognized the stranger who had suddenly appeared in our household.

Ben D. Reimer and Archie Penner were hired as teachers at the Steinbach Bible School, which announced that "new emphasis will be put on missions and English." Before long Reimer was holding evangelistic meetings in the Steinbach church, while Dad led the singing. Dad also preached at the new mission hall in East Steinbach, and although the attendance was only fair, "some sinners repented." He had a new hunger for saving souls, but temperamentally he was not a revival preacher. His sermons tended to be measured and thoughtful rather than emotional.

In the summer of 1946 Hyman Appelman, one of the speakers who had deeply impressed Dad in Indiana, was invited by the Steinbach ministerial to hold revival meetings in the tabernacle. Appelman, a converted Jew and passionate orator, took the community by storm, holding afternoon and evening meetings and racking up previously unheard-of numbers of conversions. Once he had supper at our house, and the soul-saving conversation can only be imagined. "Some people don't like this," Dad remarked of the meetings, apparently referring to traditionalists. The *Carillon News* estimated that 8,000 people attended the Appelman meetings over six evenings at the tabernacle, adding: "This has been one of Steinbach's greatest evangelistic revivals, 400 people or more decided to turn to God."

Hyman Appelman.
Credit: Wikipedia Commons.

Some of the converts were children. When Dad was young, hardly anyone got baptized before the age of seventeen, reflecting the community's view that children lived in a "saved" condition until they were old enough to make a conscious decision for themselves. By the 1940s, however, under the influence of American fundamentalism, parents began to fear that their children could be among the lost. It was imperative, then, to introduce children to a salvation experience. Children, in turn, felt the pressure to have such an experience, for the sake of their young souls, and also to please their parents. The Mennonites, ironically, had distanced themselves from one of the basic tenets of their faith, the rejection of infant baptism, for which so many had been martyred. Not that they had taken to baptizing babies, but they had reordered the chronology of adult accountability.

So it was that Dad tried, clumsily, to engineer his sons' salvation. He paid thirteen-year-old Alvin and twelve-year-old Donald a dollar each to attend the Appelman meetings. They duly responded to one of the altar calls. Al remembers that Dad seemed happy. In his diary Dad wrote: "Tabernacle full in eve & many souls came closer to Jesus. Alvin & Donald were also drawn & came to the front. May the Holy Spirit give them strength, direct and guide them & fill their hearts." But both boys returned to their normal lives soon after. The spiritual bribe failed.

Mennonites like Dad who had been raised in a religion where emotions and self-expression were subdued, and where traditions were followed "because that's how it's always been done," were hungry for renewal, for a more joyful, expressive, spontaneous Christianity. So it is not surprising that they were attracted to American fundamentalism, which seemed to possess what they felt was lacking, and which also shared a reassuring similarity to their own insistence on the Bible as the absolute and unerring authority for Christian living.

Dad may have had reservations about the unashamedly capitalist message of the American fundamentalists and their notion of the United States as a country blessed and even chosen by a partisan God who wanted his children to be rich. Devoted to Mennonite teachings of pacifism and separation of church and state, he must also have cringed at fundamentalist militarism. The fundamentalists believed they were obliged to defend Western Christian civilization with force. They also were caught up in the revenge fantasy of the "end times" and a bloody apocalypse that would conclude history on this Earth. Dad did not record his views on these subjects.

#

Dad made various trips to the United States on church business. He went to the Mennonite World Conference in Goshen, Indiana, in 1948, a Sunday school convention in Indianapolis in 1954, and a Christian booksellers' convention in Chicago in 1957. Always he took the trouble to send postcards home, mainly for the benefit of his children.

He travelled to Goshen with John D. Loewen, Ben D. Reimer, Jake P. Dueck, and John C. Reimer from the Steinbach Kleine Gemeinde. They pulled a house trailer behind their car to save money on accommodations. Dad recorded his impressions of the conference on a postcard:

This is the main street of Goshen; but, my, is this a big town, over 11,000 people. I had never thought it so large; also Elkhart is a large town. Our trailer stands about 90 feet from the R.R. tracks, but not many trains are passing to bother us during the night. The audience at the conference is a very mixed one. Overlooking from the back you just see a sea of cheesecloth head covering, some small, some large, some of the younger girls with bushy hair standing in all directions, but still with the small covering. Some with bonnets black or white. And then the men seem still more different. Different style beards, no beards, haircuts with a thick edge in the neck; different hats, and even the square box-like top buggies in black made their appearance. And then we see the different speakers from all the world: French, Swiss, Holland, Germany, Brazil, Paraguay, Argentine, Canada.

Demonstrating a writer's observational skill and descriptive powers, Dad's portrayal mixes awe, curiosity, subdued humour, and admiration. Surely his definition of "Mennonite" will have been broadened at Goshen, from the narrow version of Low German speakers of Dutch descent to a multicultural mix including many languages and ethnicities.

Mom accompanied Dad to the Sunday school convention in Indianapolis with their friends the Ed Loewens. John Peters, superintendent of the Steinbach EMC Sunday school, also went, along with his wife Amanda. Peters recalled that one of the main speakers at the convention was a woman named Henrietta C. Mears, who wore a flamboyant hat, a sleeveless dress, and long white gloves. She was the director of Christian Education at First Presbyterian Church of Hollywood, California, and possessed the panache to go along with that title. When she gestured emphatically, the loose flesh of her triceps wobbled. "What will Mr. Friesen think?" Peters wondered, expecting a negative answer. Next morning he was relieved when Dad asked approvingly: "Did you ever hear a message like that?"

Mom, meanwhile, took the speeches to heart: "Had very earnest messages and we pray that we might realize more the earnestness of time, how

we need to humble ourselves and pray, and repent of our wicked ways, so God will hear us and answer." "The earnestness of time" was probably a reference to the imminent end-of-the-world fantasies popular among American fundamentalists. Mom seems to have internalized this fear-based religion even more than Dad did.

Dad travelled alone to the booksellers' convention in Chicago by train. It was August, major league baseball season, and he sent home a postcard with a picture of Comiskey Park, the home of the Chicago White Sox, addressed to his baseball-loving son Norman. Not that he ever thought of attending a game. Instead he

Mom in Indianapolis. Soldiers' and Sailors' Monument in the background.

described his search for the Mennonite Biblical Seminary where he had lodging: "Got there safely. It was hot and sweaty work lugging that suitcase along; also passed through those negro habituated streets, but I had a nice soft bed, and slept very well." Negro-inhabited streets—we could hardly imagine. At most we might have seen the occasional black man at the railway station in Winnipeg, but here it was Dad who was the white

outsider. We knew that a few of the White Sox players were black, and to us they were heroes. Our father's posts from the urban American landscape of the 1940s and '50s piqued our curiosity about the world beyond the borders of our insular little town.

Home of the Chicago White Sox.

#

CHAPTER 15: THE LIVING WORD

For more than 130 years, ever since its inception in South Russia, the Kleine Gemeinde had shown no interest in mission work, always believing that it was Christian witness enough to create a version of the Kingdom of God in their own community. By the 1940s, however, under the zealous leadership of Ben D. Reimer, the Western Gospel Mission was formed. The first missionaries were sent to evangelize Ukrainian Canadians living in Arabella, Saskatchewan, close to the Manitoba border. Dad did his little bit for the mission cause, joining a group driving to Saskatchewan for the dedication of a new chapel. He and others got a few fitful hours of sleep on the hard chapel platform before rising early on the second morning for the return journey.

Modernists had been arguing for some time that the appellation "Kleine Gemeinde" no longer suited the realities of the times, and in 1952 they won the day: the name was changed to "Evangelical Mennonite Church" in Manitoba. Most people just used the acronym: EMC. Mission work increased dramatically, and mission conferences became annual events. At one such conference in the mid-1950s, Dad spoke on Hebrews 2: "How shall we escape, if we neglect so great a salvation?"

> For quite a while, a number of years, we always thought that this word was directed to the sinners, to those who are not yet children of God. But during these last years it has also come to me that this is not particularly directed to the unconverted, but more so to God's people. Now we have had the privilege, living in this last time, knowing salvation, perhaps more than anyone else. We have had more opportunities of having it. And we have had so many opportunities of telling it to others. Now if you and I have this salvation, this great salvation, but do not heed it as we should . . . if we think it was really something great we would talk about it. If somebody has a bargain in a store, it might only be a couple of cents, but if it's a bargain, he or she is surely going to tell the neighbour about that bargain, because they believe they have received something. And as the missionaries tell us again and again, that there are so many, that there are millions yet who do not know the

Lord Jesus Christ, who do not know salvation, how shall we escape if we do not tell them? When they talk with the heathen who have become Christians, and then they ask how long have you known it, well I've always known it, how long have your parents known it, well they have always known it, and their parents have known it. Well why didn't you come sooner and tell us?

Comparing the soul's salvation to a bargain in a shop seems crude. But Dad knew his audience, thrifty Mennonites always on the lookout for a deal. He clearly endorses the evangelical agenda which by this time had become dominant in his church. However, he also acknowledges that previous generations of Mennonites possessed a valid version of salvation: "our parents have always known it, and their parents have known it."

When missionaries came to our home for meals and fellowship, we boys, unimpressed, would vanish to our rooms upstairs as soon as possible. Yes, in church we watched the slide presentations showing brown-skinned people in exotic costumes, but some instinct prompted us to avoid personal contact with God's servants. When Dad gave me a red plastic piggy bank with the letters "Mission to the Lepers" stencilled on it, I was more interested in the realistic-looking toy pig than in helping any lepers. None of the coins I collected made their way further than to Modern Grocery across Main Street.

Dad at a meeting in the Steinbach Bible Institute,
seated between Ben D. Reimer and Don P. Shidler.

CHAPTER 16:
MAN OF THE HOUR

A few months before I was born, Dad made the following diary entry:

> February 4, 1945: Sunday. Stormy in morning but nice &
> fair later on. I served in Hospital in morn. Jac P. Dueck
> & I first went to Kleefeld, where we served the gospel.
> For dinner [noon meal] at Geo S. Fast, then to Barkfield
> where we had a little service at Nick Wiens' place, & visited
> several other places. Home at 10 p.m. tired but happy in
> the service of the Master.

"Tired but happy in the service of the Master"—perhaps the phrase
was inspired by a volume of poetry entitled *Im Dienste des Meisters* [In
the Service of the Master] by Saskatchewan Mennonite evangelist Isaac P.
Friesen. To me, it's a title with a sting—we, his family, are not included in
the account of that day. My mother, pregnant with me, probably went to
church in Steinbach and visited with relatives and friends and made meals
as usual, keeping an eye on her youngest, Norman.

Dad was at the peak of his life's work, running a business, raising a large
family, and leading a growing congregation. He had been elected pastor

of the Steinbach Kleine Gemeinde in January. Previously, the four Kleine Gemeinde churches in the East Reserve—Blumenort, Kleefeld, Prairie Rose, and Steinbach—had been administered basically as one congregation. *Bruderschaft* meetings were jointly held, and baptisms and communion services were performed only by the *Aeltester* (bishop). This arrangement was now changed, with each church becoming more autonomous, electing its own leader who could also hold communion and perform baptism. The pastor assumed parts of the *Aeltester*'s role while continuing the duties of *Prediger*, or preacher. Jacob P. Dueck and Peter J. B. Reimer were also elected ministers.

P. J. B. Reimer was more qualified for the leadership position than was Dad—he was better educated, more outspoken, more articulate. But Dad had established his credentials with the traditionalists by listening to them and working diligently to keep young Mennonite men out of the armed forces. On the other hand, he had shown progressive leanings by leading the choir and supporting Sunday school and mission work. The Steinbach congregation valued his levelheadedness and diplomacy skills. According to Ben Eidse, who later became a minister and missionary, Dad never seemed threatened by the leadership competition, maintaining a humble and unassuming attitude.

Reimer himself later said: "He was the man of the hour . . . a tactful man who was able to keep things together for the blessing of the whole conference."

In June, 1946, *Aeltester* Peter P. Reimer of Blumenort deliberately stayed away from a church service where young people were to be baptized. He wanted to signal his disagreement with the worldly direction the Steinbach church was taking. In the absence of the *Aeltester*, someone had to fill in, and Dad officiated at a baptism ceremony for the first time.

Church historian Dave Schellenberg says that Dad played a unique role:

> We were the only urban church . . . and we all know
> that urban living brings with it situations which country
> churches do not face. In a sense . . . he was our first leader.
> Great men are often not recognized during their lifetime.

> I believe Mr. Friesen was one of these. Today we bow and
> thank God for giving us this man.

That anyone would call my father "great" surprises me. When I set out to tell his story, it was not so much because his life was exceptional or heroic, but almost because it wasn't. Even though he was a leading member of the church community for twenty-five years, several people I interviewed suggested that his contributions were not sufficiently recognized, partly because of his quiet and unassuming demeanour. A part of me wants to correct the imbalance and give him his due. But then, if the lack of recognition did not really bother him, I shall have to honour this self-effacement too. Maybe he was content with being "ordinary."

Like other Mennonite congregations of the time, ours was something of an extended family. Not only did the members share a common belief system, they tended to be made up of people related to each other. If you were a Reimer or a Dueck or a Loewen or a Kroeker or a Toews, you could be sure that a genealogical map would show various interconnections between yourself and the larger "family." A pastor in this type of congregation must be aware of family history and decide how he will respond, especially when it comes to forming alliances. If he is seen to be taking sides, he runs the risk of alienating some people. If he does not take sides at all, he runs the risk of being seen as being weak in his convictions.

The pastor is also expected to minister to the spiritual needs of the congregation and provide moral direction. For Dad, this meant visiting people's homes, counselling, or confronting individuals who had broken church rules or were beset by doubts, or were simply indifferent to religion. One afternoon he and Ben D. Reimer "went around in my car hunting up Wm Fehr." Luckily for Fehr, "We could not find him." For the most part, though, Dad did not try to force himself or his opinion on others.

Dad mediated in family disputes, such as the one which arose amongst the children of well-known merchant H. W. Reimer in the late 1930s concerning the family estate. Dad, along with other ministers of the Steinbach church, met with the family on several occasions but could not broker an agreement. Eventually the estate was tried in surrogate court.

Where others were quick to judge, Dad was known to temper such inclinations. At one *Bruderschaft* meeting in which some were condemning a woman who had committed adultery, Dad "reminded the others that we all have our flaws, and we all make mistakes."

Dad was sensitive to the whole question of "belonging," and wanted to build a welcoming church community. Ben Eidse remembers being warmly greeted when he came to Steinbach from his home in Rosenort. "He made me feel right at home, even though I was from *Jantsied* ['the other side,' meaning west of the Red River]. Under your dad, nobody would be afraid any longer."

Others recall receiving positive regard. As a teenager, Mrs. Eidse (Helen, daughter of the P. D. Reimers) went through bouts of depression. One time as she walked with a group of young people into the church basement after Sunday school, he singled her out for a special greeting, as if he sensed her need.

As a young man, Art Kroeker was studying the catechism in preparation for baptism and was worried because he hadn't had a dramatic conversion experience. Dad responded with a story:

> In this life it's like we're all on a ship, all on the voyage together. And it's known that storms will come and the ship will get into trouble at some time. So some of the people practice life-saving drills, getting into the lifeboats and so on, but others don't. Then a storm comes and the ship starts to go down, and those who didn't practice become very fearful and cry out in their panic, thinking that this is surely the end. They wave their arms and shout in their fear. Whereas the others, who rehearsed the life-saving skills, quietly get into the boats. They are also joined by the frightened ones, and in the end, all are saved.

Taking catechism classes was like practising life-saving drills, apparently. Less disciplined personalities might have needed a revival meeting to frighten them into conversion. But "all are saved." Art took comfort from the lesson and proceeded to baptism, at peace.

One day Dad drove to *Jantsied* to visit people in the Rosenort area. He came upon a boy on a tractor on the dusty road and stopped to ask directions. The boy, it turned out, was Levi Dueck, a young cousin. Not satisfied with just getting directions, Dad also asked whether Levi was saved. Levi replied that he was not ready to answer, and the matter was left there.

Glen Klassen, who was in a class of thirteen-year-old baptismal candidates with Dad in the 1950s, remembers: "He did not confront each of us individually, the way some ministers did in those days. His attitude was acceptance and we had nothing to fear from him."

Another teenager in that era, Doreen Reimer, attended baptismal classes with Dad. Doreen, sincere, conscientious, nervous, found the pastor to be father-like and kindly, but not really warm. He might have erred on the side of caution, not wanting to be inappropriate with adolescent girls, but over-compensating, then, by keeping too much of a distance.

At one baptism Dad performed, he said, "I wish it was my own children kneeling here." As it happened, only Don was baptized by Dad. I would say that those of us who were never baptized wished for his blessing, but were not able to receive it in this way because of everything else we would be obliged to accept.

Dad's egalitarianism impressed a teenaged Travis Reimer:

> One Wednesday night, Young Peoples was cancelled, but Bernie Klassen and I decided that in that case we would join the adults for their prayer meeting. When it came time for dividing up into small groups, I got shuffled into a group that included both your dad and Jac. P. Dueck. Intimidating for sure! But what struck me and has stayed with me to this day is how in your dad's prayer he spoke of his sinfulness with remorse and also reveled in God's grace. Our pastor an evil sinner? That prayer had more impact than 10 sermons.

At the same time, Travis, who later became a pastor himself, recognized a lighter side to Dad, which apparently had to be suppressed for reasons of church politics:

He had a battle royal trying to act *Fromm* [pious] all the time as an ordained minister of the Kleine Gemeinde. I think he enjoyed the humorous side of life, but he had to keep it under tight restraint. When we would have visiting speakers to our church who didn't realize the impropriety of telling jokes in the EMC pulpit, your dad would show a slight smirk, although you knew that on the inside he was guffawing heartily.

The church ministerial, Dad included, frequently presented a face of concern about too much pride (*Hoffart*) amongst the membership, as shown by the wearing of jewellery or excessively stylish wedding dresses. "It is an invasive influence," Dad declared, unimpressed by the excuses he kept hearing, that "other *Gemeinden* have it or others do it." The ministers agreed on a rather impotent course of action: "We wish not to cease warning and admonishing."

And then, he made concessions. In 1942, when a young church member persisted in his intention to marry a girl from the Mennonite Brethren, he was put out of the church. He was reinstated in good standing when the young woman agreed to join the Kleine Gemeinde. When the couple asked if they could have the choir sing at their wedding, Dad responded: "I don't see why not." But he had no intention of allowing it; he knew it was against church rules. He did not want to say a direct "no." In the end a compromise was reached—the Mennonite Brethren choir came in and sang, and their minister officiated.

Dad often conducted premarital counselling sessions in the living room of our house while upstairs we boys tried to listen in through the stovepipe opening. We soon lost interest, though, at the abstract admonitions about kindness, respect, and modesty.

In the 1950s Dad counselled Elvira, a daughter of the C. T. Loewens, prior to her marriage. Somehow, he had got word that Elvira's dress was going to be wide at the bottom—a more worldly look than was approved of by the church. "*Dien Kjleet woat nich too breit senne, nä?*" he said to Elvira. Your dress won't be too broad now, will it? Elvira, since "*too breit*" had not been exactly defined, simply answered, "*Nä.*" She had a suspicion that the dress would have been judged too wide, had anyone come to measure it. The wedding was held. She wore her beautiful dress. After, she nervily asked Dad, "*Na, wea daut Kjleet dann doch too breit?*"—Was the dress too broad, after all? Dad only smiled.

Which brings us back to Mrs. P. D. Reimer's question: what did he think, but not say? Elvira concluded that the dress in fact had been more extravagant than the *Gemeinde* would have approved of, but Dad, loath to forbid it outright, said nothing. All his ministerial life, she thought, he had an inner liberal impulse, but also always felt he had to do what the *Gemeinde* expected. He lived with the pressure of "having to look for a way around," and, although he became skilled at this, he was weighed down by the burden—partly self-imposed—of not speaking his true mind.

All this earnest ministerial warning and admonishing would prove to be in vain in the long run. During Dad's tenure as pastor, the practice of non-conformity to the world, once a pillar of the Mennonite faith, steadily eroded.

A tape recording of another wedding, that of Eddie Loewen and Lydia Reimer, shows Dad's much-practised rhetorical style, in Low German–accented but correct English. He admonishes the couple to attend to each other with care and to bring their religious faith into their relations with each other. When I first listened to the recording, I was put off by what I thought was a formulaic presentation, but Lydia Loewen herself defended it: "The tone of his voice is calm and clear, just as I remember him. The account of his message is upstanding and authoritative in a non-threatening manner."

When Annie Hildebrandt transferred her church membership from the Mennonite Brethren to the Kleine Gemeinde upon marrying Elvira Toews' brother Cornie, Dad asked her for a commitment: *bauen zu helfen, und bauen zu lassen* [High German, literally: build to help, build to allow]. In other words, he asked for her participation in helping others, but also for a kind of restraint in not criticizing others.

Wilma Doerksen, who worked in the bookstore for a short time in 1948, comments on Dad's leadership style:

> He was not outspoken; he didn't have what you'd call number one P. R. He didn't go up to the pulpit to be

eloquent. But what he said was loaded . . . there was no idle word.

He did not find it easy to speak from the pulpit. He had to do it despite what people might have been thinking or saying, their criticisms. When the strong wave of evangelism hit Ben D. Reimer, and to a certain extent Archie Penner, your dad still felt he had to stay in touch with the more traditional part of the church. He always tried to be realistic; he didn't use high-flown language, and whatever he said, he said it sincerely. Although when not speaking from the pulpit he also did have a dry sense of humour.

One time I and some others organized an event on behalf of Cradle Roll, in the church basement. We wanted to make a good impression on the parents. Your dad said: *"Na joh, nu ha' wie uns en party jemoakt"* [well, now we have made ourselves a party].

Your dad was under-appreciated. Ben D. Reimer and others belonged to the new guard and they got a lot of attention. Your dad worked quietly in the background. He spread himself thin, giving attention to everyone and every notion. He gave so much in service. I think he felt alone many times, especially when it came to the battles between the traditional faction and the evangelical one. He was a bridge between the old and the new in the church. He had to find a way in between. At those times he would walk stooped, as if carrying a burden. I think it was hard on him, and it may have been why he had a stroke.

#

CHAPTER 16: MAN OF THE HOUR

One of the flashpoints for conflict between the old and the new was the question of musical instruments. For its entire history the Kleine Gemeinde had not allowed instruments in church. By the early 1950s, younger members and some ministers began arguing to have a piano. Mom described the problem in her diary entry for December 16, 1954:

> There is quite a commotion about the instrument, some believe we should just move it in while others again are more careful. It really stirs up a lot of trouble, but being such a controversial problem we are at a loss just what to do about it. So far we stemmed the idea of having one for our district alone, might agree on it more consilliable [conciliatory] but we also have to consider our other churches so may the Lord give us grace what to do about it.

The debate was pre-empted by events, according to an account by Art Neufeld:

> It happened that some of the deacons saw an ad in the paper for a piano at a good price, so they went ahead and bought it. When the truck arrived to deliver the piano no one had a place to put it, so the driver was directed to the church building. He and his helpers began to unload the piano. Just then Ben D. Reimer came back from a preaching tour. Thinking that the church had finally voted in favour of allowing the piano, he jumped out of his car and also put his shoulder into helping the others. Later he learned that the piano was not officially supposed to be in the church. Your dad was quite concerned, and became more so when he discovered that the very conservative Rev. David P. Reimer of Blumenort was scheduled to preach in Steinbach. What to do? He was on the hot seat. Your dad had the piano covered with a blanket. Reimer came and preached but said nothing

about the blanket-covered object. The moral: "why hurt somebody?" It was not seen as hypocritical.

Another church member adds that Dad, who also spoke that day, never mentioned the piano but told a story of parents who went away on a trip, leaving their children in charge of the house. The children decided that this would be a good time to introduce a new, improved heating system. The only trouble was, they couldn't get it to work right. The parents returned, alarmed, to a house full of smoke.

The traditional faction seemed satisfied that the story justified their concerns; the "progressives," while they might have felt a bit chastised, did not feel obliged to do anything. It must have been a strange service—everyone pretending that the blanket-covered object, in plain sight, was not there. But the pretence helped avoid a crisis which could have become serious enough to cause a split. In time, the rural congregations also installed pianos.

Dad eventually bought a piano for his own household from his brother and sister-in-law, Abraham and Gertie. At *Bruderschaft* one man objected strongly and repeatedly, saying it was unbefitting of a pastor to have such an instrument in his home. Dad would not get rid of the piano. The man would not let the issue go and eventually was put out of the church because of his persistence. Mary Ann taught me how to play "I Love Coffee, I Love Tea" on the keyboard, but the piano was not in our house for long; after she left home to get married the piano also went somewhere else.

In seeking the middle road, was Dad demonstrating conflict avoidance? And if so, does that imply lack of moral courage? Or did his bridge-building take a special courage of its own? Because of his efforts, quite often solutions were found where otherwise people would have been left stuck in their polarized positions.

#

As a minister, Dad often kept company with sorrowing people. He presided at funerals ranging from that of prominent merchant H. W. Reimer to the smallest and most intimate situations, as described in his diary entry for February 23, 1939:

I was called to H. H. Epps in afternoon to officiate at a funeral which was held in their home, with only the parents & their children present. A small son had been born to them but died after an hour of life. Then Mr. Epp & I went to graveyard & buried the child.

Mr. Epp, a school custodian, was a *Russländer* and not a member of the Kleine Gemeinde. Yet he turned to Dad in his time of need.

A very hard moment came when two young women, Alice Wiebe (daughter of one of Dad's cousins) and Elma Loewen, drowned at Red Rock Lake Bible Camp in July, 1947. Alice had seen Elma struggling in the water. She swam out to help her and was pulled down. The camp had been established by the Kleine Gemeinde as part of its youth ministry in 1946, and the drownings were a severe blow to the families and also to the wider community. Dad was given the task of informing Elma's parents of their daughter's death. He had to be the messenger of crushing news, and then sit with the bereaved to make funeral arrangements.

I don't know what he said or did in those moments, but it seems that no death was random or meaningless for him. When, on a mild December day in 1948, a toddler was run over and killed by a truck on Main Street, Dad commented that this loss was very hard on the parents, and then added a one-line prayer: "May this bring the results that the Lord wants it to bring." For him, every death was part of God's plan, a call for awareness. The way Dad looked at it, God's ways are not our ways; our task is to learn, accept, and obey.

That attitude was also the Mennonite way, a kind of strategy for dealing with loss. Dad suffered many losses in his life, especially when he was a child. I do not think he mourned these losses completely, and so I believe that some of his grief went underground. Suppressed grief can manifest in various ways—as sickness, anger, emotional distancing. I think that this also happened with him.

#

In 1949, after a dozen years in the ministry, Dad reflected on church life in a German-language article appearing in the church yearbook. He spoke of the "guardians"—church elders and leaders—who had been appointed in the early years of settlement. These guardians "in all sincerity took the responsibility upon themselves to fulfill God's purposes. Each guardian in whichever time he worked will have had a feeling for the task of that time, and how great his responsibilities were." Quite deliberately, he acknowledges the validity of his ancestors' spiritual path. He was surely aware that the modernists tended to dismiss these "guardians" as benighted and ignorant. He even points out that the manifestations of modernity in the community—telephones, newspapers, fast vehicles, radio—may not always be of spiritual benefit. "So we are meant to be cautious, to watch and pray."

"Before all else," he continues—and here as pastor, he is speaking personally—"the guardian must attend to himself . . . a person can speak the best words and preach himself hoarse, but if he does not lead by being a good example, all that will be of no help." Finally he speaks of community, experienced at the deepest emotional level:

> Through inner and spiritual fellowship we can at times be so closely tied to our neighbour that we have the sense of having had a glimpse into the soul of the other. With the result that both are wonderfully strengthened, in belief and in love.

So he had something in his faith community which I knew nothing about, this unity with others, emanating from shared belief. He could speak of soul glimpsing soul. No wonder that his church work meant so much to him.

One of his sermon notes is entitled "Behold the Man," based on Pilate's iconic words in the Gospel of John, referring to Jesus. German translations are inserted here and there; evidently Dad could use the same outline for different audiences. The portrait of Jesus emerging from these notes is an orthodox evangelical Christian one, of a god-man with a mission, a sinless, self-sacrificing mediator who suffered unjustly while on earth, but who will one day return in glory and triumph. We are instructed to believe in this divine man, obey, revere, and be grateful to him. Dad tried to imitate him and live a surrendered life "from self to Christ as Lord."

In 1951 the church presented Dad with a four-door blue Dodge sedan in recognition of his years of service. Our family's battered twenty-two-year-old Model A Ford was pretty well worn out by this time, and a source of social shame for us children. I was thrilled to sit in a car with actual upholstery. The Dodge's fat padded inside door handles hinted at a promise of luxury I had not dared to imagine.

Mom was moved to Biblical phrasing in her humble gratitude for the new car—"Oh God, who are we, that thou shouldst bless us thus?"—not thinking, apparently, that "we" deserved some compensation for the many years of unsalaried service Dad had provided. By comparison, the Evangelical Mennonite Brethren church had been paying their pastor since 1928.

On the last day of February, 1953, nineteen-year-old Alvin, out for a drive and a good time with his buddy Aubrey Reimer, hit a patch of ice just past Ste. Anne. The Dodge skidded into the oncoming lane. A tractor-trailer, coming from the opposite direction, swerved and the trailer jack-knifed. The car hit the rear wheels of the tractor and then the side of the trailer, peeling back its roof and crumpling the hood. Miraculously, both young men escaped serious injury. Alvin was hospitalized for a few days with a dramatic gash on his forehead that required twenty-three stitches. Aubrey suffered a bruised heel. In her diary Mom uttered a frightened prayer for her reckless son: "Oh, that he would listen to the voice of God speaking to him, and yield his life to Him, to the Saviour." The church quickly replaced the car, which must have been insured. This time it was a Plymouth.

Our wrecked Dodge on the back lot of J. R. Friesen's car dealership.

Alvin, unchastened by the accident or the gossip of townspeople, continued to frequent the Tourist Hotel beer parlour. Occasionally he would come home after a Saturday afternoon in the pub, jovially tipsy, and have a bath before going out again, often to a Ukrainian barn dance in Sarto or Piney. If our parents were not at home, he would demonstrate his polka skills on the living room linoleum, his feet moving with surprising agility for a man six feet tall and over 200 pounds. I did not know whether to be impressed or dismayed. I was not accustomed to his voice being so loud, or the strange sour smell of beer emanating from him, but I liked watching him dash around so playfully. Sometimes he would stumble and crash into the chesterfield and laugh gleefully, scaring me. I was relieved that our parents were not there to see it.

In March, 1957, the Steinbach church elected a new pastor, Archie Penner. Penner, equipped with a master's degree, had been an associate minister for several years; his election signalled the congregation's belief that a more educated man was needed to guide them in the modern age. For the first time in its history, the church now also would have a salaried pastor. On this point—of not being paid for his service to the church— Dad never complained, and Mom didn't either. Dad still gave sermons and was deeply involved in church affairs, but his role had changed. Whatever recognition or prestige he had derived from his position as pastor had to be given up. His tenure as a minister lasted twenty-one-and-a-half years, including twelve as pastor.

Dream
November 12, 2001 *Dad's Blessing*
I'm in a room full of people including my father, who is able-bodied. The idea is brought up that I should ask my father's blessing, and I agree without hesitation. With everyone watching, I get down on my knees in front of him. He places his hand on my head and says a few words of blessing, and maybe a little prayer. It is very brief. I don't feel much, but I do like this, think it is a good thing.

CHAPTER 17:
THE STROKE

Dad's life spanned fifty-six years before his stroke, and only seven-and-a-half after it. So, for the much larger part, he was physically whole. When I first thought of writing an account of his life, I did not think I would give the stroke and its aftermath a lot of space, because that might not do him justice. Upon reflection, though, I decided that I would give this "invalid" part of his life full attention. As a family we have tended to look away from his difficult last years, and in that way we have also looked away from our father.

When Mom and Dad celebrated their twenty-fifth wedding anniversary in the EMC church basement in late 1956, Mom was moved to declare that it was "a highlight in our life." The next spring Dad was relieved of his pastoral post. Maybe Mom was allowing herself to dream of the contented retirement they could have together.

But even after he had relinquished church leadership, Dad's agenda was very full. Every Wednesday evening he went to Bible study and prayer meeting; every Sunday was a church day, and then there were ministerial meetings, "convert" instructions, baptisms, Invalid Home services, missionary conferences, and the occasional sermon to be given. He made regular business trips to Winnipeg and one long bus trip with Archie

Penner to St. Catharines, Ontario. He participated actively in planning meetings for the construction of a new church building.

Mom acknowledging anniversary gift; me looking on, hair carefully plastered onto my skull.

In the summer of 1957 Mom and Dad were invited to Detroit Lakes, Minnesota, by their friends the Ed Loewens. They rented a cabin, went boat riding, and ate restaurant meals. They even tried golfing—for Dad, the first time since 1933, when he first played on Cornelius Kroeker's pasture. Back then he had scored 78 over nine holes, which he had judged "a good game." Mom was happy in Detroit Lakes: "The lake is beautiful. We thank God for friends like the Loewens. Wonderful day, nice weather. We enjoy the fellowship."

Shadows encroached on this dream. On July 12, 1957, Dad's sister Catherine, a sweet-natured, much-loved woman, died of bone cancer. A week later my sister Mary Ann gave birth to a premature infant who lived just four hours.

In the fall Mom and Dad took an extended trip to the United States and Norman and I got to go along. This was in September, at the beginning of the school year, so not the best time, but of course I wanted to go. Especially since Dad had bought a new car that year, a robin-egg-blue Ford Custom sedan.

When Dad bought that car, Vern complained. "Why do we have to have the cheapest model? Why couldn't we get a Fairlane?" The answer, of course, was that we didn't need anything fancy. Nevertheless, Vern wheedled and argued until Dad agreed to get whitewall tires and chrome wheel covers. I think Vern paid for these himself. He searched the Bible for evidence that a radio should be permissible and came up with "make a joyful noise unto the Lord," from Psalms. Dad drew the line at a radio, however, and even Vern's inspired persuasion was not enough to win that battle. We younger brothers, however, were impressed. It was possible to argue with our father. It was even possible that Scripture could be interpreted in more ways than one.

Our 1957 Ford Custom with whitewall tires.

Off we went on our trip, without Vern, but Aunt Marie and her two boys came along. Dad allowed Norman to convince him to buy a plastic transistor radio in Kansas so that we could listen to World Series baseball games en route.

Heading west toward Colorado, Dad challenged us boys to a competition: whoever would see the mountains first would win a prize. We thought this was great, and for a while studied the horizon intently. Seeing nothing in the first ten minutes or so, we lost interest and fell into our private reveries until jolted by Dad's announcement: "There they are." And sure enough, we could see the faded purple outline of peaks in the distance. We had not considered that Dad, as the driver, had a distinct advantage in this game. We

Me with a beheaded corn snake in Kansas.

never found out what the prize would have been. For Dad, directing his gaze into the distance for hours must have been a welcome change from the close work with watches and sermon notes he was accustomed to.

In Oregon we waded in the ocean, visited relatives, and then drove north to British Columbia for even more visiting with various transplanted Manitoba Mennonites before driving east across the prairies and back home. Dad gave Norman, only sixteen and a novice, much of the driving responsibility, even on the mountain roads. He put a lot of trust in his young son. Norman proved a quick and skilful learner; he got us all home safely. Now he says, "I got the real sense that Dad was treating me as an equal in all our conversations. I felt proud that I could feel like an adult with him, rather than 'just a kid.'"

Back in school in Steinbach after a month away, I had fallen behind in mathematics, missing some basic concepts everyone else seemed to have mastered. In subsequent grades I managed to pass the subject, barely, but then in the later grades of high school, I would run into deeper trouble.

#

In February of 1958 Dad hit a tree stump beside the home driveway he had negotiated a thousand times before without incident. An odd thing to happen; the stump was well off the road. In July, while I was away at Red Rock Lake Bible Camp, he was hospitalized for three or four days with symptoms of a severe cold. The doctor was concerned about his heart, and wanted to keep him under observation.

In the early morning hours of Monday, August 11, Dad fell out of bed and was not able to move. Mom tried briefly to help him back up but could not do it. She went upstairs to wake Alvin, and with her big, strong son doing most of the lifting, succeeded in getting Dad back into bed. Al remembers that it wasn't easy; Dad could not help himself at all. Mom called the doctor: "Only Dr. Giesbrecht home, so he was there in a hurry." Dr. Giesbrecht gave Dad an injection and said: "He has a fifty-fifty chance." At 2:00 a.m. an ambulance took him to the Bethesda Hospital in Steinbach and Mom stayed with him until 4:00 a.m.

It was an ischemic stroke. A clot had formed in an artery and blocked the flow of blood to the brain. A certain population of brain cells, starved of energy, died. The diagnosis was almost exactly the same as the one Dad recorded for Grandfather back in 1942: "Dr said it was a stroke, an artery burst in head, left side paralysed."

These days, the effects of an ischemic stroke can be ameliorated if medications are given quickly, breaking up the clot and lessening the extent of brain damage. At that time no such medications existed, and the speed or slowness with which Dad was taken to the hospital probably made little difference to the outcome.

Dad's own description of events, in a note he added to Mom's diary after his stroke, was this: "Had a heart attack about 1:30 a.m. shortly after retiring and I rolled out of bed onto the floor & was taken to hospital with an ambulance." It was, of course, not a heart attack, but a "brain attack." Did he not understand that? Or did he understand correctly, that there often is a connection between a poorly functioning heart and a stroke? Or that his heart—his feelings, his love, his courage—had been altered by this event?

He fell, or rolled, or slid out of the bed, onto the floor. His eyes jerked to the right, toward the site of the stroke. Surely he must have been conscious and wondering what was happening. Vancouver Island writer and stroke survivor Ron Smith describes his experience this way:

> You are in slow-motion free fall. Perhaps it's resignation. Whatever happens will happen. There seems to be an inevitability about this event that you don't comprehend but that you curiously accept. Your body and spirit have been deflated in an inexplicable way. You are experiencing a mystery. And you are terrified.

You are brought down to the floor; your upright status gone, your mobility gone. I had never imagined my calm father as capable of terror, but now I can.

The next day Mom visited Dad—"my dear husband," she called him—in the hospital and found that he "talked much." Saying what, and with what kind of clarity? Sometimes stroke victims experience a kind of thickness of the tongue which impairs their intelligibility. A week later, G. G. Kornelsen commented in the *Steinbach Post*: "He speaks with difficulty." Kornelsen pointed out the harsh irony of the situation: "On Sunday morning he gave a weighty sermon in the German language in the Evangelical Mennonite Church, and now he is himself helpless." Seven weeks after the stroke, his ministerial colleague P. J. B. Reimer also visited him in the hospital and remarked: "His talk and behaviour is somewhat childish, so his thinking is not quite what it was before."

He talked much, he spoke with difficulty, his talk was childish. He, who had always been a judicious man with a dignified demeanour, who had run a bookstore, who had delivered hundreds of sermons in German and English—he could not speak properly. Those who suffer a left-brain stroke may be completely aphasic, unable to speak at all. Dad, his right brain damaged, rambled and struggled to stay on topic.

Or? Shortly after his stroke, Ron Smith found that he could access long-buried memories, some from early childhood. These memories came to him in sharp sensory detail, as if he was again able to be present in that earlier time. This was not supposed to be possible. Smith says that stroke survivors may not tell their story because they fear that others will judge them to be crazy. To my knowledge, Dad never spoke of his thoughts and emotions when he had his stroke. He might not so much have feared the judgement of others; he may simply have thought that sharing his experience was not important, or that it would be a form of self-indulgence. If he expressed his emotions and thoughts to Mom, she kept it to herself.

Ron Smith's advice to every stroke survivor is that they demand to be heard. Dad made no such demand.

For a little while Mom thought Dad would die, but he remained in Bethesda Hospital for several months, bedridden. From August through to December Mom visited him almost every day, while still running the household and trying to run the bookstore as well. Friends and relatives also visited Dad, and he was gratified to receive twenty-nine cards on his fifty-sixth birthday. During these months he seemed neither to progress nor regress, although he suffered from bladder issues, or possibly an enlarged prostate. A catheter had to be put in, causing him a lot of pain.

Ron Smith speaks of wanting to weep, of being aware that, deep down somewhere, "a cord had been severed." He felt as though he was lost at the heart of a maze, unable to find a way out. Mom described Dad as "depressed." Today, stroke victims are routinely given antidepressants.

"The one thing I knew for certain," writes Smith . . .

was that I was losing something . . . the confusion was
overpowering and the loss profound. I wasn't finding or
becoming anything, I was pretty sure. I knew where I was,
but not why I was there. Everything seemed so vague.
So intangible. So mind-bogglingly alien, as if I was from
another planet.

A few weeks after entering the hospital, Dad wanted some pictures
taken of him, so Vern came by with a box camera and flash. Why did he
want pictures taken? Was he thinking of a before-and-after scenario, of
some day looking back on his disabled self from the perspective of one
who had recovered? Or did he think that something life-changing had
happened, so pictures were in order?

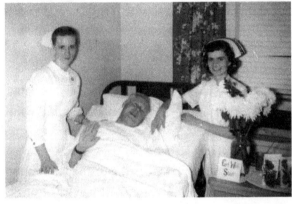

Picture one: Dad lies in the hospital bed, propped up, looking straight at the camera, his mouth open a little. He is not wearing his customary glasses. He looks stricken. His body is invisible underneath the glaringly white bed cover, except for his right hand, his good hand, the fingers arched as though he's about to play the piano. Beside him stands Mom, in a print dress as usual, smiling happily as if nothing in the world is wrong. Behind her is Al, large and bulky as he was in those days, also wearing a smile, but his eyes conveying a detached awareness of something absurd in all of this. A fruit bowl sits on the food tray, piled high. The hospital walls are stark, undecorated except for an emergency pull cord.

Picture two: Four smiling, pretty nurses line up on one side of the bed in their starched, winged caps. They seem tickled about something. Did Vern make a funny comment? Mom, leaning in from the right of the frame, smiles, too. Dad gazes at the camera with the same stricken expression as in the first photo. The fruit basket maintains its place of honour on the food tray, but there also seems to be an angel food cake there, in which case these pictures were taken on the occasion of Dad's birthday, when we—Al, Norm, Vern, and I—came to his room to sing "Happy Birthday."

Picture three: The food tray is gone. It's just Dad, with a nurse on either side of him, each with a gentle hand on one of his shoulders, a touch that would never have happened in ordinary life. A bouquet of chrysanthemums stands on the night table, along with get-well cards. Dad waves at the camera and manages a brave, slightly crooked grin. He wears his watch on his right wrist instead of on the paralyzed left one. If I could guess at what he was thinking, I would say it was, "I will get better."

I think the fruit basket had been sent by our neighbours, the "Hotel Peters." I was impressed. I'd never seen a fruit basket. Although I was a sometime friend of young Peter Peters, I knew that my parents didn't approve of his family's business. Nothing personal, probably—they were not bad people. But Al had been a regular customer of the men's-only pub in the hotel, and in our strict religious town that was a sin and a cause for shame for my parents, even more so since Dad was a minister. Also, as I discovered later, my grandfather had launched a petition against the opening of the beer parlour back in 1937. It had been unsuccessful. But had there been hard feelings? My mother said something critical about the basket. I have the impression she sent it back, but then, where did the basket in those pictures come from?

Tourist Hotel, circa 1955. Credit: Winnipeg Free Press.

One day, maybe a week after the stroke, I was skipping on the concrete walk behind our house, trying to see how far past 100 I could go, imagining myself a boxer in training, when I was called to the phone. I picked up the cylindrical black plastic listening device that dangled on its cord from the phone, a rectangular wooden box on the wall. Breathless, I listened. It was Mom. She said I could come to the hospital and see Dad. I set off immediately, running. I didn't exactly know why I was running; I just wanted to get there fast. Although the hospital was several blocks from our house, I was there in minutes, breathing heavily and sweating a little and oddly elated. The hospital smell, of sickness and antidotes, burned in my nose. Mom greeted me and said, smiling, "You didn't need to run." This was true. Dad, his body covered by institutional sheets, one corner of his mouth looking frozen, wasn't about to go anywhere. He hadn't been around very much before. I sometimes had thought that he was running away from me. Now it seemed that I would have him. Frozen. I didn't think I wanted him this way.

During this time, Mom struggled, overwhelmed by events and responsibilities, and stunned by what had happened. Norman remembers her "sitting in the blue rocking chair for long periods of time, her gaze in a far-off place."

That summer, the new outdoor swimming pool in Steinbach opened. Alvin, a member of the Kinsmen Club, had put in a lot of hard hours helping build it, pushing heavy wheelbarrows full of asphalt after working full days at Friesen Machine Shop. Mom agreed to sign me up for Red Cross swimming lessons and I was an eager student. Al came to watch when I took my test for the first level. I passed, and Al praised my achievement, and for me that was almost like having my dad come and witness my success. I felt proud of myself.

In fall I started Grade 8 in a new school, Elmdale. The teacher had a temper; when my toes were sticking too far out of the line before entering the school, he stepped on them. One recess I was hit in the head by a soccer ball and knocked unconscious for a minute. When I came to I looked up at a circle of worried faces and felt half-embarrassed and half-pleased to be the centre of attention. I did enough schoolwork to get by. I could not memorize the dates in history class. I tried to fit in. No one asked about my dad, and I would not have known what to say if they had.

#

Dad stayed in the hospital in Steinbach until December, when he was transferred to the St. Boniface Hospital in Winnipeg, where he had an operation on his prostate, alleviating some of his discomfort. And he finally started to get physiotherapy.

He was able to write a letter, in German, to the EMC church publication, the *Christlicher Familienfreund*, updating the membership on life at the hospital. The letter will have been edited for clarity and coherence, but its poetic tone was surely his own:

> Some time has passed since I have been in touch with my dear friends and acquaintances and fellow believers, except that some have visited me, and some have written letters, which I have greatly treasured. Thanks very much, too, for the get well cards, etc.
>
> My time away is rather monotonous; most of the time I sit in my chair. In the morning I am usually given treatment for my left arm and leg to bring some more life into them. And it does help, if only slowly; but it also serves to remind the patient to be patient and hold up one's head.
>
> One encounters a lot of religion here, but not true Bible knowledge. The religion is observed more outwardly than in the heart. If you ask Catholics whether they have Christ in their hearts they usually answer yes, they ate him when they took communion.
>
> I found out that the cleaning girl was a former Mennonite, now a Jehovah's Witness. And another patient did not want to carry the conversation further, as we were such good friends. He was German, and did not want to disturb our friendship. Sometimes, very early in the morning, we get into quite a heated discussion in which almost everyone takes part, but one doesn't know whether it was helpful. Usually it concerns the only name, Acts 4:12 and here they appeal to Holy Mary, and this is where

I cannot always keep silent. She is also made into a mediator. 2 Tim. 2:5.

But it has to be said also, that much good is done here.

It is Christmas, but I am lonely and pining for my loved ones. There is the sound of lively celebration in the next room. There are many expressions of "Merry Christmas" while the bells play "Silent Night."

My thoughts go to my home, what are they doing just now, probably they are all at the Sunday school program, or by now they have gathered as families and presents are being given out. A powerful homesickness grips my innermost soul.

My thoughts rush further back to my own childhood in my parents' house, when Father and Mother were still there, and how we would observe our Christmas then. What marvellous memories! But with a jolt I am back in reality, as I hear the loud groaning of a sick person somewhere, and the voices of the nurses. They wish us all "Merry Christmas." We return the wish and feel a little better.

So, it is Christmas, Christ is born, the world was lost. Peace on Earth, goodwill to men.

On the first day of Christmas I had the joy of being together with my loved ones, at the home of my married daughter Mary Ann, the Dave Goertzens. That was really something else. They brought me there by car, and it went very well.

Now I wish all of those who read this much courage and happiness in the spiritual battle. It is really not worthwhile to throw away one's trust, for it has a great reward, as we have experienced.

A happy new year and God be with you to the editors and all the readers.

-- P. D. Friesen

Christmas at Mary Ann and Dave's, 1958. Back row: Don, Norm, Vern, Al. Front row: Anne, Mom, Dad, Mary Ann, Dave. Me seated in front.

In this unfamiliar hospital environment, away from home and with Mom no longer able to make daily visits, Dad had to find his way. Ron Smith writes of being buoyed by his wife's visits but also of needing to be reassured that he would get better, and that she still loved him. The words "I love you" were not spoken in our house, and it is not likely that Mom spoke them now, though she may have conveyed her love for Dad by her manner and presence. I very much doubt that she ever told him that she thought he was going to get better. She did not think that, and the doctors were not saying that. As for us, his children, we were fatalistic, or in some way indifferent. It did not occur to us to offer our father encouragement.

So he was on his own with his thoughts and uncertainty, not knowing if he could dare hope for recovery. "It does help," he says of the physiotherapy, but he doesn't seem convinced. He kept hoping that he would be able to come home after his "time away."

Uncharacteristically, in this public letter he confessed his personal pain: "A powerful homesickness grips my innermost soul." His innermost soul—what did *Familienfreund* readers, or, for that matter, what did we, his family, know of that? We were accustomed to a private man who did not readily share his thoughts and feelings. We did not read his letter when it was published, and it is only now that I am struck by his naked nostalgia for his childhood home. Did he, like Ron Smith, have vivid recall of childhood memories? An innocent and happy part of him can be glimpsed here.

His ability to remember the past was not just an indulgence in nostalgia, however—it was an essential element of his being. Without it, how could he have an ongoing sense of self? His long-term memory seemed to work fairly well, but his short-term memory had become unreliable.

Dad did not give up. He, who had always been known for his patience for others, now counselled patience for himself, and courage. In the Catholic hospital, where he was confronted with crucifixes and images of Mary, he could not keep silent, could not restrain his evangelical impulses. Apparently a group of patients would regularly get into emotionally charged arguments on religion, with Dad rejecting the elevated role of Mary for Catholics, since, for him, there was "none other name" than that of Jesus. He was perceptive enough, however, to notice that these "I'm right and you're wrong" discussions were generating more heat than light. He does concede to being well treated by the staff.

Dad might well have despaired, and no doubt he did, at times. But early on he decided that his new circumstances actually could be an opportunity "to contact different people and do some personal work." "Personal work" was an evangelical euphemism for trying to convince sinners of their lost condition and need for salvation through Jesus Christ. This work had structured a good part of Dad's life, and through it he had found, or created, personal meaning. Now he tried to hold onto this structure, to carry on in the service of the Master, despite his brain impairment, and despite the resistance he encountered: "With some people it just seems impossible to make contact, some are so impossible. With one for instance I'm with now I got at odds right away."

It seems that Dad was not as diplomatic as he had been before his stroke. Yet, even with this "impossible" man, he realized that "if I wanted to win him for Christ I would also have to win his confidence." In this he succeeded to the point that the man "asked many questions which were hard to answer and caused me to do a lot of thinking & praying." They talked far into the night but without conclusion—"so finally I told him there was one thing he could not forbid me in doing and that was to intercede for him." The man agreed, and so the matter was left.

Dad had hoped to return to Steinbach but instead, on January 23, 1959, he was transferred to the King Edward Hospital in Winnipeg, where he began a more extensive rehabilitation program which continued for more than half a year. Mom could not visit him as often as he would have liked. She had to make the drive into Winnipeg and then negotiate city streets, which made her nervous. She delegated the job to Norman, who was glad to be of use, driving even when the roads were bad in winter. A dozen times or more, according to Mom's diary, I went along, but I don't remember much about these visits. Mom found the King Edward dreary and depressing, and so did we. She would talk with Dad while Norm and I waited.

King Edward Hospital. Credit: Mennonite Archival Image Database.

For Dad, the King Edward must have been a dark abyss. He only wanted to come home. Yet in personal work, he could at last count a success: "He had a lift by leading one soul to Christ there," Mom noted.

That winter I got scarlet fever, which got so bad that I became delirious and had a crying bout. I stayed home from school for a week while Mom did her best to care for me on top of everything else she had to do.

The married siblings living in Winnipeg, Don and Mary Ann, made regular visits to the hospital as well, and sometimes would take Dad to a city park or on some other outing. In late March he came home for Easter. On Good Friday he was in the Steinbach church for the first time since his stroke. He was given the opportunity to say a few words to the congregation, and this must have meant a great deal to him, as he connected briefly to his pre-stroke life.

Mom, centre, with her friends at our house. Aunt Marie kneeling, front.

Mom's friends, led by her sister Marie, rallied around her and helped with laundry, cleaning, or running the store. Socializing with them helped keep her sane. Whatever hopes she might have had for Dad's recovery seemed to fade quite quickly, and soon she resigned herself to his gradual, inevitable decline.

For Dad, real meaning now was less invested in religion and more in Mom. In May he wrote to her:

> My Dearest, sweetest charming brown eyed Darling Margaret. Sweetest name I've ever come across the only girl that ever meant anything to me and everything to me oh how often have I thanked God for this wonderful woman and no flattery meant. Today is Saturday and we hardly know what to do with ourselves so my thoughts were with you again my love so dear so dear we didn't talk anything about Monday Victoria Day well we can plan on Sunday if you come here maybe you have something good up your sleeve nothing extra though whatever you would favour.
>
> So my dear sweet honey we have 3 days of rest now with our exercises Saturday and Sunday and Monday. Thank you again for the way you treated me when I was home last I have to laugh in between "John" is giving instructions to one of the other patients who is roaming around the hall and he seems quite excited must look what he is up to let me kiss you my dear tulips and embrace you oh how I love you believe me. As ever your old Peter & loving you more than ever believe me.
>
> Oh my dear Marge I hardly know how to quit or to tear myself away from such a dear woman you my wife my sweetheart, my mate. Oh I can't express myself the pen is not good enough for that.
>
> Come to mee
>
> As before but more loving than ever.

He completely opened his heart to her, holding back nothing. As his son, reading the letter I almost feel as if I'm intruding on an intimate moment, not intended for my ears. And I am amazed; I had no idea that he loved her with such an epic love.

A telling phrase of psychiatrist Irvin Yalom comes to mind: "The lonely 'I' dissolves into a 'we.'" I think Dad's flight into romance rhetoric helped him escape the pain of his actual situation.

Mom was not lifted up by this adoration. At home she tried, heroically, to keep the show going. Rose Penner, our bookstore clerk, stayed on. But Mom had to assume managerial tasks, such as making book and card orders and keeping track of accounts, which Dad had previously always done. She still had all her housework, the cooking, laundering, and cleaning for her family at home, and somehow also fitted in socializing and church meetings.

Early that year our banker, T. G. Smith, had let Mom know that the business account was overdrawn. Apparently she had thought that red ink meant there was money *in* the account. At the same time, the roof began to leak in the part of the building that had housed Kehler's barbershop and was now a dress shop. Pipes got plugged and needed a plumber, and the furnace went out for a while. Overwhelmed, Mom sought advice from Steinbach businessman and family friend Cornie Loewen and Dad's brother Henry. Since none of the older children was interested in running the business, Mom decided to sell it. The decision was promptly carried out: Evangel Book Shop was sold to Peter and Susan Martens as "a going concern" for $21,000 as of June 30, 1959. Cornie Loewen acted as Dad's representative.

In June, Norman graduated from Grade 12. He was the first in our family to finish high school, and he would be the only one until I did, a number of years later. Dad got leave from the hospital to attend the graduation ceremony in the EMB church. He must have been proud of his son's achievement.

I was a regular at the Kinsmen pool, and in August I got "swimmer's ear," an infection serious enough to put me in the hospital for five days. Mom visited me faithfully, even though she was preparing to move us to a new place while also getting ready for Dad to come home.

On the 11th of August, Mom wrote: "It's exactly a year today since my dear husband took sick. What a long and dreadful year it has been." To which she added: "But I thank the Lord He has helped and carried us through." I did not have the sense of having been carried through by God;

if anything, I felt I was being carried along by the stream of events. Around me, the adults made their decisions—selling the store, selling our house, releasing Dad from hospital—and I lived with the consequences, trusting that they knew best.

Chapter 18:
Post-stroke:
It all takes time

On August 23, 1959, almost exactly a year after his stroke, Dad was released from hospital. His left side—leg and arm—remained paralyzed and his cognitive functioning scrambled. He got about in a wheelchair, although he was able to walk for short distances with the help of a person steadying him by his dangling left arm. The shoe of his paralyzed foot would scrape along the floor and he would struggle gamely along, his skin slightly damp and clammy from the effort. He could feed himself, but needed help getting to the toilet. At night he needed help putting on pajamas and getting into bed. Did the doctors prescribe exercises to be done at home? I never saw him doing any.

Almost immediately upon Dad's return home, we moved to the Woodlawn Park suburb in east-central Steinbach. Woodlawn was a C. T. Loewen company development, and I believe that Cornie and Ed Loewen, both EMC church members, will have given us a good price for our new house. Using the proceeds from selling the store and the old house, Mom bought a three-bedroom bungalow with full basement, a yard, and a garden—nothing fancy, but well-suited to our new situation. We moved piecemeal, through September and October. Helped by Aunt Marie and some church friends, and sometimes by Al and me, Mom conducted a massive cleanup of stuff from the old house. Jake Dueck, Dad's ministerial colleague and a farmer with a truck and trailer, made several trips to the "nuisance grounds," as the town dump was known. "Moving is horrible," Mom complained, "out of the house which Peter's Dad built when he first married, where they raised a big family and brought up some other people's children, and things were stored away, from that time on."

A steady rain fell through September, turning the as-yet-unseeded lawns to mire. Dad commented: "We begin to call this place 'Mud-Lawn' instead of Woodlawn."

One Spruce Crescent, Woodlawn Park.

The plan was for Mom to draw some income from the room-and-board paid by Al and Vern (and, later, Norman and me), and also from Dad's disability cheques. She was able to manage this way, supplementing her income by taking in ironing, mainly for neighbours George and Ed Loewen, businessmen with lots of white shirts.

For Mom, the move was a giant headache, but once complete, a godsend. It was much easier for her to clean and manage a smaller, new house. Mom sold Dad's roll-top desk to a local furniture store; there was no room for it in the new place. As to what Dad felt—we didn't know. The old place had been a part of the original lot on which his pioneer grandparents had settled in 1874. The place where he was born and raised, and also where he raised us, his children. Three of his brothers and their families remained in the old neighbourhood and Friesen Machine Shop was still there. But now the geographic continuity of our part of the extended Friesen family ended.

Four of us boys—Al, Vern, Norman, and I—lived with our parents in the new house. My older siblings had jobs and girlfriends and social lives, while I, aged fourteen, began high school. Now, for the first time in our family history, Dad would be home with us every day. But I had already decided that the damaged man in the wheelchair was not my father.

On Sunday mornings I helped him up the church steps, holding his slack arm as he went, as if he were a large, slow child. His suit flapped baggily around his changed body, his tie hung crooked down his caved-in chest. I didn't think people wanted to see their former pastor this way. I turned away in shame when he greeted them in the lobby with a cheerful imitation of Billy Graham: "God bless you real good!"

On a cold, windy day in early March, 1960, the old EMC church building on Main Street went up in flames. A new church was already almost complete, and this was saved from the fire. But the 50-year-old wooden structure, along with years of church and Sunday school records, burned quickly, and there was little the Steinbach volunteer fire department could do. Most of the town's populace rushed to witness the conflagration. A bunch of us from high school also went.

My friend Patrick Friesen, an across-the-garden neighbour whose parents attended our church, offered a theory for the origin of the fire: "Maybe Pastor Penner was smoking behind the church." I giggled and replied: "Maybe he got his wires crossed." "Or Mrs. Reimer burned her buns in the kitchen," said Patrick. We hooted and laughed. Some of the bystanders gave us disapproving stares.

The EMC church on fire, 1960. Photo courtesy of Marcella Fiola.

That evening as I took my seat at the supper table I listened to Al describing the fire and the heroic but futile efforts to put it out. Suddenly, unaccountably, my father put his fork down, pushed back his wheelchair, and began to laugh. It was not ordinary laughter: it welled up inside his chest, lifting his round shoulders in rhythmic convulsions and driving the blood into his head until his face was purple. He heaved and heaved. I had seen him laugh this way before, but never with such alarming force, and now I saw it was not laughter. Mom, making remonstrating noises, wheeled him away from the table. "Now stop," she said worriedly, in Low German. She removed his glasses. His cheeks were wet with tears.

I could not swallow the food in my mouth.

Now I began to see the rift between us more clearly. The church had meant so much to him! And I had laughed and rejoiced in its burning, as at the burning of the effigy of a hated tyrant.

Barely a month later, on April 10, Mom got a phone call from Alvin at the machine shop, to say that "our" store and house on Main Street were on fire. "Got us all shaking again," said Mom later. The fire ignited when the augur carrying coal to the store furnace accidentally reversed, carrying live coals back to the bin. The flames spread quickly and leaped to the stairway so that the young couples renting apartments above the store had to jump from the second-storey windows to escape.

Our old house, with the wreckage of Evangel Book Shop in the foreground.

Now the old church was gone, and the old house and store also. Mom, unsentimental as ever, rashly declared in a letter to her siblings: "I often wished the house would have burnt sooner, then we wouldn't have near as much junk here." Dad's thoughts are not on record. His social world became drastically smaller after his stroke, and now his physical world had shrunk, too: the environment in which he had grown up and later made his mark as a preacher and businessman no longer existed.

For most of any given day he sat in his wheelchair, reading, writing, or receiving visitors. Sometimes he would sleep in his chair. He and Mom went to church on Sundays and he still attended the occasional *Bruderschaft* or ministerial meeting. But he could not truly participate in church affairs, and he did not get out nearly as much as before.

Mom described her routine—and also Dad's—in May of 1961:

> We are still five [herself and Dad, and Al, Norm, and me] at home to cook, wash and iron for, and Peter needs some of my time too, now that it gets nice outside he sits outside a lot. I walk him out first, then I make him lean on the house and his cane, then I get the chair out, and getting him in the same, and if it's nice in the evenings, I do this three or four times a day. Then he needs some help in the bathroom once a day, and dressing and undressing etc. It all takes time, we never rush, it doesn't work, and just can't be done.

On some of those sunny days outside, Dad, in his wheelchair, would rake the driveway, holding the rake handle in his good hand. It was a semblance of useful work. Part of me wished he wouldn't do that. The raking had no effect, and just made him look ridiculous in my eyes. Then again, I did understand that he wanted to feel useful. Sometimes he would watch Mom work in the garden and laugh at himself and the absurdity of the situation: "I am spending a lot of my time sitting outside looking at other people work . . . and act as if I am the boss or the manager or overseer slave driver or whatever you want to call it."

He would dig into a genealogy book, looking to see whose birthday it was:

> I have made it a habit of phoning people on their birthday [and wishing] them God's blessings and usually Psalm 103 and also Psalm 25 and other verses. Some will shout back: how do you know my birthday and I keep them wondering & guessing for a while then I finally tell them I have a "Reimer" book ah! Oh I make it kind of a ministry to cheer up people and I get a kick out of it too.

I cringed when he greeted the unsuspecting victim on the other end of the phone line. Only later could I appreciate that he was carrying on, as he was able, with the pastoral work he had performed for so many years.

His tone did not always wax adoring toward Mom. In a letter to her siblings he is clearly trying to get a laugh at her expense in describing her broken slippers: "the rear of these slippers at the heels they will open & close in exact harmony to her walking so that to the ones who'd watch her from behind it would appear as it some animal was snapping its jaws open and closed":

> And then you should see her toes they look battle worn (war scarred) because they stick out just like a rooster spurs and every once in a while she'll catch these toes on the legs of our kitchen chair because the legs of the chairs I mean stand out diagonal and so they very easily catch anything that's sticking out . . . and then she has chicken eyes yet on these toes so you can imagine about how it looks. Well that's that aren't your hearts stirred to compassion already?

Dad held to notions that Mom thought delusional—that he could still drive a car, for example, or, if not that, ride a bicycle. Perhaps he even thought he would recover completely. This thought was not supported by the facts—Mom did not believe it, friends of the family did not believe it, we children did not believe it, and the doctors did not believe it either. It was skewed thinking, typical of right-brain stroke victims, who often do not have a realistic measure of their limitations. But then, perhaps we were *too* realistic, lacking in faith. Stroke survivors today insist that the hope of recovery is essential for them. They take strength in knowing that others have this same hope.

At first Mom argued with Dad, trying to get him to understand the permanent nature of his disability. "You cannot drive a car," she said. He was annoyed but helpless to prove the contrary. "How would you ride a bike?" she asked. In Low German he replied that he would just *schlacks* (flip) his paralyzed leg over the bar and go. He could not be convinced of the impossibility of such a thing, and eventually Mom learned to humour him.

Right-brain stroke sufferers commonly have difficulties in reading a clock. I do not remember whether that was ever an issue with Dad. How ironic that would be for someone who had spent countless hours repairing watches.

"He just wants thousands of books anyways."

For Christmas, 1961, Dad "gave" Mom a cookbook and a pair of leather gloves. That is, Anna (Mrs. Ed) Loewen, a close friend to Mom, bought these with Mom's money and wrapped them as gifts. "I just hope he doesn't start giving me too much," Mom commented, wryly. She in turn gave him a "book of the Mennonites," since "he just wants thousands of books anyways."

Despite our father's reduced condition, we continued to respect the old prohibitions in our house. At Christmas, we still did not have a tree. According to Dad, a Christmas tree was pagan. Vern, persistent as he was about such things, smuggled a three-foot evergreen into the house and placed it on a chest of drawers in the bedroom he and I shared. He strung the tiny tree with a few decorations. I don't think Dad ever knew.

#

Dad set himself the monumental task of transcribing selections from his diaries into Norman's old science scribblers, alternating blue and red ink in a random pattern. His title for this project: "important events & happenings taken from my diary." Watching him, I thought it meaningless, a way of killing time. Why would anyone want to go back over what he had written? I see now that it gave him the opportunity to review his life, the years in which he had been active and productive, and so also was a means of escaping the oppression of the present moment.

More than that, I believe it was a way of building a bridge to the past in the hope of reconnecting with his lost self. He must have had many associations and emotions through this structured way of remembering. He also went through his father's memoirs and began a genealogical chart, which he soon abandoned, as it proved too difficult. After a time he transcribed some of Mom's diaries, too, sometimes interjecting clarifying comments or even grammatical corrections. But he could not keep the dates straight.

Sometimes, to amuse us, he would pound on his feeling-dead left hand with his good right one, in a display of bravado. Maybe this also came from the perception right-brain stroke sufferers sometimes have that the paralyzed left side does not really belong to them. I was kind of impressed, but also worried that he would hurt himself. I had grown up thinking of my dad as someone to be taken seriously, as someone who took himself seriously. It was slightly liberating to see him laugh at himself in his straitened circumstances.

Increasingly, Dad lost the ability to read and remember, and to write coherently. In January, 1964, Mom wrote one of her regular letters to her siblings, and Dad insisted on adding to it. She included his page, commenting: "seems he gets nowhere." Indeed, his eccentrically punctuated, repetitive ramblings give the impression of a mind going in circles:

> Just happened to read this out of a booklet Psm 118, 19-29
> Just read this out of a booklet so do according and likewise & so you have a good reason to be really happy & do likewise and come home & do likewise and we shall all be happy! So there is a good reason to so also mom is quite busy with her Saturday work so I almost have no room in the house but there's room to come home & visit for a change the sun is so bright it bothers my eyes don't say we have no sunshine we have plenty of it today as a fact even if we are in good old Manitoba she has lots of sunshine today & it's just bountiful & glorious & we're all happy! To be sure, are you too?!! Sunshine to because P. C. is supposed to have lots of it don't you know? Mom is more than busy now with her Saturday work and Ralph helps her at times like a good boy! So there don't say that he isn't! its so bright that my eyes are affected a bit it seems so now I just took a bit of a nap but I feel good though so if you want to feel good come here & do likewise this province is good for it to be sure, I found it so! A & so you would too

The script runs at a pronounced angle, each line climbing to the upper right corner of the page, as if aspiring to be uplifting, but having instead the effect of suspending the meaning in space. One day I read this passage aloud, for amusement. Vern, with surprising heat, told me to stop. He didn't want to be exposed to this mixed-up stuff, this rank nonsense. But reading it now I can parse it; there is meaning.

As he had done when still a minister, Dad speaks encouraging words, urging his readers to be grateful and of good cheer, even reminding them that "you have a good reason to be really happy." His own reasons for happiness were not obvious. Nevertheless he extols the benefits of the wintry Manitoba sunlight which hurts his sensitive eyes.

I think he was also reaching back into the pioneer Mennonite world-view of his childhood. The world belongs to Satan, so we must expect to face hard times. It is altogether for the best to be patient and content, no matter what the circumstances. Our place is not to complain, but to remain faithful.

Dad references Psalm 118:19, which reads: "The Lord hath chastened me sore: but he hath not given me over unto death." Oh. The Lord had not given him over unto death—but he had suffered a partial death. He would never be "himself" again and that was a sore chastening indeed. Was he happy for that?

Dad echoes one of his father's often-quoted Bible verses: "For whom the Lord loveth he chasteneth, and scourgeth every son whom he receiveth" (Hebrews 12:6). Grandfather was referring to the death of loved ones, but Dad's scourging took the form of his own marginalization, his assignment to a peripheral life. He never talked this way, though. Perhaps he didn't want to reveal anything that looked like doubt. Had he voiced such doubt, he would have caught my full attention.

After his stroke, Dad couldn't keep his lines straight. They would tend upward or downward.

In the midst of all the literal and metaphorical sunshine of his words, a few shadows fall. He almost has no room. He takes up space. Life goes on around him. He is not needed; rather, he is needy. He needed Mom. She had always been his hard-working helpmeet; now she became his caregiver. Yet his great need, an old need preceding his illness, preceding even his marriage, was emotional, or perhaps spiritual. Shortly after coming home from the hospital, he wrote:

> to have such as my Margaret to be close at hand to care
> for me yes I'm very thankful & pleased to have her & own
> her & love her and be owned by her yes its just too good
> to be so and to come home too yes its just wonderful to
> have her around and carefree & be loved and see how she
> moves about in our home dear, dear

"See how she moves about"—his adoration moves him close to poetry. To own her, and be owned by her—this is his claim. Is it uncharitable of me to think this is a fantasy arising from desperation? Then he could never lose her. But the sad truth was, he *had* lost her. Not that Mom would have considered leaving her invalid husband. Social and religious rules and her personal morality excluded that option. But emotionally, she could not connect with him as she had before. He was no longer her equal, physically and mentally. And perhaps there had always existed an imbalance of love between them, even at the beginning.

He did not love us children as he loved his wife, with that same open heart.

When I was a child, Dad would sometimes sing to Mom a verse or two of a popular song of his youth, "When You and I Were Young, Maggie." It was one of the few non-religious songs he ever sang, and its melody and words touched a melancholy chord:

> I wandered today to the hill, Maggie
> To watch the scene below
> The creek and the creaking old mill, Maggie
> As we used to long ago

Child that I was, what did I know of a lost past? Yet I was moved. Dad sang of a "you and I" from which I was excluded and drawn into all at once.

Reality belied Dad's claim that we were all happy. I, for one, was a highly self-conscious and self-doubting adolescent with a bad complexion, girlfriend-less, failing core subjects in high school. Mom, famous for her good humour and her pealing laugh, presented a cheerful demeanour, but struggled with grief and worry. She worried especially about the spiritual welfare of her sons. On top of everything, her aging father, aware that we boys were not all good church-going Christians, blamed her for not being a good enough mother. Hardly knowing how to defend her children or herself, she wrote:

> Pa hates sinners, and our children are among them, and he even has no use for us, thinking we are at fault, and that's what's continually eating me to think how much we are at fault. But I can't understand it, here are quite a few unsaved parents, where all the children are saved. I'm sure the parents didn't even try to help them . . . . I know he is old and it shouldn't bother me, but with a hard life, being tense always, seems one can't take all things which did not bother me before.

Grandfather Peter F. Rempel, with a display of wooden animals and toys he made by hand.
"Pa hates sinners."

She felt that she and Dad had failed as Christian parents despite all their efforts. This, more than anything else, perhaps even more than her husband's stroke, undermined her happiness. She could not prove to her family and friends that all her children were saved. Sorrowfully, repeatedly, she spoke of giving this problem to the Lord.

What we all needed, Dad especially, was encouragement, not criticism. Reading the repeated injunction to "do likewise" in his letter, I am put in mind of the story of the Good Samaritan in Luke. A man is beaten by thieves and left half dead by the roadside while "good" citizens walk past, until finally a stranger stops to help. "Do ye likewise," said Jesus to his listeners. We are to help the fallen, even if they are strangers or sinners.

Dad must have preached on this parable many times. I was surprised to find a highly allegorical interpretation of it in his sermon notes. He is strangely unsympathetic to the man beaten by thieves, comparing him to a "sinner" tempted by "the lust of the flesh" and wounded by a bad conscience resulting in "fear & fright & cruel doubtfulness." The thieves are equated to "Satan with his companions." The Good Samaritan is a stand-in for Christ; the oil and wine he pours on the man's wounds symbolize the shed blood of Jesus.

Now, I think: "*You* were the beaten man, left alone at the side of the road. The world passed you by. Who stopped to bind your wounds?"

Yet there were Good Samaritans. Men like Henry B. Peters and Ben H. W. Reimer and others from the church membership were faithful in picking up Dad and Mom for church every Sunday. Dad received visitors and valued their company even though his ability to keep a connection was compromised. An uncomfortable silence would descend in the middle of conversations with him; the track was lost, and his companions had to work at re-establishing it.

Sometimes Dad was the object of pity or even of mockery. A Steinbach townsman, Rollin Barkman, recalled chatting with Dad as he sat in front of the post office in his wheelchair. Some young boys passed, and, seeing his crooked body, the curled-up fingers of his left hand, or perhaps a trace of drool running from a corner of his mouth, laughed in derision. Rollin was angry and wanted to reprimand the rascals, but Dad said, "Oh, no, they're just young." A different response from what he once gave, in pre-stroke years, to our cousin Leroy who was visiting from Kansas. Leroy had the nerve to say: *"Na joh, Peeta,"* (well, yes, Pete) and Dad, suddenly angry, scolded him: "I am your Uncle Peter. Don't you ever call me 'Peeta' again." Children were to respect their elders, and that's what Dad demanded.

Mom relied on her sense of humour to help her through the days. She had a way of telling stories of ridiculous events in which she was at the centre. One day she walked to the post office and was surprised to find herself limping, though she felt no pain—then she looked down and saw that she had lost the heel of one shoe. She accompanied such accounts with high-pitched, unrestrained shouts of laughter. Without her laughter, without her sense of life's absurdities and her own absurdity, our household would have been dreary indeed. Perhaps I learned from her how to find renewal in embracing mistakes and accidents. As a teenager, though, I had a lot of trouble with this lesson.

#

Aged fourteen, accustomed to my father's absence all my life, I now had to get used to his presence. He was at home almost all the time. But to me he was a ruined version of himself, a version I did not really recognize and did not want to recognize. This shrunken bent man in a wheelchair was an imposter.

Trying to get homework done.

And yet he was my father. For a few years, I became his secondary caregiver. Mom needed some breaks from her routine and called on me, since I was home more than anyone else. Nothing very arduous: often I stayed with Dad while she went out for a few hours in the evening or on a weekend. Mostly Dad and I would sit quietly at the Formica kitchen table Mom had bought for the new house. He would read the *Carillon News* while I made half-hearted attempts to do homework in my weak subjects, mathematics and the sciences, or played at a baseball board game. Sometimes he would read aloud a piece that interested him, and then, minutes later, having forgotten, read it again. My stomach would clench. The repetition demonstrated that his brain was irreparably damaged. I could not bear to know this.

Once Mom assigned me the task of trimming Dad's toenails. I was reluctant, but sitting on a low stool at his bare feet, started in. I misjudged the angle of the clipper blade and Dad's foot jerked back abruptly. A red line of blood formed on his toe. Mortified, and hurt because I had hurt him, I stopped and refused to go on.

When Dad had to go to the washroom he would wheel himself down the corridor and call on me to help him stand, turn, slide down his pants and undershorts, and ease him onto the toilet, where I would leave him. He would sit there for a while and then call again to be helped up. I would come, and he would be standing with his shirttails covering his private parts and his shanks, and from behind I would carefully pull up his underwear and then the trousers before swinging him back onto his wheelchair. He could wipe himself. It never occurred to me that I would have to help him with that.

Or, if Mom was out late, he might declare it was time for bed, pivot the wheelchair and drive off, back rounded, head bent, the crown of his skull pink and vulnerable. I would follow him into the bedroom, where he had stationed his chair at the side of his bed. They had single beds now, since the stroke.

I pulled the covers back and swung him out of the chair to a sitting position on the sheet. I unbuttoned his shirt, stripped off his undershirt, put on his pajama top (starting always by inserting the paralyzed arm into the left sleeve), removed his shoes (the left one with a metal brace on it, to help stabilize his paralyzed foot), tipped him back on the bed to a half-lying position, pulled off his trousers, and, together with him, put on the pajama bottoms, over his shorts. This strenuous exercise over, I covered him with blankets while he shifted into a comfortable position, we wished each other good night, and I left the room, turning out the light.

At first he used to laugh, out of embarrassment, when his pants were pulled off, and he tugged at the top of his shorts with his good hand to avoid "indecent" exposure, but after a time the two of us got accustomed to the routine and it was all done efficiently and soberly.

After a childhood of missing my father's physical touch, I held him, steadied him, helped him stand and sit. This was not equivalent to an embrace or a caress. And it was me taking the initiative, not him. But still, it simulated a certain physical intimacy that we'd never had—or, if we ever did have it, that I could not remember.

Fathers of his day, Mennonite fathers especially, were not given to kissing and hugging their children. Still, children need loving touch, and not just from their mothers; the embrace of the father, whether heartfelt or playful, imparts a kind of blessing to the child, a sense of confidence that "you can do it." Dad was not physically playful with us; he did not wrestle with his sons as did the grader operator P. K. Neufeld, according to son, my friend Wayne. Rather, we felt there was a kind of invisible fence around him.

#

During a 1955 trip to Kansas, we were staying at the farm of my aunt Liz and uncle Jake Bartel, and we must have been out all day visiting. It got dark, and I, in the back of my uncle's car, fell asleep. When the car stopped moving, I woke up but did not let on that I was awake. My uncle reached into the back seat and easily lifted me out and carried me in his muscular farmer's arms to a bedroom upstairs. The truth was that I did not need to be carried, physically. It was my baby self that wanted it. Wanted to give itself over, surrender, entrust itself completely.

I fell asleep again and did not awaken until the next morning, with the sun streaming through the window. I let my gaze travel to the wall where a calendar hung, with a picture of a smiling American family in a gleaming new sedan, travelling along some rural road, blue sky overhead. The picture stirred something in me—happiness, and longing.

#

One evening I overheard my parents talking in their bedroom, a subdued sense of urgency in their muffled voices. My father's voice alternated between complaining and pleading, while Mother's responses were patient but determined. I guessed that he was hoping that she might come to bed with him. Part of me did not even want to admit the possibility of such a topic. I thought that the stroke would have made such a thing unmanageable, and also, at their age, how could Dad be interested in sex? I could not bring such a thought together with my own "dirty" sexual desires, now burgeoning in adolescence. I never knew what happened that evening, but my intuition would say that the door on that part of their life stayed shut.

As a child I occupied a crib in my parents' bedroom in the old house. I remember arguing with my mother that I was old enough to wear a belt instead of suspenders, so I might have been six. Sleeping in that metal frame crib in one corner of the bedroom, did I ever awaken to the sounds of love from my parents? If I did, it's blocked from conscious memory. As in so many Mennonite households of that time, sex was never talked about; it was a secret the adults were keeping. A dark and dangerous secret, and whatever you found out, you kept to yourself. Among my father's sermon notes there is this: "So often our senses are our undoing. Lust of the eye, the flesh." This lust so powerful, apparently, that it was best not even to make reference to it.

Every Saturday evening my mother gave Dad a sponge bath on his bed, having first closed the bedroom door for privacy. One time she was trying to turn him over and he slipped off the bed and fell to the floor, completely naked. Mom called me in to help, but we couldn't lift him; he was wet and slippery and blubbery, like a large seal, and he was incapable of cooperating with us because he had to laugh so much. It wasn't a real laugh, but a sort of high-pitched, drawn-out heaving. He wheeze-laughed like this until his whole head was positively purple. We gave up trying to lift him and left him lying on the floor, covered with towels, while Mom phoned my uncle Barney, who soon arrived. The three of us then managed to hoist Dad back onto the bed. I felt embarrassed for my father and for myself, and aware of being inadequate to the situation.

I did not draw close to my father during those years when each of us was "ill" in his own way—he with his stroke, and me with the confusion and insecurity of adolescence. But when I saw how close he was, or tried to be, to my mother, I felt jealous. Sometimes, even if she just went out for part of an evening, he would lament that she had left him alone. Alone? But I was there! Admittedly, though, that was almost all that could be said: I was there, and he was there, and there we were, each of us in his own world.

Dreams

October 8, 1996 *Helping Dad with His Catheter Bag*
I am taking care of my father, who is paralyzed. He is sitting on an elevated chair; the setting has some similarity to the living room in our old house, and the chair to the old blue rocker in the corner. He is partially covered by a blanket. There is someone else in the room, so it is necessary to be discreet; Dad doesn't want to be exposed (or I think he doesn't). I look under the thin, pale green blanket. There is a sort of rubber sack resting on his legs above his knees, about the size of a hot water bottle. I am to fasten it onto his penis so that he can urinate into it. I look inside the sack; it is more than half full of urine already. But then Dad gets up and I walk partway across the room with him, supporting him. I say a short phrase in High German to him, something like—"Das ist ja aber nicht leicht zu ertragen." I imagine that he will be surprised that I am able to speak German, and will wonder how I learned it. I also wonder if he finds my correct German accent somewhat pretentious—a giveaway that I learned the language not from fellow Mennonites, but in university. I feel sympathy for him.

July 21, 2007 *Young Child or Dad Alone*
I have a dilemma: I'm meant to look after a young child, but, in a house at the top of the hill is my father, who's been left alone. If I go to look after him, the child may run away or something may happen to it. I see my father in my mind's eye—he is paralyzed, alone, and he'll need help climbing the stairs to his room. I envision myself beside him, helping him up the stairs. If I don't go, there'll be no one else. Maybe he'll have to soil himself . . . I used to help him onto the toilet. He may survive but he'll wonder why I haven't come. But I don't go, there is this child . . . . I feel trapped, guilty.

CHAPTER 19:
DON'T FORGET TO STOP

Whenever you see a white-haired traveller
bent, all petered out
plugging along the road
that's me
that's me, probably asking for a lift

Don't forget to stop and take me along

I'm afraid the walking stick
would be worn short
because that's me
I'm afraid the soles of the shoes
would be worn through
and toes sticking out hungrily
that'd probably be me

Don't forget to stop
I'd beg most heartily for a ride
or don't you stop for hitchhikers

and bums like that
That's me

*Found poem by Ralph Friesen from a letter by Peter D. Friesen, undated,
circa 1961*

Chapter 20:
No turning back

In early July of 1960 my mother arranged for me to go on my second "tour of duty" at Red Rock Lake Bible Camp. I was of two minds about going: I didn't much look forward to being re-immersed in the religious pressure cooker, but I also thought I was now better at defending my views. And there were other things I liked—the great granite rocks, the calm lake, the pine-scented air. And there would be girls.

I believe the word was out—counsellors were aware that I was the recalcitrant son of a minister, and by this time I had acquired something of a reputation among my peers in Steinbach for arguing about religion. I knew I would not escape testing. But at first it seemed that I might. I took part in the softball games and swimming and boating. One of the counsellors challenged me to swim around Turtle Island and I did that, with him accompanying me on a rowboat and offering encouragement. I felt proud, and stronger than before. (I did not know then that "Turtle Island" was the Indigenous people's term for North America as a whole.) I stayed out of confrontations and contented myself with mocking the counsellor assigned to my cabin, who invariably exclaimed, "Isn't that precious?" when he would hear the bugle sounding at sunset. My friends and I adopted the expression for all situations, however mundane. If someone announced, "We have porridge for breakfast today," we would respond: "Isn't that precious?"

One evening I was leaving the dining room when a figure emerged from the shadows under the stairs that led to the second level of the building. It was Mark Gripp, the evangelist on duty that year. He was a small, compact man with a confident manner. He said he wanted to talk to me about salvation. I glanced around, looking for an escape route. There was none. So we stood under the stairs and talked—or rather, he talked, presenting the story I had come to know so well, but holding my attention with his eloquence and urgency. Would I not take this opportunity to come to Jesus, who loved me and had died for me? Would I not set my armour down at last?

This time I was readier than I had been two years before. I offered my usual objections to the "only true way" concept, but he parried them with surprising vigour, until I was not sure that I had any strong rational argument left. When I still did not soften, Reverend Gripp reminded me that, when the Judgement Day came and I found myself standing before Christ, I would bitterly regret my stubborn refusal to accept him now. A part of me wanted to give up, finally, and become a Christian. How happy my parents would be! But I suffocated that impulse, and with a combination of slight desperation and absolute determination, I surprised myself by playing a trump card I did not even know I possessed. "Even if everything you are telling me is true, I still would not accept it," I said. "If I have to go to hell, then I guess that's what I'll do." I refused to believe what he wanted me to believe, because . . . well, I did not quite understand why.

At this, Reverend Gripp released me. He had argued with reason, intimidation, gentleness, threats—but he could not bring me to my knees. Perhaps he was able to tell himself that he had done due diligence, and could wash his hands of my soul. I had given him blank intransigence, and gone somewhere that neither logic nor eloquence could reach.

What was behind my irrational defiance? What was the heart's dumb hope or yearning? I must have had an intuition that salvation was not something achieved through argument or proofs, not a state to be induced through fear of punishment, and not even a matter of right or wrong. If I was motivated by fear, then my choice could not be genuine.

I think of these Bible camp encounters now as initiation events. The male elders take the adolescent boy out of his home environment, away from his parents, but with his parents' consent and even with their active endorsement. They subject him to frightening trials, placing terrifying images in front of him, testing his courage and perseverance. He must "die," his ego must temporarily be dissolved. From this passage into darkness he will emerge as a new creature, born again, an adult male now ready to participate fully in the life of the community.

For me, it didn't work that way. My ego did not dissolve; it hardened. I was not born again but I had stood up for myself. Mark Gripp had been a stand-in for my dad; I had fought him to a draw and that was as good as a win. I had learned that I had a reservoir of strength I could access. I even recognized that there was a voluntary quality to all this, that I was complicit. I could have refused to go to Red Rock, but I went of my own free will, as if sensing that I needed to face these trials entirely on my own, without parental protection or help. So that I could become a man. What kind of man? Of that I had no very clear idea. My silence and my negation took me a certain distance along my journey, but they also formed a barrier to the expanded life I was seeking.

My first time at Red Rock, I had been held a spiritual hostage, surrounded by religious zealots trying to extract an emotional confession. When it happened, I thought it was just me. Years later Al told me of being surrounded by badgering teachers at Steinbach Bible Academy, of how he had refused to give them any answers. And in 2004, long after these events, my brother Norman sent me this account of a dream he had. I had never told him of my Red Rock experience.

> I'm sitting in the living room of our old house on Main Street. Mom instructs me to go into the summer kitchen to see Dad. I do so, wondering "What the heck does he want?" I must be around 20 years old.
>
> I enter the summer kitchen area and the door to the regular kitchen is closed. It is somewhat dark in there. No lights on. I can see what appears to be a circle of about eight shadowy figures. It seems like quite a

cross-section. . . Dad, perhaps a local preacher or two, a Sally Ann guy, could there have been a priest? Their identities remain unclear.

Suddenly I feel very uncomfortable. All eyes appear to be on me. Nothing is spoken. I remain silent.

Finally Dad comes to me and impels me to join the others, locked arm in arm in a circle. Now I'm really freaked! Dad or one of the others then speaks, beseeching me to come into the fold and pointing out the folly of my life. At first, I think I might just wait them out . . . let them say their piece, and then I'll leave, none the worse for the experience. Then, suddenly, I think no . . . I must speak. Almost out of control, heeding not the consequences of what I might say, I utter, "This is NOT gonna work! This is not the way to approach me on this. I'm not going to co-operate and I refuse to participate! I insist you leave me alone. If ever I'm ready to do your bidding, I'll make that move myself."

Mom, who I'm not sure was in the room the whole time, comes up to me in a conciliatory tone and suggests they leave me be, for now. I leave.

I wake up wondering "What the heck was that?"

"That" was an echo, in dream form, of what actually happened to me, and to Al. In the dream, Dad takes a leading role in applying the pressure for religious conformity, whereas, in reality, he did not do that. But in putting him in that role, the dream seems to hold him to account, making him do the work which, in life, he had assigned to others. The work of breaking our spirits, arising from his fear that we would not find our own way. And then, quite wonderfully, the dreamer finds his voice, the voice Al and I did not have, and speaks the truth for us all.

#

After we moved to Woodlawn Park I soon struck up a friendship with Patrick Friesen. We had known each other previously, as our families went to the same church, but hadn't had much to do with each other because he was a year younger. Now we found that we had interests in common, like music. He was avant garde, a fan of the Beatles and Bob Dylan; I was still listening to my brothers' Kingston Trio and southern gospel quartet records. We both loved baseball, and would play on the corner lot, throw-

On the social committee at Steinbach Collegiate, 1963-4, Patrick in front. Yearbook photo.

ing each other hard-to-get ground balls or "batting out." In this we achieved a kind of physical grace and personal confidence. Patrick took me up, becoming my friend when I very much needed a friend.

Our greatest shared energy and joy emerged in mocking and criticizing the earnest religion and sanctimoniousness of the town. In Sunday school, Pat and I were placed in the same classes, and I was delighted to have a fellow debater on my side. He was quick-witted and daring and funny. When mild-mannered Jack Klassen became our teacher, Patrick and I, drumming on our Bibles, sang, "Hit the road, Jack," the Ray Charles tune popular at the time. We didn't dislike our teacher; it just seemed fun to do this.

We also took our fight to the streets, as it were, arguing theology with other teenagers, and even with the adults of the town, such as the owner of Pete's Inn, the café where we hung out after school. It was not long before we acquired something of a reputation, not like the usual "bad" boys who drank or smoked or drove fast cars or had sex, but as argumentative unbelievers, which was somehow worse.

We called ourselves infidels, with a kind of nervous pride. I liked the word because of its association with religious warfare. From childhood on, I'd been taught that to *schpott*—to mock or scorn religious belief—was a grave sin, possibly even the unforgiveable sin of the New Testament. Now I blasphemed, and laughed and waited, half-curious, to see what punishment would befall me.

Patrick thought of things that would not have occurred to me. One day as we walked home from school, talking religion as we often did, he mused, "What if there *is* a hell?" I was shaken. After all we'd been through together, how could he say that? But that was Patrick—he questioned received wisdom and notions of having a corner on the truth, wherever these came from. I decided he wasn't serious, but also that I needed to be clear about my own thinking.

My brother Vern happened to be reading Sinclair Lewis's novel *Elmer Gantry*, the story of a predatory American evangelist. Vern and I shared a bedroom, but he was often out, and it was easy for me to read the novel myself. I was astonished and excited that a man of God could act the way Elmer Gantry did, carrying on with the church pianists and such. But what really caught me were the contradictions in the Bible that Lewis exposed. In one place in the Bible it said: "No one has seen God at any time" (John 1:18). And in Exodus 33:20, God said to Moses: "You cannot see My face; for no man can see Me and live." But Genesis 32:30 records Jacob as saying: "For I have seen God face to face, and my life is preserved."

Here was something to take to Sunday school! Later, I would become less literal in reading the Bible, but at that time I imitated the polarizing literalism of my teachers, and fought fire with fire.

I did not dream then, as University of Toronto English professor Magdalene Redekop once did, that members of my family formed a jury and sentenced me to hang for not believing in the literal truth of the Bible. I was only beginning to get a feel for myth and metaphor and to imagine reading the Bible that way. How to approach the text was still a life-or-death problem, deeply steeped in fear and judgement. I was starting to understand the meaning of "murdering literalist," to use Redekop's phrase—the inherent violence in such an approach to the Bible or any other book.

Once a churchman made the effort to reach out to me. My teacher had kicked me out of Sunday school class one summer Sunday for my insolence. I think word got back to Mom, who didn't say much to me about it, but she must have talked to the pastor. I was surprised and immediately suspicious when the pastor phoned our home and wanted to speak to me. After a few preliminaries he said, "Would you like to go on a date?" I smirked. I knew what he meant, and was embarrassed for him. "A date?" I said, trying not to laugh. "Do you like to golf?" he went on, in a slightly strangled voice. "Sure," I said.

So it was that he came round to pick me up in his car and we went over to the service station which rented out clubs and on from there to the golf course, which was only a slight improvement over the communal pasture it had once been. We got to the first tee. The pastor selected a club and got set to hit a drive. I did a second take—he had a *putter* in his hands. "That's a putter!" I warned him. "It looks like a good one," he said, and swung. The ball travelled thirty yards or so, which I had to admit was not so bad, considering.

He must have tried to raise "spiritual matters" with me. I must have deflected his attempts. It was terribly awkward for both of us. But I had to give him credit for trying.

With Patrick, I went to a Max Solbrekken tent meeting. Solbrekken, a veteran evangelistic campaigner, noticed that we were laughing at his mini-dramas of healing the sick on stage. He picked me out from the audience and called for repentance. I was embarrassed, but impervious. "Who can know when that mocking young man might be hit by a bus?" Solbrekken wondered aloud. As there was no transit service in Steinbach, my chances of avoiding this fate were pretty good, but the next day schoolmates asked whether I was keeping a lookout for buses. I laughed, but looked both ways before crossing the street.

For years we fought this way, Patrick and I. Our fathers were lined up somewhere with the enemy. We did not think of them as betrayers, because we knew they were doing what they believed they had to do. As sons who departed from their religion, *we* were the betrayers. This is how we moved toward manhood, by fighting our own battles, not looking for parental support.

#

As I wrestled with religious questions, at first I did not think of my dad's stroke. I knew and accepted that sickness and accidents happen, and it's not always necessary to find out who is to blame. Maybe no one is. The church and my parents, however, taught that God is in control, that he has a plan for everything and everyone, and all is for the best. Suddenly I became angry. My father had faithfully done the Lord's work for many years, often putting this work ahead of his family. He had made a sacrifice for a higher cause, and so had we, his children. And *this* was the reward? Irreversible brain damage. Irreversible paralysis. What sort of plan was that? Even if there was a divine mystery to explain this, I, with Dostoevsky's Ivan Karamazov, cried: "I renounce the higher harmony altogether." Either God was a capricious tyrant, indifferent to justice, or he didn't exist at all.

My father's situation was an unanswerable argument against the very religion whose servant he had been.

In his sermon notes from the 1940s and '50s Dad conveys the certainty of a literalist. The fate of unregenerate sinners is "eternal death – the lot or share of the lost in hell – 'where their worm dieth not, & the fire is not quenched.'" That line is from Mark, quoting Jesus. Elsewhere, setting down his numbered points in columns, Dad contrasts what believers have to what unbelievers do not have. Seen that way, the sheep beside the goats, a stark polarity emerges. Where believers have the guidance of the Holy Spirit, the promises of God, membership in the body of Christ, and the comfort of the Bible, unbelievers "have no faith & no excuse," no hope, no freedom, no peace, no love—no life.

In another note, Dad characterized the rebellious soul: "Prayerlessness, not reading, independent, offended, pride, not first love, own will, stubborn." All this could have applied to me as an adolescent—except for "not reading," because I loved to read, but then, I wasn't reading the uplifting material he had in mind.

All these years later I read my father's words and find myself condemned. But I'm not angry or worried about it. I'm sure he wasn't thinking of me when he gave that sermon, and I certainly don't take his judgements personally. In the words of someone in the church back then: "Too bad he had to front a religion that was very threatening."

My behaviour constituted infidelity not just to the church, but to my parents. I knew that my unbelief could bring shame to them and raise questions about their spiritual credentials. This part I did not like, or want. I still wanted to be their son; I still wanted them to love me. So I directed most of my rebellion against other authority figures, leaving my parents out of it as much as possible.

You don't stage an open rebellion against a stroke-damaged man. Still less do you stage it against his long-suffering wife whose burden is really too heavy to carry as it is. Strangely, they too avoided religious discussions with me; we all colluded in avoiding the subject in our house. Yes, they urged me and my brothers to go to church and Sunday school and to attend revival meetings. But we were never asked: "What do you believe?" Nor did our parents share stories with us of how they came to believe what they did, or of any doubts they might have entertained. On this most important question of all—"are you saved?"—we kept silence. The topic was too dangerous.

Even good people could be lost. Mom almost allowed herself to question the logic of such an idea: "it's hardly graspable that a decent person, that lives a decent moral life, if the person does not accept Christ, that he is just as much lost as the worst of sinners."

Dad must also have had such questions. We were all in a kind of psychological double bind. My parents "had" to believe in hell, had to believe that anyone—some of their children included—who was not a Christian, was condemned. Yet they loved us. Had they been able to articulate this dilemma, they might have been obliged to say: "I love you. And I believe that, as things stand, you are going to hell." This could be crazy-making. Maybe that was why we didn't talk about it.

How could they handle the cognitive dissonance? Only by resorting to the age-old answer to things which have no answers: it's a mystery. And one great day all mysteries will be made clear, and all contradictions resolved.

In Mom's words, "All we can do is pray and trust the Lord." She said nothing of her puzzlement to me, and I said nothing about my unbelief to her or Dad. I feared their disappointment and grief. But not talking about it did not relieve us of the emotional burden each of us carried. We developed our individual strategies for dealing with that burden. I wanted to be freed from it entirely, and had the intuition that, for this, I would need to find a new level of consciousness.

#

In high school, I did not do well in mathematics and chemistry and physics—all subjects which, for me, had no emotional content or connection. I spent anxious hours in the classroom and at home, chastising myself for not being able to catch on. I suffered from acne which worsened in the senior grades, and, studying my ravaged face in the mirror, I imagined that others saw only my blemishes, as I did. I tried to divert myself from those self-condemning thoughts by making smart remarks in class, or playing after-school sports, or dreaming about a girl who would love me. I looked for love from exactly those pretty girls who were not interested in a complicated boy who could not find his place in the material world, and of course they easily deflected my uncertain advances. Failing physics and mathematics, I spent an extra year in school after my cohort graduated, and, although I pretended not to care, I was ashamed. I had always thought I was intelligent; now I had doubts. In literature class we studied *Hamlet* and I compared myself to the brooding, half-mad, misunderstood prince of Denmark.

I was braver when fighting false religion. But even here I could not find truly solid ground. I ordered *The Origin of Species* through the University of Manitoba inter-library loan service. It came in the mail, a thick book, and although I started it with enthusiasm, I quickly found it heavy going. Nor did it directly take on the story of the six-day creation as recorded in Genesis, and so it did not fulfill the purpose I had hoped, of providing stronger arguments against the idea that the Bible was a scientific text. Darwin provided an alternative narrative to the Bible's, and that gave me inspiration. But I was not truly interested in the science of evolution, which lacked the poetry and the drama of the moral tales I had grown up with. I also read Spinoza, the optical lens grinder who dared question that the Bible was divinely inspired. I was thrilled at his explanations, which clearly articulated ideas that were only half-formed in my mind, but here, too, the going got heavy, and I sent the books back half-read. The God of the Bible might be absurdly jealous and wrathful and tyrannical. But also, I had to admit, he was far more interesting than some abstract First Mover who had set the universe in motion and then quietly withdrawn.

Key components of the worldview of my parents and most members of my community had fallen out of place, and I did not have a new system to replace the old one. If I did not believe in original sin, then how did I explain human evil? If heaven and hell did not exist, then how should the demands of justice be satisfied? If there was no all-powerful God directing events, then how would I live without that security?

What salvation might truly be, then, I did not know. I began to realize that life was not just about saying "no." Gradually, fewer adults bothered to engage with me, and as I understood that I had become a lost cause for them, I felt a pressure begin to build. It was not the external pressure I knew so well, but a less familiar one from within me. "What must I do to be saved?" What could I say "yes" to?

All of these questions reverted to a larger problem of personal meaning. I had once unthinkingly absorbed the church's teachings as true. I could not hold them that way anymore. Not simply that I would not—not simply that I was being *jäajenaun*, contrary for the sake of being contrary, although I was capable of that—but I *could* not. I had stepped outside of my childhood faith story, and, looking back, saw that an unbridgeable gap had widened behind me. No longer: "I have decided to follow Jesus." I was unsure of what or whom to follow. But I knew this: "no turning back, no turning back."

CHAPTER 21:
FREED FROM THE PAIN-BODY

Dad had travelled frequently all his adult life. After the stroke, there were no more trips. Mom sold our car, making travel even less likely.

Mom felt chained down and lonely for her siblings. A few came for visits but most did not, perhaps thinking that she had enough to handle as it was. At last, in July-August of 1964, she took a month-long trip to Oregon and British Columbia, leaving Dad at the Rest Haven Home in Steinbach. Her days were filled with visiting relatives and friends or trips to forest waterfalls or the ocean. She had no cleaning or caregiving to do, others cooked for her, and she found it all quite wonderful. One Sunday at church "all of us seven sisters sat on one bench." They recreated the bonds of childhood. She was home.

In Steinbach, I was left in charge, paying the bills and visiting my father from time to time. Or so I wrote in a brief note to my mother—I do not remember these visits, except in a vague and general way. To my surprise, my note also says that I spent a weekend at Red Rock Lake with the EMC young people. I must have wanted companionship. And, evidently, some part of me was still drawn to the structures of the religion I purported to reject.

The Rest Haven charged $80 for taking care of Dad, which was a lot for Mom at the time. But it wasn't much compared to the emotional price of guilt she had to pay:

> Marie and I went to pick up Peter from the Old Folks Home. He cried much when he saw us, and said he had been just terrible lonesome, and that he has told me a hundred times over, since I'm home. Now he acts terrible, he doesn't want me to be in another room, till I have dressed and combed myself, to say nothing of walking out of the house. He sure can act childish. I didn't think I would find it quite so hard to get back into the groove again. But I hardly feel as if I have been away from it at all, I sure have put him on the toilet, I don't know how many times since I'm home, it's outrageous. In that way he figures he gets more attention.

Dad's loneliness had truly been terrible for him. Without Mom, he was left to his own devices—and he could not find much comfort within himself, or even in his religion. Mom was his all, and without her he was nothing.

In the summer of 1964, having spent a makeup year in Grade 12 and still without the credit in mathematics that would have given me my certificate, I walked into the offices of our local weekly newspaper, the *Carillon News*, and asked to see the publisher, Eugene Derksen.

My father had been a founding member of the credit union, along with Mr. Derksen, almost twenty years earlier, but I did not know that. I was shown to Mr. Derksen's office. He asked me what I wanted, and I told him that I wanted to write for the paper. He said: "*Wem sien Jung best dü?*" (Whose boy are you?) I believe he already knew the answer. "Peter D. Friesen," I said. "Okay, we'll give you a try," said Mr. Derksen.

Founders and charter members of the Steinbach Credit Union got together again in 1964 to commemora the organization's beginnings. (Left to right) A.T. Loewen, Herman Neufeld, Joseph T. Penner, Eugene Derkse K.J.B. Reimer, Jacob H.W. Reimer and (in front) Rev. Peter D. Friesen. Missing were P.J. Reimer, Paul Friesen a Aaron Reimer, the latter two being deceased.

Credit: Carillon News.

I think now: did he have any idea about my writing ability? Did he decide to hire me out of compassion, knowing my family circumstances? Did he simply believe that P. D. Friesen's son would prove trustworthy? Whatever the answer, whenever I think of this man I feel deep gratitude toward him, and toward my father.

Dad was getting weaker. Something was wrong. In September he was hospitalized with pneumonia and x-rays showed a cancerous tumour on his left lung. Again he was moved into the Rest Haven.

Mom made another trip to Kansas in March of 1965. Upon returning, her routine was both the same as before and profoundly different: "Ironed and helped quilt at a few places, had company etc. and of course I go to see Peter ever so often." When she saw him, she found him confused and able only to talk about how lonesome he was. The loneliness, like the cancer, had taken up residence within him, a chronic condition of his confined life.

He did have some warm human contact. One of his caregivers at Rest Haven, Glen Klassen, recalls helping him: "He would have to use his good arm to embrace my neck so that I could swing him into bed or back onto the wheelchair. It felt funny to be that intimate with an authority figure but he cooperated nicely and probably liked it."

Dad found some friendship at the nursing home. At least one resident, Lily (Mrs. Peter) Keating, sought his company—she would later complain to her son Wes that the institution would not allow her to visit him alone in his room. That was against the rules.

Uncle Nick and Uncle Abe were already dead of heart attacks. Then in September, 1965, Uncle Henry suffered a stroke, becoming paralyzed on his right side, and losing his ability to speak. By then Dad had little awareness of outside events, as he was shuttling back and forth between the Rest Haven and the hospital, and had been operated on for cancer. Health deteriorating, away from home and his beloved Margaret, Dad, who had always gamely emphasized the sunny side of life, fell into low moods. Darkness was closing in.

#

At the *Carillon News*, Eugene Derksen put me in charge of covering sports. I knew nothing about journalism but was not aware of how much I did not know, and got right to work, writing stories and a column. I made mistakes. I showed my ignorance. But I could write, and was open to instruction from the experienced reporters on staff. I learned something about taking photographs, getting the focus and distance and light settings lined up. My employer seemed happy with me.

The local dentist did some work on me and commented that I might get a cap on a front tooth "when you're writing for the *New York Times*." To that point, I had barely allowed myself the thought of writing for a Winnipeg daily some day, but now I started to wonder whether I should be more ambitious.

I had always loved baseball but never shown much skill at the game, so I became the scorekeeper for the local senior team, the Steinbach Millers. One June evening the team was short-handed and I was picked to be the starting pitcher in a home game against Niverville. I surprised everyone, mostly myself, by pitching well enough for the win, striking out fourteen batters, including three with the bases loaded. At the end I felt a new kind of joy, having excelled when so often before I had failed. No one from my family was there to watch my success, but in the stands that evening was Peter "Hotel" Peters, who said, "You did a good job out there." His words warmed my heart.

An evangelist, one of many who kept coming to Steinbach even though it was almost entirely a devoutly Christian town, arrived for a series of revival meetings. I wrote a critical and scornful letter to the editor of my own newspaper and the letter caught the attention of Professor Jack Thiessen at United College (soon to become the University of Winnipeg). Thiessen, himself a Mennonite from southern Manitoba, came to pick me up from work and take me to the Tourist Hotel, where we had lunch. This was an entirely new experience for me: no one had ever invited me for lunch anywhere, much less at the Tourist Hotel, which was better known for its men-only beer parlour.

On no more evidence than my letter, Thiessen thought I was fit material to come to university, study German (he was the head of the department), and go on a student work exchange to Germany. I was alarmed. I had been a poor student in German, and had not seriously considered going to university. Besides, I still did not have my complete Grade 12. Thiessen grandly brushed these objections aside with a sweep of his curved-handle pipe. I would take a summer makeup course in mathematics at United College. Germany would be the experience of a lifetime and I would become fluent in the language. I was smart and thoughtful; the Mennonite world needed me, and needed me with a university education.

His arguments swayed me. That summer I took three weeks of vacation time to go to Winnipeg each day for mathematics classes. I passed the exam. But I was too late to be admitted to university that fall, so I had a year ahead of me before that would happen.

But I was restless. I had met a local girl, not Mennonite, a sweet-natured, good-hearted person. I was at ease with her, and she with me. I said, "I love you," to her, and she said the same words to me, and we started talking about our future together, and a part of me felt happy about this, but another part felt a hint of despair. I thought of myself as a searcher, alone, a seeker of adventure like Jack London. But working at the home-town newspaper, thinking of marriage, even university—where was the

DAD, GOD, AND ME

adventure in that? I could see my life fitting into a prescribed pattern of safe domesticity. Of Steinbach, I declared: "Nothing ever happens here." Impulsively, I answered an ad in the paper, quit my job with the *Carillon* and took a DC-3 to the northern town of Lynn Lake, thinking I had a job working underground in the gold mine.

In preparation, my mother accompanied me to Rieger Clothing, where she helped me choose warm underwear, a parka, and winter boots. She sewed my name into my underwear. She said little about my decision, but I'm pretty sure she could see I hadn't thought it out very well. She would no longer have whatever help I had been to her in caring for Dad. Still, she supported me.

I told my girlfriend I would be back within the year. That would turn out to be true, but the relationship did not survive this absence. We went our separate ways.

When I got to Lynn Lake, I failed the eyesight test for underground workers. I tried to get a job in the mine office, but there was nothing for me there. So I returned, by slow train, not wanting to see the people to whom I had so recently waved farewell. I stayed in Winnipeg with my brother Al and his wife Connie, and weighed my options. I answered another ad, this one in the *Canadian Mennonite* newspaper, for a job as a "psychiatric aide" in a Mennonite Central Committee (MCC) mental hospital in Reedley, California. To my surprise I got a response, and was called in for an interview. A providentially broad-minded man gave me the job even though I was not a church member and my faith credentials were weak. Most MCC work was voluntary service, but they let me work for minimum wage because I needed to save money for university the following year. In November, 1965, I boarded a Grey Goose bus for California. Mom cleaned my room and wrote in her diary: "I miss Ralph terrible."

I felt guilty, leaving Dad in deteriorating health in the Rest Haven, and leaving Mom, who seemed to need me. I was the last child to leave home. I knew that Dad might not have much longer to live. He was in a nightmarish ward with a senile man who groaned incessantly. Dad had complained about this unnerving noise at my last visit, but it seemed that not much could be done. The groaning man had to have a bed somewhere.

250

At the U. S. border, customs officials examined my papers, interviewed me briefly, and let me through. Safely back inside the metal capsule of the bus, I slept fitfully as we headed south and west. In the morning light the landscape had changed, the snow was gone, in places the grass was green. I was going to a new world and a new life. My guilt receded with each mile.

Stepping down from the bus in Fresno, I felt the California air on my skin, as gentle as the first embrace of a new lover. I was given a room at the MCC volunteer unit house in Reedley. An orange tree grew in the backyard; I had come to paradise. Every day at Kingsview Hospital held new experiences, and I did not think about home overly much, or about Dad's ongoing pain and discomfort. His urine flow was blocked, and Mom commented in a letter to her siblings that "the doctor has to fix him up every week already, something always clogs up."

"Once in a while, when I'd come and see him, he would say, he was dead," wrote Mom. He would have spoken in Low German: "*Etj sie doot.*"

In the MCC volunteer unit house in Reedley, I did not endear myself to my American counterparts who were doing alternative service so that they would not have to serve in the military. I suggested to them that they didn't really believe in the Mennonite principle of non-resistance, as they couldn't even articulate it properly. An MCC staffer said to me, "You don't scare us."

In Steinbach the Rest Haven had a Christmas dinner for the patients, inviting spouses as well. By this time Dad was mostly bedridden, but the nurses dressed him and put him in his wheelchair for the meal. "But you could see," wrote Mom, "he hardly could get any food down, nor could I hardly get mine down. He was so tired soon after, that they had to put him back to bed." Dad's old friend Klaas J. B. Reimer visited him and asked if he had pain. He nodded. And "he spoke very little."

I will let Mom continue the story here, as she told it in a letter to her siblings:

> He never felt well anymore. On Jan. 4, he got rather short of breath, so I stayed with him afternoon and eve. The next day he was more calm again. From Jan. 4, I went to the Home every day, except for just a few odd days. Even in 40 below, and in stormy cold days. He always looked

quite sick during this time, but didn't complain, he often was short of breath, and he did complain some about that. Since he only always talked in a whisper, I didn't talk to him very much, I sat and did some handwork, and in the last weeks, I often sang for him, which he liked.

On Jan. 12, I phoned to the Home, and asked how he was doing, they said he seemed to be quite calm, and maybe much the same, so I told them I wouldn't come that day, as it again was so awful cold, but then at 9:30 in the eve they phoned me, he had suddenly turned for the worse. So Mr. Reimer, the boss there came and picked me up, he was very short of breath, and the doctor came there too, he said, they would take him to the hospital the next day, they had to discharge somebody before they could take him in. They had put him on Oxygen already at the home, I stayed with him all through the night, and the next day, Jan. 13, they took him to the Hospital, he was very sick by now, always on Oxygen, and even then he was short of breath, which bothered me terrible, it was hard to see, how he would turn all sweaty, and big sweat drops on his forehead. It was very hard for him too. He looked real bad that nite, and we phoned the children. Al & Mary Ann came out. On Friday morning they phoned me from the Hospital, and said Peter wanted me. So when I came there, he was very confused, asking one thing over and over, he didn't know where he was, and he was very restless all day, also very short of breath, that nite the doctor gave him a good needle, and told me to go to bed and have a rest, the nurses would phone me for any change there was, they phoned me at 15 minutes to 5 in the morning, he again was very short of breath, and perspiring terrible.

Later in the morning, when the Nurses took care of him, he had answered one question, but after that he was in a coma, all day Saturday, Jan. 15. It was very hard to see him breathe so deep and with a jerk, and his mouth open and gurgling all the time. I went and sat in the corner so as not to see him all the time, it was unbearable. He kept this up till about 3 in the morning, when they turned him again, then he didn't breathe so hard anymore, but very fast, and from then on he started to breathe less every hour, till 15 min to 9, when he went to be with the Lord, he passed away so quietly, that I wouldn't have noticed it, had I not stood close and watched him. Sis Marie was with us from Sat. afternoon, until he passed away on Sun. morning. The weather was cold.

My siblings had come to the hospital in those last days to say their goodbyes. My eldest brother remembers leaning over the bed and hearing Dad say one word: "Alvin." When Al told me this, tears came to his eyes. He realized, in that moment, that Dad's last utterance to him was a declaration of love.

"He complained some" about shortness of breath. But in general, he did not complain, and in this was true to his forebears, the pioneers for whom complaining would have been a temptation of the Devil, a failure to acknowledge the wisdom of an almighty deity. If you could go through the valley of the shadow of death without complaining, you demonstrated your faith. You were supposed to remember the suffering of Jesus; your courage in dying was the last and maybe most crucial part of a life of imitating Christ. My mother could hardly bear witnessing Dad's dying and I can hardly bear reading her account.

On that Saturday when Dad was nearing death, I was called to the phone in the MCC volunteers' unit house in Reedley. Long-distance call from Canada. It was my mother. "Dad is going," she said in a tremulous voice. Her emotion actually surprised me; I had judged my father to have been a burden to her for so long that she would be relieved when she no longer had to care for him. I sought for words to comfort her.

She called again the next morning to say that Dad had died. I had been working night shift at the hospital and was alone in the house. I hung up the phone, went to the living room, and picked out a Peter, Paul and Mary LP from the stack on the table beside the record player. The trio of voices, so harmonious, celebrated Stewball, the legendary race horse: "Oh way up yonder / Ahead of them all / Came a prancin' and a dancin' / the noble Stewball." Tears started in my eyes; I did not know why. Today I think of the song as an ode to my father, who had always put himself second, who had abjured dancing, who was humble and slow-moving. Now, released from his pain-body, he was a beautiful thoroughbred, dancing proudly, crossing the finish line first.

The next day I took the bus to Vancouver where I joined my brothers Norman and Vern and Vern's wife Irma, and rode with them on the long trip through the mountains and across the prairies, back home. When we arrived in Steinbach we went to see Dad's body at the funeral home. It was a shock. His jawline was sharply defined, his nose pointed, his cheekbones prominent. This was not the face we knew, which had always been full and rounded. His sickness had transformed him, as if he had literally gone through some refining fire, melting away the familiar flesh.

We were gathered at last in the presence of our father, all of us children. But "he" was not there. I don't think any of us wept then, or at the funeral. Only much later did the tears come.

Our family at the time of Dad's funeral. Having travelled in a rush from California, I had no formal clothes and had to borrow a suit jacket from my friend Patrick.

Dad's long-time friend and colleague Peter J. B. Reimer gave the sermon at the funeral, comparing Dad to Moses. From my point of view the comparison was bewildering. The "In Memoriam" card read: "For the last seven-and-a-half years the Lord also saw fit to permit His servant to suffer. Away from the main stream of life, apart from the busy throngs, to an entirely different life."

Different life? I thought. A monumental understatement. The Lord saw fit to permit his servant to suffer? To me such explanations and consolations, however well-meant, were hollow and dishonest. After the service, we drove to the cemetery southwest of town, where a grave had been dug in the deeply frozen ground. There was no more room in the Pioneer Cemetery, where Dad's parents and grandparents were buried. Another former colleague of his, Jake P. Dueck, spoke at the graveside, and his words were snatched away by the wind in the near twenty-below Fahrenheit temperatures. The wind swept swatches of snow onto the plain grey coffin that hung suspended above the grave. We did not see it lowered and we did not see the hole closed up.

The following week, Mom received 134 sympathy cards and many visits. Archie Penner, studying at Mennonite Biblical Seminary in Indiana, wrote a letter of condolence:

> I remember the years we spent together in the ministry and how benevolent and considerate he always was. I have said on many occasions that no person would have treated me better than Peter did when I took his office and ministry at the Steinbach church. Transitions like this are difficult for all of us, but I felt no aversion, no rancor in the attitude of your husband . . . . We trust that you are persuaded that it is the Lord Who has done this, and, therefore, even your husband's death is a mark and evidence of His care over you and of His victory.

His death was evidence of God's victory! I balked at this absurdity, but my father himself would probably have agreed. Six years earlier, Mom had summarized the events of Dad's stroke and hospitalization:

We never dreamed what this last year would bring to us, but we know it's the Lord's leading, and we thank Him who keeps His promises. He has given strength for the day, and has helped us. We again commit ourselves to Him as we are about to enter the new year. All things work together for good, to them that love the Lord.

To which Dad added: "God's blessings, may His name be praised for everything that has happened." This was my parents' faith: faced with catastrophe and great hardship, they saw it all as God's will, and praised him.

Mom found that adjusting to Dad's death was not easy, but not as hard as it might have been. In the year before, he had hardly been at home, and she had become accustomed to not having him there. His stroke, more than his death, shattered her life.

In a sense, he passed away for me 7-½ years ago. It was then I was much more deeply hurt, than I am now, it was then, that the world crumbled away, from under my feet, and I dangled into nothing, it also was then, that I had to make hard adjustments. And now, nothing seems very real to me, not yet, tho, I have seen Peter suffer so, and also saw him take his last breath, I was relieved, he was over his suffering, but then too, I realized this was final, and the parting hurts, regardless of how you wish the Lord would end his suffering. And now it doesn't seem to have been such a long time, and to tell the truth, it doesn't seem real to me that he is not in the Rest Haven Home. I still feel as if he's there, even though I know well and good he isn't.

I read Mom's letter again after all these years, and I marvel at these words especially: "the world crumbled away from under my feet, and I dangled into nothing." I never heard her speak this way. She sounds almost like the madman in Nietzsche's parable who proclaims the death of God: "Is there still an above and below? Do we not stray, as though through an infinite nothingness?" Mom kept her faith after all was said and done, but she looked into the abyss.

For Mom, Dad had "died" at the time of his stroke. So it had been, too, for us, his children. We had all lived that way, more or less consciously, for seven years, unwilling or unable to embrace Dad as a whole human being. When our neighbour Margaret Friesen, Patrick's mother, told Mom that her husband was going to lose his diseased eye, Mom replied, "Be thankful it isn't his mind."

Near the end Dad said, "I am dead." Part of him was aware, and likely had been aware all along, of a previous self which had died. The new self—emotional, sentimental, humorous, forgetful, repetitive in think-ing—could try to express itself, but could not flourish. Dad tried his best to be whatever he could be after the stroke, and maintained an attitude of good cheer for a long time. But we did not give this post-stroke person welcome; we did not validate him. I am deeply sorry for that.

Within a year, Mom sold the house and moved into an apartment. With her small savings and, after a few years, her Old Age Pension, she no longer needed to take in ironing, and was able to travel and live modestly but comfortably. She was highly social and enjoyed the company of her friends at quilting parties. Eventually she moved into a two-bedroom apartment with my aunt Gertrude Friesen. The two of them bought a TV so they could watch *Hymn Sing* and the news.

Mom died in 1983, seventeen years after Dad. She lay in her bed in Bethesda Hospital and declared herself *doodeskrank* (sick unto death). I asked her if there was something she wanted, thinking she might ask for water or a little ice. "I want all my children to come to the Lord," she said. An electric current of guilt ran through me, and I made no answer.

Dream
March 22, 1995 *My Dad Died*
I am standing in our garage with a woman. I tell her that I've just received news that my father has died. And this is a good thing, because he had been hanging on for a long time. I'm free now, I tell her.

CHAPTER 22:
BEYOND RIGHT AND WRONG

Returning to California after Dad's funeral, I was detained at the border, where the U. S. officials told me that I would have to register for the military draft, and they would be checking to see that I had done so. They hadn't said anything about this the first time I had entered the country, but now they insisted, and as I reboarded the bus, I felt a watery fear in my guts.

The U. S. was sending increasing numbers of young men to fight in the Vietnam War. The prospect of being one of those men did not appeal to me. I was a dual citizen, Canadian and American (on account of Mom having been born in the U. S.) and thought that this status might exempt me from military service.

I decided to write a letter to the FBI, explaining my position, saying that I had no intention of breaking any laws, and asking for advice. Two months passed; I heard nothing. Then one afternoon while at work I was called to the day room, where two men in suits sat at a card table. They introduced themselves brusquely, placing their identification badges on the table, complete with J. Edgar Hoover's signature.

After a brief interrogation during which they told me that a Canadian of my age working in the States would be drafted even sooner than an

American, and that evading the draft was a felony punishable with a jail sentence, I asked what my options were. They wanted me to register. But, failing that, I could take the first bus back to Canada.

MCC volunteers from Reedley on a trip to the mountains. I am second from left.

The next day I was on the bus, leaving behind the patients and staff at the hospital, my friends in the volunteer service unit house, and the promise of the coming California spring. I went to Vancouver, where I stayed with Vern and Irma until I got a summer job working on a road-building survey crew. That fall, I enrolled at the University of Winnipeg.

I majored in English Literature. My first-year teacher, Carl Ridd, assigned the essay topic "The Shape

Student at the University of Winnipeg.

of My Life." I dove in—did my life truly have a shape? If so, who did the shaping? Random events? God? Me? I wrote about my father's stroke. Ridd responded with enthusiasm and wonder, as if my story really mattered. He gave me the recognition I had missed in high school, and my confidence was bolstered. At the end of the academic year I went to Germany as an exchange student, just as Jack Thiessen had promised.

I also took courses in Religious Studies and encountered teachers who were believers, not in the narrow literalism with which I had grown up, but in a more universal and generous spirituality. I found that I could slip out of the sacred text straitjacket and study religion just as I studied languages or social sciences. I took a class from Rabbi Zalman Schacter, who opened new possibilities with his talks about his experiments with mind-expanding hallucinogens and meditation in the Eastern tradition. Meanwhile, my friend Patrick attended services at a Zen Buddhist temple and gave me accounts of worshipers who believed, but not in a Biblical God. I looked at the medieval Scholastics' proofs for God's existence and the skeptics' proofs against his existence, all laid out in logical, even brilliant arguments. But reading them was for me like watching a display of mental gymnastics—impressive, but pointless. I lost interest in fruitless debates with literalists, and tried to keep an open mind to various religious expressions.

On weekends I would go home, my briefcase—a brown leather briefcase with a brass clasp that had belonged to Dad—filled with laundry. Hoping to assuage Mom's fear that university would turn me into an atheist, I told her that some of my professors were ministers.

At the end of the academic year in 1968, some of us in Rabbi Schacter's class went for a weekend retreat at Camp Arnes on Lake Winnipeg. Some students invited their friends, and so it was that I found myself in the back seat of a Travel-All van with a bunch of Oblate initiates and a girl wearing a button on her jacket which read: "Reality is a crutch." "How true," I said, and she smiled, a bit uncertainly, as if she wasn't quite sure herself of the meaning of this upside-down aphorism. Her name was Hannah Hofer, and before long I discovered that she had left her life in a Hutterite colony not far from Winnipeg and was completing her Grade 12 so that she could get into university.

In the morning of the second day at Camp Arnes we were all seated in the common room listening to Rabbi Schacter explain the meaning of the Tao. I noticed that Hannah quietly left the room and decided to follow her outside. She walked over to a set of children's swings and sat there, spinning around slowly. Her brown hair shone in the sunlight. We talked about religion. "Why do you believe in God?" I asked her. "Because I'm afraid not to," she replied, and I laughed, pleased with her honesty.

Hannah on a winter visit to the Winnipeg Zoo.

We were married that same year, in December, between semesters.

At university I was partially conscious of the fact that I was seeking a father. Jack Thiessen and Carl Ridd believed in me and my abilities. They invited me into their homes and showed me kindness, and a part of my father-wound was healed through their nurture. I won the gold medal for highest standing in Honours English, and I was proud.

I carried on to graduate school and got a master's degree in English Literature at the University of Alberta. My thesis topic, "Metamorphosis in *A Midsummer Night's Dream* and *The Tempest*," explored all manner of changes and transformations. Was I subconsciously trying to solve the problem of my dad's "transformation" by stroke? Of all of Shakespeare's sublime poetry in those plays, it was Ariel's song that most captured my attention, and does still:

> Full fathom five thy father lies;
> Of his bones are coral made;
> Those are pearls that were his eyes:
> Nothing of him that doth fade,
> But doth suffer a sea-change
> Into something rich and strange.

Hannah and I attended the General Conference Mennonite Church in Edmonton and were "adopted" by Jake and Hella Harder, who seemed to sense that, away from home, we were drifting a bit. Jake gave us work at a camping ground so that we had a place to live and a source of income. Again, I felt that Jake believed in me, like a good father.

In 1971 our son Nathan was born, and I became a father myself. I still wanted to be a fiction writer, but found that I just didn't have the energy to do that and also be a father and husband and scholar. I told myself that, if I could not excel at the creation of art, I might at least teach literature, and that would feed my hungry soul and put bread on the table, too. But the road to a PhD, strewn with research of minutiae, became a slog.

When the federal government came to the campus on a recruitment mission, I applied and was accepted and we moved to Ottawa, where I went to French language school. Whatever would come after this, I couldn't lose by acquiring another language. After nine months I was declared officially bilingual and assigned to the Secretary of State Department. Soon I asked for a transfer to the Winnipeg office and found myself working as a "social development officer," assisting Indigenous, ethnocultural, and other community groups, facilitating project funding.

Having no training in community development, I was out of my depth. But I was given the opportunity to learn, and I did learn, especially from the minority communities themselves. I felt I was contributing to the good of these communities, and that my efforts were in line with my egalitarian values.

In 1974 our daughter Zea was born. Hannah and I invested ourselves in being the best parents we could be. We enrolled our children in special schools and music programs, read to them, went camping, took them on trips to other provinces.

November, 1976; Zea had just turned two.

I wanted to live fully. As a teenager I had developed the ambition to be a writer, a novelist, or at least a short story writer. As an adult my attempts at living out this vision were erratic and undisciplined. When I sat down to write fiction, I kept going back to my memories of actual events, and I lacked belief in my own inventions. Historically, the Mennonites had been dismissive of fiction, which they regarded as *ütjedochte Jeschichte,* or "thought-up stories." If the stories were thought-up, then they were a form of lying, and lying was a sin. I had thought I was far beyond such dull literalism, but maybe a part of me still operated from it.

Hoping to honour my creative urge, I got a job with the National Film Board—not as a filmmaker, but in distribution and marketing. I wanted to learn film editing, but wasn't sure how to make that happen. I was afraid to step outside the boundaries of my daily life. Still, I was hounded by what Colin Wilson calls "the religious appetite." Like my father, and like everyone else, I suppose, I had a notion of some part of myself that could be extraordinary and even heroic—and this notion would not leave me be.

Unlike my father, I could not claim to be doing the Lord's work. But this was still what I wanted to do. Not in the way that my father had done it, not *his* Lord's work, but in my own way, pursuing a higher purpose in the secular world. Yet as time passed without significant writing output, I began to feel a dull despair, which I mostly kept to myself since it held no promise of change. Whatever my father's failures or shortcomings, he had been bold enough to claim his values and live them, with Jesus as his helper and leader. Now I feared that I would never become what I was meant to be, and Jesus was not on my side. Now *I* was the imposter.

I left the Film Board and Hannah left her teaching job and we took a three-year assignment in Zimbabwe with World University Services of Canada. We took our children with us and taught in a rural secondary school, befriended the Zimbabweans and travelled around southern Africa between terms. It was an adventure, as we had hoped it would be. I think it was also an attempt to live a more meaningful life. Was this my secular version of mission work? Had I heard Ben D. Reimer's call in the tabernacle after all?

On our return to Winnipeg I again found work in government, earning a decent salary, doing a decent job. In my family life, with my wife and children, I tried to be a good listener and to support them in their dreams. Middle-aged by now, I had not escaped from my never-ending slow-motion wrestling match with my own unfulfilled dream. I was not fully present with Hannah and the children, or with myself. I also had an unrelenting Inner Critic and at times succumbed to a sense of being defective, inadequate, and unworthy. At times I said: "I can't do this anymore."

By the time of my fiftieth birthday, my marriage was in deep trouble. A part of me reasoned that my elusive dream could somehow be fulfilled if I could be single again. But confusion and intense emotional pain for my wife and my children ensued. I went into therapy, with Hannah and also on my own. I exiled myself from our home, hoping to find clarity and a way forward by myself, in a one-room apartment on Stradbrook Avenue on the edge of Winnipeg's Osborne Village.

My life had come to an impasse. I had swallowed a hot coal that had lodged halfway down my gullet; I could neither swallow it nor spit it out. I wanted to be someone else. I wanted to be relieved of the burden of being myself. When I was a child, Dad had warned me against self-pity; now I felt sorry for myself, and tried to "balance" the self-pity with self-hatred.

#

On the night of Father's Day, 1995, alone in my rented room, in the midst of writing in my journal, I stopped, suddenly aware of . . . a ghost. My father! I could feel him in the room. I got up, vibrating with anger and triumph. Gazing into the dresser mirror, I spoke to my reflection:

> Hi, Dad, recognize me? Maybe not. I know you didn't expect to see me at this age, when I'm fifty. But here I am. It's Peter Ralph. Your last-born, that afterthought who wasn't really thought of, whom you weren't expecting or hoping for. But I arrived anyway, and I'm still here.
>
> And I've found you. I bet you thought you'd gotten away. You've been hiding all this time. From me, and not just from me, from all your kids. Well, guess what, you bastard? I've got you now. You can't hide anymore.
>
> You let God bully you and order you around and you never said "no." And all the time I was there and I wanted you on my side but I never said anything because I never thought I could ask anything of you. I still don't know if I can.
>
> I've messed things up, as you can see. So, now that you have me in front of you, and now that you see who I really am, what are you going to do? If you tell me that you'll only accept me, only love me, if I'm that certain kind of Christian (we both know what I mean), then I guess you won't accept me or love me. And that would be too bad.

That would hurt. But let me tell you something, Dad—it doesn't matter. If you can't accept me this way, I can still accept you.

I love you, Dad. No matter what you do, or did. And if you can love me, just as I am, I will be very glad to take your love. But if it's too much for you, with all you've been taught about right and wrong, and after all this time has gone by, then I still want you to know that I am accepting myself, loving myself.

So it will be all right. I will be all right. God loves me. You don't have to worry. Are you scared? Don't be. Fear not, said the angel. Remember?

Goodbye, Dad. It was so good to talk to you. I miss you. I love you.

I emerged from this conversation with fresh energy. All my adolescent and adult life I had not had a father to speak with. Now I had conjured up that father, and uttered words which had long been latent in me. I was not telling myself that I had done nothing wrong; I knew that I had grievously wounded those closest to me, and I took responsibility for doing that. But I was claiming my birthright, a kind of unconditional acceptance of my own being. This acceptance went beyond the religious categories in which I had been raised and evoked an innocent "self" unburdened by shame—the person I was meant to be. My parents could have their dreams and wishes for me, but they could not decide who this person was, or bring him to life. I had to do it.

In researching this book, I found that Dad had written about fear, post-stroke. He wrote in German, beginning with a quotation from John 16:33: "*In der Welt habt ihr Angst . . .*" *In the world you are afraid, but be assured, I have overcome the world.* Dad takes "fear" as equivalent to "worry," and says that worry is unnecessary, because God has overcome everything, including all of our troubles. Our task is to put our trust in God.

Dad had done just that, in facing his stroke. I did not think he had managed as well with me, his son. I was asking my father to listen to his own counsel—to set aside his fear and worry, even the fear that I would not become a born-again Christian, and to have faith that I would be saved, even if my way of salvation did not conform to the four steps in the tract I had been handed on Steinbach's Main Street so many years earlier.

#

My path now led me to the Interfaith Marriage and Family Institute in Winnipeg (now Aurora Family Therapy Centre), where I was accepted as a student therapist in a master's degree program. There I learned to recognize my own emotional experience and to search for the wisdom residing within that experience.

At one point a prospective client requested "a Christian therapist." My supervisor, Dick Dearing, assigned this person to me. "I don't know if I can take this client," I said to him. "I doubt that I qualify as 'Christian.'"

"Of course you do," said Dick, without hesitation, and handed me the file.

I worked with that person, and I don't remember the issue or the outcome, but I do remember that we did not encounter any problem related to my Christian credentials or lack of them. This scenario repeated itself several times later on, when I was working for a large employee assistance counselling company. I think I was able to help most of these clients, and I did not mind quoting Scripture or exploring prayer life and questions of faith. I was able to establish a bond with them, using the language that spoke to them. In turn, more than once, they wished me God's blessings.

I have been present with people in despair, suicidal, frightened, and angry. People who panicked and could not breathe, or lost control and smashed a fist into my office wall, or fell on the floor weeping. It wasn't easy to keep my balance. Often I was at a loss, and prayed for guidance and understanding. My work required courage and faith.

My work as a family therapist, engaging with thousands of clients over the years, was a kind of spiritual practice. I tried to help people, and when I succeeded, felt gratified. I tried to maintain an attitude of curiosity and reverence and humour. I believe that I was called to this work, and I answered the call, and fulfilled my purpose.

My ancestors came to Canada, a land inhabited by Indigenous people with a sense of the sacred alive in the physical world, including animals, plants, and stones. I am strongly drawn to this way of seeing, but hardly know how to practise it. I've placed myself in situations that demanded the suspension of disbelief—from talk therapy to cranial-sacral massage to marginal participation in an Ojibway Sun Dance ceremony. I've done dream work and non-dominant-hand writing. I have sung gospel songs, all my life, with a fervency I do not bring to secular songs.

At the Sun Dance, when the elders stood around me, fanning the air with eagle feathers, singing, I felt deeply grateful. They offered their blessing and healing to an anonymous, undeserving descendant of the very settlers who had displaced their people. I received grace, that time. In First Nations stories, Coyote is a creator god, mischievous, playful, and exuberant—far from the perfect Christ of my father's religion, but somehow an expression of what I needed then and still need now.

Unlike the poet William Blake, I do not see angels, and I sometimes fear that scientific materialism has drained the world of transcendent meaning. My father was a rational thinker, and I don't think he saw angels, either. He did, however, embrace the idea of Absolute Truth and of one path only to that truth. What a comfort that must have been to him! And what an unadmitted arrogance behind it. It is a comfort impossible for me to accept and an arrogance I hope to avoid. But I can, I do play along with my inherited religion, like a charlatan with claims to sincerity.

When my brother Vern lay dying in the Steinbach hospital, I sat at the foot of his bed and sang "Jesus won't you come by here," reciting the words I'd learned off an old Reverend Gary Davis record, long before. Something greater than Vern or I was present in those moments.

A few times, I've taken communion in Mennonite and Baptist churches, always with a sense of inner turmoil. I have reasoned this way: *I am part of the body of Christ, if "Christ" is the spirit of love and transformation.* My ancestors would never have accepted such a weak rationalization. For the church in which I grew up, communion was the most solemn of occasions; people prepared themselves beforehand. Only believers could participate, and then only if they could do so with a clear conscience. Anyone taking communion "unworthily" would have to answer at the Last Judgement. Well, one more thing on my accountability list, I guess.

Have I turned out to be some kind of Christian after all?

If this were a conventional "coming home" story, I would tell you that, at last, I came to accept my father's religion and took it for my own. I would tell you of being converted, getting baptized, joining a church.

It hasn't quite turned out that way. In my own way, though, I believe I am on my journey home.

My heritage is imbued with Christianity. My ancestors were Mennonites for generations, going back to the 1700s in Prussia as far as genealogical researchers have been able to find, and almost certainly further back to the 1500s in the Netherlands.

The Mennonites refused to carry arms, on the grounds that Christ had taught his followers to love their enemies. They also believed that each person could come to religious truth through the study of Scripture, without the benefit of priestly intervention or church tradition. For their stubborn adherence to such radical beliefs, they were severely persecuted in the sixteenth and seventeenth centuries, a story which is documented in *The Martyrs Mirror*, first published in Holland in 1660. This thick volume, with graphic illustrations of the faithful being tortured, beheaded, drowned, and burned at the stake, was found in Mennonite households for hundreds of years. It has lost its central place now, with the assimilation of most Mennonites into mainstream Protestant Christianity. But I have a copy in my bookshelf, and consult it from time to time.

I am not a Mennonite, if that status is bestowed through formal church membership. But "Mennonite" is also a name for the ethnic, linguistic, and religious world into which I was born. And if the martyrs held so bravely to their faith, and gave up so much for it, is it not my obligation to take their sacrifice seriously?

Thanks to Professor Jack Thiessen, without whom I would never have learned sufficient German, I have been able to research and write books and articles on Mennonite history. I have written a family history—*Abraham S. Friesen, Steinbach Pioneer*—and a history of Steinbach—*Between Earth & Sky*. I co-wrote the life story of my maternal grandfather, Peter F. Rempel, for still another family history. I have written numerous articles in *Preservings*, a magazine published by the D. F. Plett Historical Research Foundation, of which I was a board member for many years.

I discovered ancestors my parents probably never even knew about, recorded stories they themselves had never heard, bringing those otherwise lost lives into the light of day. So I think, yes, I have taken the ancestral story—in large part a religious story—seriously, and given it its due. This book, now, is for me the last part of the process of engaging with this story, narrowing the focus to my parents, my siblings, and myself. It is a vital part of my answer to the ever-present question of personal salvation.

In *The Varieties of Religious Experience* William James says that medieval Europeans required some cruelty and arbitrariness in their deity, since that was what they were used to from their reigning monarchs. Perhaps my Mennonite forebears and their persecutors needed that God. And large numbers of fundamentalists still seem to need a modern variation of him today. I will concede that cruelty and arbitrariness cannot be extirpated from our planet, and even that they might be essential to some mysterious divine order or disorder beyond my understanding. But I deplore the use of religion to perpetrate suffering and hatred and the dehumanization of those we perceive as "other."

What about a loving God who controls the universe? When Dad says, "May his name be praised for everything that has happened," a part of me revolts. God ordains a stroke, and the victim says "thank you"? No! But then, Dad surrenders to "everything," including his stroke; he accepts that which he cannot change, and even elevates his acceptance to a kind of approval, if praise implies approval. He sets aside the logic of the ego. Is this what Dostoevsky meant by "higher harmony"? Dad did not demand justice for himself, and I am caught here, wanting to demand it for him and also recognizing I am over my head; this stuff is beyond my understanding.

In Freudian terms, by killing the god of fundamentalist religion, I had also killed my father, who embodied that religion. But did he, really? He was not confined to rigid fundamentals of abstract doctrine; there was much more to him. In fact, many people I interviewed say this—he was not judgemental, and he calmed their fears. Of my eighteen-year-old rebellious self he had said: "Ralph helps Mom at times like a good boy! So there don't say that he isn't!"

He meant that humorously, but I also choose to take his words at face value: he believed I was a good boy, and was ready to defend me against the naysayers.

When I was 50, my therapist said to me: "You are a faithful man of God." Still, today, these words stay with me. I am a faithful man of God, even though I don't believe in the God who shows up in Bible stories. But God, it seems, believes in me.

Dad fell short in fathering me. I have also fallen short in being a father to my own children. That is another story. I forgive my father his failings, and ask to be forgiven for mine. We do our best with the light we have. I acknowledge, also, how much Dad gave, how much he did, and I am grateful.

Dad believed that he and Mom would meet after death, in heaven, "to go on in eternity forever and ever." They would be there, Mom and Dad, and Vern would have joined them, and we other children would eventually join them too, if Mom's dying wish could be realized. Every time I hear Steve Earle sing "I expect to hold his hand, boys," tears come to my eyes.

Who knows? The Bible itself has an intuition that eternity is not time marching on endlessly; rather, "Time shall be no longer," says the writer of Revelation. And wherever Dad and Mom are now, in some transpersonal non-place in non-time, are they not also beyond all earthly religious categories?

Always, whatever else has happened or is happening or will happen, there is love. "*Gott ist die Liebe*," sang the ancestors. God—or goddess, or the divine, or the light, or the true self, whatever you want to call it, is love. "*Er liebt auch mich*"—he, or she, or it, loves me also.

I'll give you the last word, Dad. Or next to last: "October 15, 1942: Thursday. Lovely weather. It seems that each fine day is an extra present from the Creator, but that is really what each & every day is to us, good or bad."

We call weather, people, events, "good or bad." It's all a gift from the Creator. In this field, beyond good and bad, beyond true and false, beyond right and wrong, we can meet. In this field we are dancing, Dad and Mom and all of us children, on a warm summer evening, the stately moon hanging in the soft sky overhead.

Sources

- P. 1. *The First Man in My Life: Daughters Write About Their Fathers*, Sandra Martin, ed., (Toronto: Penguin, 2007).
- P. 166. Quoted by Ken Reddig, "Judge Adamson Versus the Mennonites of Manitoba During World War II," in *Journal of Mennonite Studies*, vol. 7, 1989.
- Pp. 198-9. Ron Smith, *The Defiant Mind: Living Inside a Stroke* (Nanoose Bay: Ronsdale Press, 2016).
- P. 207. Acts 4:12: "Neither is there salvation in any other: for there is none other name under heaven given among men, whereby we must be saved." 2 Timothy 2:5: "And if a man also strive for masteries, yet is he not crowned, except he strive lawfully."
- P. 211. Irvin Yalom, *Staring at the Sun: Overcoming the Terror of Death* (San Francisco: Jossey-Bass, 2008).
- P. 239. Magdalene Redekop's story appears in "Through the Mennonite Looking Glass," in *Why I Am a Mennonite*, Harry Loewen, ed. (Kitchener: Herald Press, 1988. I have also borrowed the phrase *ütjedochte Jeschichte* from her.
- P. 256-7. Quoted in Karen Armstrong, *A History of God* (New York: Ballantine Books, 1993.)

ACKNOWLEDGEMENTS

Thanks first of all to my wife Hannah, for inspiring and supporting me through the long journey of writing this book, and to my siblings for their stories, without which this account would be far less rich. I hope they will forgive any inaccuracies or misrepresentations.

Thanks to all the folks I talked to who knew my dad and for their stories, which added greatly to my understanding.

Thanks to the Monday morning men's coffee group for all their father stories, which helped me greatly to gain perspective. Thanks to Scott Simpson and Arthur Bartsch for our discussions about Eliade and Tillich—some of the insights I gained found their way into the book. Thanks to the writers' group in Nelson—Ross Klatte, Diana Cole, Brian d'Eon and Vera Maloff—for your input, which led to definite improvements in the text. Thanks to Dan Schellenberg and Faith Eidse for your editorial input, early on.

A special shout-out to my brother, Norman Friesen, for his many hours of labour in transcribing Dad's and Mom's diaries and letters. Your interest encouraged me and your work made mine much easier.

I am grateful to Ron Smith for his marvellous account of dealing with a stroke—his book gave me information and wisdom I had long been seeking.

Acknowledgements

Thanks to the Mennonite Heritage Archives in Winnipeg for access to journals and newspapers to which my father contributed.

I am grateful to my editors, Rita Moir and Heidi Harms, whose suggestions made a very significant, positive difference.

Finally, I very much appreciate the D. F. Plett Historical Research Foundation's financial support, which made this publication possible.

CPSIA information can be obtained
at www.ICGtesting.com
Printed in the USA
LVHW011919171219
640838LV00001B/1

9 781525 560880